The Continuing Story
of Point-to-Point Racing

MICHAEL WILLIAMS

The Continuing Story of Point-to-Point Racing

PELHAM BOOKS

First published in Great Britain by
PELHAM BOOKS LTD
52 *Bedford Square*
*London, W.C.*1
1970

7207 0409 X

Set and printed in Great Britain by
Tonbridge Printers Ltd, Peach Hall Works, Tonbridge, Kent
in Baskerville ten on twelve point on paper supplied by
P. F. Bingham Ltd, and bound by James Burn
at Esher, Surrey

This book is dedicated to my wife,
without whose encouragement it
would never have been undertaken;
and to point-to-point enthusiasts
everywhere

Acknowledgements

So many people have helped me at various stages of this book that it is impossible to name all of them. They do, however, have my most sincere thanks, particularly those who gave me the information which has enabled me to write the chapter about the courses, and whose names it would clearly be unpolitic to mention.

I would like now to express special thanks to Mr F. E. Jervis Foulds, Mr Harold Charlton and Mrs Mary Cole for their invaluable assistance; to Mr Charles Weatherby for his help and encouragement; to Mrs Harold Rushton for so kindly lending me her old Worcestershire Hunt racecards; to Mr J. Lloyd Philips for parting with two prized possessions, Quarrell's history of the Worcestershire Hunt and the clipping from the *Birmingham Post* containing the report of the present Duke of Windsor's performances at the Harkaway Club in 1928; to Mr Edward Cazalet and Mrs Nina Guilding for the loan of books; to Lord Daresbury, Capt. Harry Freeman-Jackson, Mr Wilfred How and Mrs Joan Makin for the information about their horses; to Miss Julie Turner for information about the horses owned by her grandfather, Mr Edward Turner; to Mr Len Coville, Mr Brian Thompson and Mrs Sheilagh French for telling me some very good stories; to Mr Jim (Frank H.) Meads for most of the photographs that appear in this book; and to Mr J. M. Turner, M.F.H., and Col. Arthur Clerke-Brown for the information about the new courses they are building.

I would also like to thank the publishers of the books I have quoted from; and the Editors of *The Field*, *The Sporting Life*, the *Birmingham Post* and *Horse and Hound* for permission to quote from these publications and, in the case of the last-named journal, for the additional courtesy of being allowed to spend hours browsing through the files.

My final thanks are to my wife, for her forbearance; to Guy Cunard for his Foreword; to Messrs. Weatherbys and the Jockey Club for permission to reprint the point-to-point regulations in full; to John Hopwood for compiling the Index; to Mrs Jane Gutierrez for typing the final draft against the clock; and last, but not least, to Bill Luscombe of Pelham Books for cracking the whip over me.

Thanks are due to the following for permission to reproduce photogaphs in which they hold copyright: John Hopwood, 3, 4; *Hereford Times,* 12; Frank H. Meads, 7, 8, 10, 11, 13, 14, 17, 18, 19, 21, 22, 23, 24, 25, 26, 27, 28, 29, 30, 31, 32, 33, 34, 35; Greyhound Racing Association, 20.

M.W.

Contents

Illustrations

Foreword

by

Major Guy Cunard

When Michael Williams asked me to write the Foreword to his book I said I would be both honoured and delighted, and asked him what he was going to call it. A conversation which went something like this then ensued:

M.W. '*The Continuing Story of Point-to-Point Racing.*'

G.C. 'What a damned silly title!'

M.W. 'It's after Peyton Place, you know.'

G.C. 'Never heard of Peyton Place. I suppose it's one of those dark horses from the West Country or the Welsh borders. I shall look it up in Geoffrey Sale's annual and the "The Pointer".'

M.W. (patiently) 'It is not a horse, Guy. It's a T.V. soap opera. Surely you must have seen it?'

G.C. 'I don't watch T.V. serials or Wednesday plays. I hope it is not as smutty, and that you don't intend to present your point-to-point customers with a soap opera!'

M.W. 'That remains to be seen.'

I have never written a Foreword before. So I read up everything I could find about them, and was disconcerted to find much that was derogatory, and nothing complimentary. I also discovered that nobody ever reads them anyway.

But it seems to be usual for the writer of a Foreword to say a few words about the author; so it pleases me to be able to say that Michael Williams has done a very great deal to put point-to-point racing on the map with his writings in *The Sporting Life, The Horseman's Year* and other publications. Readers (and I am one of them) who regale themselves on Thursday mornings with the extensive point-to-point reports in *The Sporting Life* owe it to Michael Williams. At one time – he may even do it still – he used to type every word himself. What is more, he gets things right.

There was a time when a harassed point-to-point Secretary, glad to get the whole thing over, used to scribble on a race-card and send it off. Mistakes were frequent. When I won the adjacent hunts' race at the York & Ainsty on Cyril Chapman's Jeremy II in 1951, I was very surprised to read that I had finished unplaced, and that the race had been won by a horse who figured among the also rans. When I pulled dear old Trianon up with a broken leg at the Goathland in 1953 I was surprised to read that I had finished second. Having won the members' race at the Bramham Moor on Britomart in 1936, I was most elated to read that I had also won the open race at the Fife on the same day, especially as I possessed neither an aeroplane nor a fast car. Three mistakes in the case of a single rider makes one think that there must have been many more in other instances.

In those days, before Michael Williams came on the scene to put one in the picture as one had never been put there before, the reporting was mainly done by local papers, and usually not very well. On Easter Monday 1950 I rode three winners at the Staintondale. If dear old King of Kilcash's steering had been a little better round the bend before the final fence, it would have been four. To borrow a Gillette Cup term, I thought I was 'the man of the match'. In my vanity, I bought the local paper, the *Whitby Gazette,* to read all about my great feat, etc. Alas! The only event which had captured the imagination of the reporter and which he thought worthy of comment was the fact that a hare got up between the second and third races and careered down the course. He found the hare's antics, which he spent several paragraphs reporting, a great deal more interesting than mine.

The title *The Continuing Story of Point-to-Point Racing* leads me to say a few words about what I have considered to be a very definite threat to its survival in this age of inflation. The vast majority of those who own and race point-to-point horses would gladly race as the Romans did, for a laurel wreath alone, *if they could afford to.* The bugbear is that not enough people can afford to do so to make the sort of racing at all the meetings scheduled which enough people will pay to come and see.

With modern sponsorship, I feel certain that higher stakes could be given. Spurious arguments are raised about all hunts giving the same prize money. That is nonsense.

Stake money in steeplechasing varies a great deal from meeting to meeting. The better horses go for the better prizes and usually the larger number go for the smaller prizes. People who assert that all the horses will go for the bigger prizes and that there will be no runners for the smaller prizes are talking nonsense.

There is a body called the M.F.H. Point-to-Point Advisory Committee who advise the Jockey Club, with which the old National Hunt Committee has been enveloped. I have the impression that this committee which represents the hunts which have to find the stake money, except when sponsored, do not feel it is in their interest to raise it very much. I firmly believe that this is a very mistaken policy, possibly even a suicidal one. I think that if they could put to the Jockey Club the case of raising the stake money as sharply as I would – at the same time a great deal more diplomatically! – it would be raised!

But on then to point-to-point racing, and long may it continue.

1

Beginnings and Musings

Ever since I sat down to write this book I have been haunted by a remark made by John Blis in *The Sporting Life*: 'Why do books about horses one has never seen seldom come to life?' I hope this book is not going to be one of those. But I must leave it to my readers to deliver the verdict.

Since the origins of point-to-point racing are also the origins of steeplechasing, let us begin there. In the *History of Steeplechasing* which he published in 1901, William Blew gives Ireland the credit for being the birthplace, with the match between Mr O'Callaghan and Mr Edmund Blake which took place in 1752 'over four and a half miles of hunting country' from Buttevant Church to St Leger Church; and this race might equally well be described as the precursor of point-to-point racing, were it not for the fact that similar matches were staged in England a hundred years earlier. Such as the one between the Duke of Richmond and Lord Suffolk at Newmarket in 1662, described by a certain Thomas Ross, a member of the Duke of Monmouth's staff, in the following terms:

> This day the first race was run between the Duke of Richmond and Lord Suffolk who lost the day, and the Duke won an 100lb though in the morning hee got a very terrible fall in running a horse of my Lord Tumonds, who teeke up the Duke bleeding at mouth, and dead for a time, but hee got home, let blood, took Sperm-cete and went after dinner to see his horse run . . .

Some 150 years later, another Ross, but no descendant of the earlier one as far as I know, matched his horse Clinker (the same Clinker who was to engage in an even more famous match with Squire Osbaldeston's Clasher) with Lord Kennedy's Radical for 2,000 guineas over four miles. The match was won by Clinker, with his owner riding. But what is more interesting is the ungentlemanly spirit in which it was ridden. After Lord Kennedy had laid down his idea of the rules, Capt. Horatio Ross was moved to remark, 'In short, I understand that we may ride over each other and kill each other if we can.' 'Just so,' said his lordship, who was not riding his own horse.

Personally, I don't think that it matters two straws which race one takes to be the original one, because the probability is that there were many others unrecorded; and in any case, they all seem to have been matches between two parties.

The first recorded steeplechase (i.e. between more than two people) took place in Leicestershire in 1792, when Mr Charles Meynell (whose father, Hugo Meynell, hunted the Quorn for half a century), Lord Forester and Sir Gilbert Heathcote raced against each other over an eight-mile course from Barkby Holt to Billesdon Coplow and back for 100 guineas a side, Mr Meynell winning.

The first steeplechase over a properly constructed course was at Bedford in 1811. The original intention was to stage a three-mile flat race for hunters and exclude *racehorses*. But Mr George Tower, of the Oakley Hunt, had a better idea, namely to introduce fences. So eight obstacles, each measuring 4 ft. 6 in. (the height of N.H. fences today), were constructed 'with a strong bar at the top'. Eleven starters duly declared themselves but in the end only two of them went to the post. One of them was Mr Tower, riding his own mare Cecilia; and the other was Mr Spence, who won the race on his mare Fugitive. *The Sporting Magazine* of the period reveals that 'Fugitive and Cecilia had certificates gained by being in at the death of three foxes in Leicestershire, the certificates being lodged with the Clerk of the Course.' So here is a real link with the point-to-points of the present day.

It is not George Tower, however, but Thomas Coleman who is generally reckoned to be the father of steeplechasing; and of this gentleman, Michael Seth-Smith says in his contribution to *The History of Steeplechasing*, which was published by Michael Joseph in 1966, 'it is highly probable that, where villainy, skulduggery and sharp practice were concerned, he was no better or worse than many of his contemporaries', which seems a rather back-handed compliment.

Coleman, who started his professional career working under the stud groom of Lord Arthur Wellesley (later the Duke of Wellington), and then became a trainer in his own right, first at Brocket Hall, the home of Lord Melbourne, and then on Lord Verulam's land at Gorhambury, near St Albans, was an ambitious character who successfully combined training racehorses with hotel-keeping. After acquiring the Chequers Tavern in St Albans he promptly pulled it down and built a more imposing one on the same site, with stabling for thirty horses. This was appropriately named the Turf Hotel and among its patrons were such notabilities of the turf as Squire Osbaldeston, John Gully the prize-fighter, Prince Paul Esterhazy and Mr Tattersall. This establishment still stands today in St Albans where, since 1852, it has been known as the Queen's Hotel. Osbaldeston lost £3,000 at billiards there in a week.

Coleman it was who first put steeplechasing on an organized basis, and from 1830 to 1839 he ran the race that became known as the St Albans Steeplechase. The initial venture, said to be inspired by a group of officers of the 1st Life Guards, after a dinner they had held at the Turf Hotel, attracted sixteen starters and was won by Captain Macdowall on Wonder, a grey horse owned by Lord Ranelagh. The course was from Hartlington Church to Wrest Park, Silsoe, a distance of about two miles, and, to quote the late Col. Ted Lyon's article in the Lonsdale Library volume on steeplechasing, 'Coleman had so arranged the course that he was able, by riding across country, to act both as Starter and Judge. As often happened later in point-to-points, the field rode two miles out on a straight line and returned over a parallel line of fences a few fields away from the outward-bound route.'

The riders, in fact, were not given the line beforehand, and Coleman had helpers concealed in ditches who were instructed to raise their flags to indicate the line of the course just before the race started. Not unnaturally, some people lost their way and, as Col. Lyon records, one of them, Mr Stretfield on Teddy the Tike, fell over a gate and was killed.

The St Albans Steeplechase continued for nine years, and in the meantime its rivals were popping up elsewhere. It finally fizzled out in 1839, the year the first Grand National was run; and in this connection it is interesting to note that Jem Mason, who won the first Grand National on Lottery, made his début on a racecourse in the 1834 St Albans race, which he won on The Poet. Another rider in those early races of Tommy Coleman's was the celebrated Capt. Becher, who was later to give his name to Becher's Brook. Capt. Becher first rode in the race in 1831, when his horse Wildboar fell exhausted in the closing stages of the race and is said to have bled so badly that he died the next day. That was the year the famous Moonraker won for the first time. Capt. Becher won the race in 1835 (the year The Poet was destroyed after staking himself) on Norma, a mare he remounted after a fall.

One of the other races which sprang up during this period is of particular interest because it has left a legacy behind on the point-to-point scene. This was the Vale of Aylesbury Steeplechase which was first run in 1835, and won by Capt. Becher on Vivian, a horse bought in Dublin by his owner, Capt. Lamb, for sixteen guineas. Today the open race at the Whaddon Chase point-to-point at Great Horwood is known as the Vale of Aylesbury Steeplechase.

The first Vale of Aylesbury race was the brainchild of a party of hunting men who were dining together at Crockford's. 'It was considered,' writes Michael Seth-Smith, 'that the wide and deep brooks which intersected the Vale were eminently suitable for a race. A four mile course [this is rather longer than the Whaddon Chase one, which, although an undoubted stayers' course, is three and a half miles] was agreed upon between Waddesdon windmill and Aylesbury church. A cup valued at £50 was added to a sweepstake of twenty guineas each. The second to save his stake.'

In the 1850's Surtees expressed some strong feelings about steeplechasing in *Mr. Sponge's Sporting Tour.* 'Steeple-Chases,' he wrote, 'are generally crude, ill-arranged things . . . There is always something wanting or forgotten. Either they forget the ropes, or they forget the scales, or they forget the weights, or they forget the bell, or – more commonly still – some of the parties forget themselves.' And he went on to say :

> In the early days of steeple-chasing a popular fiction existed that the horses were hunters; and grooms and fellows used to come nicking and grinning up to masters of hounds at checks and critical times, requesting them to note that they were out, in order to ask for certificates of the horses having been 'regularly hunted' – a species of regularity than which nothing could be more irregular.

The opinion Surtees held of amateur race-riders was equally strong: 'We know of no more humiliating sight than misshapen gentlemen playing at jockeys. Playing at soldiers is bad enough, but playing at jockeys is infinitely worse – above all, playing at steeplechase jockeys, combining as they generally do, all the worst features of the hunting field and racecourse – unsympathizing boots and breeches, dirty jackets that never fit, and caps that won't keep on. What a farce to see the great bulky fellows go to scale with their saddles strapped to their backs, as if to illustrate the impossibility of putting a round of beef upon a pudding plate!'

In one way or another these sort of things have been said off and on over the years, and will no doubt continue to be said. Thus in 1946 the late Capt. Lionel Dawson, at that time the hunting correspondent of the *Daily Telegraph*, was writing in *The Horseman's Year*, 'the point-to-point has become a species of bastard race-meeting, run for profit and with prizes competed for by horses principally kept for the purpose, and barely qualified as hunters (even under the very lax rules imposed for such qualification) frequently, whenever conditions permit, ridden by jockeys who seem to get about quite a lot'.

A few years later, that great amateur rider, Frank Atherton Brown (brother of the revered Harry who finished second on The Bore in the Grand National of 1921 with a broken collar-bone) was letting off steam in his entertaining book *Sport from Within*, which had its serious moments:

> As well as introducing flat races into the N.H. programmes, it might be a good move to cut out hunters' races. These races have been rather a farce for many years, as no one even pretends that nine out of ten of the horses with hunters' certificates are seriously used for fox-catching. Hunters' races are even more of a farce now that Point-to-Points have become so "professionalized". It might be as well to confine hunters to Point-to-Pointing, instead of encouraging racehorses to masquerade as hunters at race meetings.

And there were some who found it difficult to forgive amateurs for looking like amateurs. Such a one was Capt. Sandy Carlos Clarke, the Lambourn trainer, who started a raging controversy in the correspondence columns of *The Sporting Life* in 1961 with a letter which seems to owe something to Surtees:

> I know of no worse sight than seeing those enormous men, many with turnip heads and oversize bodies, dressed in ill-fitting clothes from some lease-lend tailor which fit only where they touch, bumping round like half-trained mounted policemen on some wretched animals, with whips singing off them for the last mile and no chance of finishing anywhere!

This letter provoked some splendid replies which must have kept the intrepid Captain busy licking his wounds for quite some time. One correspondent was unkind enough to refer to the Captain's somewhat undistinguished record as a trainer, and quote statistics; while Major Cunard told a delicious story of how the same Captain had tried unsuccessfully to sell him a 'hitherto remarkably unsuccessful animal' as 'one bound to win hunter chases'. Another indignant correspondent remarked that he had 'never read such rubbish' in his life. And there were telling letters from two well-known owners of point-to-pointers. Mr Harry Dufosee, writing from Stalbridge, Dorset, deemed the letter to be 'in very bad taste, and not to be expected from one who signs himself "Capt."'; and Mr John Robarts, who farms the land at Kimble, in the vale of Aylesbury, where several point-to-point fixtures are held, demanded 'a public apology to one of the greatest band of sportsmen in the world'.

At the risk of seeming caddish, by adding to Capt. Carlos Clarke's discomfiture at this late stage, I would just like to say that at the time he wrote his now notorious letter among the 'turnip heads' riding in point-to-points were: Guy Cunard, Bob McCreery, Gay Kindersley, Ian Balding, Clive and John Straker, John Lawrence, Michael Tory, Tony Biddlecombe, David Moore, Derrick Scott, Peter Brookshaw, John Bosley, Edward Cazalet, Sir William Pigott-Brown, Ted Greenway, John Daniell, George Small, the Australian Olympic gold medallist Lawrence Morgan, Michael Bloom, and a young rider who in later years was to become the leading professional under N.H. rules, Bob Davies.

2

The Early Point-to-points and The First Ladies' Races

It is virtually impossible to pin-point the first point-to-point meeting. Col. Lyon put the date of it 'about 1885 or a little later'. But it is certain that there was some kind of hunt racing even before that. According to one source I have consulted, that invaluable *Point-to-Point Calendar* edited by the late Arthur Coaten in the thirties, Mr W. E. Oakeley, Master of the Atherstone in the early 1870's, 'used to claim that he was one of the first Masters of Hounds to have an annual Hunt point-to-point meeting pure and simple', with the races run over natural country, and hunt members paying all the expenses out of their own pockets. The same source reveals that, in 1883, Philip Muntz won the hunt race at the Pytchley on Sir Robert carrying 16 st. 9 lb. and giving away 65 lb. to most of his competitors.

The most authentic claim I have come across, however, is contained in a history of the Worcestershire Hunt which was compiled from original sources by Thomas Read Quarrell (Hon. Sec. of the Hunt from 1917–1922) and printed and published in 1929 by Phillips & Probert at the Caxton Press, Worcester. This book gives the date of the first Worcestershire Hunt meeting as March 2nd, 1836, 'over a course on the west bank of the Severn from a point at Frieze Wood by the Old Hills on the Madresfield Estate of Earl Beauchamp, to the centre of the Lower Powick Ham, where Capt. Lamb's Vivian ridden by Capt. Becher won'.

The next meeting of this hunt was at Crowle on March 28th, 1841, when it appears that there were two races, won by Cotton Ball and Fairy. The first meeting to have more than two races was on the April 30th, 1851. There were sundry other meetings up to Easter Monday, 1864, and then nothing until the memorable meeting in 1883 which is very often taken to be the first of the Worcestershire point-to-points, and of which Quarrell writes:

> The Meeting was attended by an enormous crowd of people mounted, who rode alongside of and behind the competitors, with the result that much confusion occurred, and Mr. E. Woodhouse, the Judge, had great difficulty in deciding the winner of the Red Coat Race and ultimately the result was given as a dead heat between Messrs. F. Lort Phillips and R. V. Berkeley.

One of those who rode at this meeting was Tom Andrews, father of Mrs Nina Guilding and grandfather of the present-day riders Roger and Diana Guilding; and in his book, *Fox Hunting Reminiscences,* written under the pseudonym of 'Gin and Beer' and published by Phillips & Probert in 1930, this stalwart of the Croome Hunt has left us a vivid description:

> Johnnie Widger sent me a good powerful hunter, going in his wind, and bred by Sir Robert Paul, Waterford. This horse I rode in the first point-to-point in Worcestershire in 1883, arranged by Mr. F. Lort Phillips and Mr. Arthur James. They selected a course at Hill Croome, and a real course it was, very different from the course of today. We jumped Jack's Paddock brook in two places, and it is now thirty six years since I saw it cleared by "Bruiser" Woodward. There were also five big bullfinches to go through, and two stiles with footboards, also three roads to cross. Nine started in the Farmers' and Tradesmen's Race and the horse I was riding was the only one that kept on its legs, but I must admit that I was whispering in his ear on two occasions, and was leading at one time by a quarter of a mile, then only to get third, with three to finish!

Mrs Guilding tells me that her father weighed 16 st. and stood 6 ft. 1 in. when she was born in 1907 and that he often rode bare-backed, so that on one occasion when he was riding in this manner in the farmers' race at the Croome he heard someone shouting 'Look at that fool, he's lost his saddle'. Before he rode in that race in 1883 (when he did have a saddle, as he was only eighteen years old at the time) he got a friend from Cheltenham to try his horse out over some fences and, on asking for the verdict, received the reply: 'A very big jumper. I could light a cigar while he was in the air and smoke it out before he got to the next fence.'

It was in 1888 that the Midland Sportsmen's Races were started at Kineton, Warwickshire, by the then Lord Willoughby de Broke. These races were so styled because they were confined to five hunts in the area, the Warwickshire, North Warwickshire, Pytchley, Bicester and Heythrop, and they were run over a four-mile course with 'fences of fair and proper hunting type'. It was at this meeting that the House of Commons point-to-point used to be held. Sir Elliott Lees, M.P., won the House of Commons race three years running, between 1888 and 1890, on his big bay gelding Damon. But this race was never run after 1892, the year that Capt. 'Bay' Middleton and the Rt. Hon. James Tomkinson, Liberal M.P. for the Crewe division of Cheshire, were killed. The latter was seventy years old and had hunted with the Cheshire for half a century.

The Stock Exchange point-to-point races, which alas are held no longer, date back to 1892; and the Pegasus Club (Bar) races, which survive today at Kimble, to 1895, when the Pegasus Club was founded with the object of encouraging riding and hunting among members of the legal profession.

The first Bar point-to-point was held at Coombe, near Malden, over a three-mile course; and in his book *Bench and Bar in the Saddle*, which has been kindly lent to me by Edward Cazalet, who had his first ride in a point-to-point when he was still at Eton, C. P. Hawkes says that there were two races, one for heavy-weights and one for lightweights, both confined to hunters 'belonging to H.M. Judges, practising Barristers or Students of one of the Inns of Court reading in the Chambers of any practising Barristers. No horse that had won a steeplechase under N.H. Rules was considered eligible, and winners of open races at point-to-points had to carry 14 lb. penalties. The lightweight race was won by Mr A. Gee on his seven-year-old Defiance (a horse reputed to have been trained on turnips), and the heavyweight race, in which one horse broke her back and another his neck, by the Hon. Alfred Lyttelton (later Colonial Secretary in H.M. Government).' Lyttelton, however, declined to receive the cup on the grounds that the runner-up, Mr J. G. Butcher, Q.C., M.P. (afterwards

Lord Danesfort, K.C.), 'was worthier of it as he had entered and ridden his own horse'.

The most famous of the Bar riders in those days was H. G. Farrant, who subsequently became His Honour, Judge Farrant. Farrant rode his last winner at the age of fifty-nine, in 1923, the year he was elected President of the Pegasus Club. He was then, writes Hawkes, a 'County Court Judge on a Circuit which included the metropolis of racing and all the best hunting country in Bedfordshire and Cambridgeshire'.

The Cambridge University races must also have a fairly long history, since there is in existence a painting of Mr J. G. O. Thomson winning the Farewell Cup for the university heavyweight race on his grey Ballymore II in 1904. But that was well before these races were run on the permanent course of the Cambridgeshire Harriers at Cottenham, where the first fixture took place in the 1930's.

Sir Alfred Pease, who was Liberal M.P. for York from 1885 to 1892, and died in 1939 at the age of eighty-one, rode in many point-to-point races during his term of office, and in the article he wrote for *The Field* in April, 1933 this is what he said about the courses of his youth:

> Those who selected the course guarded their secret jealously; the only indication the entrants had as to the district was the announcement shortly before the race of the "rendezvous". Competitors, restricted to members of the Hunt, were mustered near the winning flag, the only flag in those days. They were then escorted by roads to a point four, five or six miles away and dispatched on the journey. I cannot remember one of those early races in which one could see the winning flag, until at least half the journey had been accomplished; but that did not matter, as the line was a bee-line, provided you could ride it.
>
> ... The rules were simple; the chief thing to remember was that to open a gate or to ride more than 100 yards up or down a road was to be disqualified. Every good hunter had a chance, and many a clever horse deficient in pace scored a victory.

There was little or no attempt to cater for the public (it was the necessity for this in later years that played a large part in changing the character of point-to-point racing), and the racing was so hazardous, and took such a toll in casualties, that some hunts (including the Hurworth and the Cleveland in the North) abandoned their meetings for several years. Sir Alfred records that 'you saw men arrive home after a succession of bullfinches and other rough obstacles with clothes and faces in rags'.

Although there were rules and regulations of a kind before the turn of the century, it was not until 1913 that point-to-point racing got its own charter. This was when the Masters of Hounds Point-to-Point Association was formed and a committee set up to regularise the position of point-to-point racing and frame a new set of rules.

These rules were not, however, so tight that they precluded ladies from riding against the men, and in the early 1920's quite a number of them did so, notably in East Anglia, where Miss Wentworth-Reeve was the pioneer and Miss Joan Parry and Mrs Cooper Bland were also well to the fore.

Whether or not any of these ladies rode side-saddle, I do not know; but one who certainly did was Mrs Mabel Aitken, who was over seventy when she rode her horse Ware Wire into third place in the members' and subscribers' race at the Old Berkshire meeting at Faringdon. In order to ride at 12 st. 7 lb. Mrs Aitken had to carry 5½ st. of lead; and I am told, by someone whose memory is rather longer than mine, that she presented a splendid picture in a green habit and silk hat.

Another lady who rode side-saddle against the men in those days was Miss V. Selby-Lowndes, who subsequently married Col. H. N. H. Wild. Riding her mare Pandora, Miss Selby-Lowndes won the lightweight race at the West Street Harriers in March, 1929 on the same day that her brother, Brig. (as he now is) M. W. W. Selby-Lowndes, won the members' race there; while Mrs A. Heald won the open nomination race on her noted Shepherd's Pie, and soon afterwards won a similar race on the same horse at the Ashford Valley.

The Kent ladies, in fact, were almost as strong as the East Anglians, and another lady to win races there against the men was Miss J. M. Magee. Miss Jean Sanday was similarly successful in Cheshire, as were Miss Melvill and Miss Sylvia Spooner in the West Country. Miss Spooner, the leading lady rider in

England in the early thirties, was probably the last lady to win against the men for nearly forty years. A week after she had won on her pony Mohun at the East Cornwall banking fixture on April 24th, 1929, the Masters of Hounds Association passed a new rule rendering ladies ineligible to ride except in races confined to their own sex, and it was not until 1967 that this rule was relaxed. In Ireland, however, the ladies have been riding against the men in point-to-points since time immemorial. But that is another story.

The first ladies' race seems to have been at the South & West Wilts at Motcombe, near Shaftesbury, in 1921; and someone who trusts his memory writes: 'I recall that the favourite was Slauntha, who was saddled up by Geoffrey Phipps-Hornby. In this race Lord Stalbridge, the Master of the South & West Wilts, rode behind the competitors in case any of them should need assistance. To the best of my recollection, he was left far behind!' The race was won, in a field of twelve, by Lady Jean Douglas-Hamilton (the aunt of Anneli Drummond-Hay), who rode her horse Cavalier II side-saddle and went like the wind. The next ladies' race – one that I have seen in several reference books named as the first – was at the Berks & Bucks Staghounds' fixture at Sonning in 1925, when Mrs Weatherby won on Reggie. But it was only after the ladies were forbidden to ride against the men that these races gathered momentum.

3

Some Soldiers and a Prince

For a number of years the point-to-points were supplemented by the *bona fide* hunt meetings, which were introduced in 1912, and the *bona fide* military meetings which came on the scene in 1927. These were, in fact, little more than glorified point-to-points, although in the case of the military fixtures the courses were often semi-permanent ones.

The rules in both cases were very similar, and the ceiling of prize money was always 20 sovereigns. The main difference between a *bona fide* hunt meeting and a point-to-point was that, whereas there was no charge for admission to the latter, apart from the car-park fees, hunts holding *bona fide* fixtures were empowered by the N.H. Committee to hold their fixtures over an enclosed course and charge a modest fee to each member of the public. The horses that ran at these meetings were more or less the same ones that were to be found contesting point-to-points; and by comparison with the number of point-to-points held in a season, *bona fide* hunt meetings were few and far between. Thus, in 1937, when 163 point-to-point fixtures were held, only the following hunts were holding *bona fide* meetings: the Badsworth and the Rockwood Harriers in the North, the Eridge, Southdown, East Sussex and Old Surrey & Burstow, in the South; the Brocklesby in Lincolnshire and the Tedworth and Royal Artillery Harriers in the South West.

The *bona fide* military meetings were meetings for hunters held under National Hunt Rules by units of the Regular Services and all horses running in these races were required to be 'the property of serving Officers of the Regular Army, Navy or Air Force, except that Regimental Races confined to one Regiment may be open to Officers serving or who have held permanent Commissions in the Regiment'. And, as in the case of the *bona fide* hunt meetings, the courses had to be officially approved by the National Hunt Committee's inspectors.

When point-to-point racing acquired 'a new look' after the war, and a great deal more attention was given to the courses and to the needs of the public, there was no longer any necessity for the *bona fide* hunt meetings, which became submerged in the point-to-point scene. But I am sure I am not alone in regretting the passing of the military fixtures, which disappeared at the same time, along with those delightful courses at Windmillhill and Hawthorn Hill. Tweseldown, where there was National Hunt racing up till 1932, has, however, survived, and is now the setting for a number of point-to-points; and for this we must be thankful. I never set foot on this permanent course near Aldershot without having my imagination stirred by memories of the past; and some of these memories were vividly brought back to me not long ago when an official there pointed to one of the obstacles and declared with obvious pride: 'This is the fence where H.R.H. usually came to grief.' He was, of course, referring to the present Duke of Windsor, who, as Prince of Wales, was more enthusiastic than skilful as a point-to-point rider, though he rode thirteen winners.

In the spring of 1928, the Prince had a momentous afternoon at the Harkaway Club races at Chaddesley Corbett, and a particularly delightful account of it appeared in the *Birmingham Post*, which I now propose to quote from:

> The news that the Prince of Wales was a competitor attracted, of course, a gathering that was unusually large for this annual event. Thousands of people splashed and struggled about on the precarious footing offered by the muddy hillside, which, in places, soon became a quagmire. It was essentially a day for top-boots, and luckless, indeed, were those numerous members of the fair sex who were not so equipped. Their thin and elegant shoes of suede, and lizard and alligator, and whatnot quickly became shapeless repositories for liberal coatings of Worcestershire soil. As for the men, one saw here and there some of the type which one naturally associates with a point-to-point meeting: the jack-booted, heavily overcoated, hardbitten and rubicund sort, somewhat terse of speech, who suggest, by their very

> appearance, that a good sample of horse-flesh may be accounted the most important figure on their horizon. But there were others to whom a gathering such as this was a new experience, who looked for, and expected – in vain – the comforts and conveniences of an up-to-date race-course. They had obviously come there to see, not the racing, but the Prince of Wales.

But if they hoped to see H.R.H. ride a winner, they were doomed to disappointment. In the first race, he rode a brown mare, Lady Doon, who had been hunted with the Quorn, and about this animal odds of 2–1 against were offered. 'The Prince of Wales led to the fifth fence, when his mount refused, and shot him off. He remounted and jumped it, but fell. He went on very strongly for another three-quarters' circuit of the course, when he pulled up.' The winner was Possible, ridden by Sir John Grey, so at least spectators had a titled victor to console themselves with. The fence where Lady Doon refused was a rather notorious one, somewhat euphemistically known as the Open Ditch. Its reputation for causing disaster was apparently well known, and around it were crammed a group of expectant onlookers. The writer in the *Birmingham Post* goes on :

> 'He's leading,' said a man with a pair of field glasses; and, of course, there was no need to ask who he meant. So the horses came to the fence, and then it seemed – although one could not swear to it – as though something shot over it; but it was not a horse. 'His mare has refused,' said the man with the field glasses. Another man – one who looked as though he might be knowledgeable about horses – started in surprise. 'Are you sure?' he asked. 'Quite sure,' said the first one. The knowledgeable man stood with the pained expression of one who has been dealt a buffet in the face by a friend. 'Well, I've known Lady Doon for years,' he said. 'I've seen her hunting all over the Quorn country, and never before have I known her to refuse. Never!' He kept repeating the assertion at intervals in a dazed kind of a way.

'When the Prince rode into the paddock,' adds the writer, 'he was covered with mud from head to foot, and it was difficult even to distinguish his features through the caking. He retired and changed, and about half-an-hour later walked into the paddock spick and span as ever.'

But this was not the end of the Prince's adventures at the Harkaway Club races. He rode another mare from the Quorn, Degomme II, in the open nomination race; and once again he was leading until he got to the Open Ditch, only to be decanted when Degomme pecked in the treacherous going as she landed and rolled over on her side in the mud. Nothing daunted, H.R.H. eventually resumed his partnership with the mare, some way behind the field, and did well to survive another mistake before finishing fourth. But how many runners there were, and who received the challenge cup that was presented by Lord and Lady Ednam is not revealed. The article ends with a splendid peroration, however: 'Here was the Prince of Wales, one reflected, a tremendous asset to the Empire, risking life and limb not once but several times at a country point-to-point, going down before a lot of flying hoofs, any one of which might have dealt a fatal blow.'

The military meetings of the twenties and thirties brought out many fine riders and horses, the like of which will never again be seen in soldiers' races, which today are but a pale reflection of the past. The names roll off the tongue like poetry, and many of them have their echoes in the present: Major-General Sir Richard McCreery, Capt. Sir Peter Grant-Lawson, Peter Payne-Gallwey, Geoff Phipps-Hornby, Ronnie Holman, Dickie Courage, Peter Herbert, Harry Misa, 'Babe' Moseley, 'Roscoe' Harvey, Frank Cundell, Capt. G. H. Smith-Dorrien; Herbert Lumsden with More Magic and Silver Gill, Sir John Pigott-Brown with The Stroller, Capt. A. G. Martyr with Ablington; Capt. the Hon. C. B. Bernard with that beautiful little mare Brownly, a grand-daughter on her dam's side of the 1910 Derby winner Lemberg; W. Scott-Plummer, with the two full brothers March Brown IV and Canfly, both bred by his father in Scotland; Capt. Mark Roddick with the trio that won him three Grand Military Gold Cups at Sandown, Buck Willow, Kilstar and Fillip; Capt. M.P. (now Sir Michael) Ansell, and the post-war Olympic horsemen Harry Llewellyn and Henry Nicoll.

Enough is enough. But I must mention two more names: Capt. Neville Crump, the present Middleham trainer, who won the 4th Queen's Own Hussars' Challenge Cup on John de Moraville's

King's Cross II at the Aldershot Military Meeting in 1936; and Guy Cunard, who had his first winning ride at the military meeting on Salisbury Plain in 1932 on Golden Light, a horse who cost him only 28 guineas and won thirteen races for him.

And here's a remarkable thing. At the Garth point-to-point at Arborfield in 1930, Fulke Walwyn, the present Lambourn trainer, won the Royal Military Academy (Sandhurst) lightweight race; Frank Furlong, who was killed while serving with the Fleet Air Arm during the war, won the lightweight race; and Bobbie Petre, then still a schoolboy, won the hunt heavyweight race. Three riders who all went on to win the Grand National, Frank Furlong on Reynoldstown in 1935, Fulke Walwyn on the same horse the following year, and Bobbie Petre on Lovely Cottage in 1946.

4

Administration in the Thirties

As a result of the growing difference of opinion between the Masters of Hounds Point-to-Point Committee and the National Hunt Committee as to how to administer point-to-point racing, at the Annual General Meeting of the M.F.H. Association in May, 1934, Lord Lonsdale proposed the following resolution :

> That a Select Committee be appointed with a view to having a conference with the National Hunt Committee to consider the whole question with the Point-to-Point Committee of the Masters of Foxhounds Association.

Lord Lonsdale was not the sort of man to keep his thoughts to himself and he expressed some strong, if somewhat incoherent, views at this Meeting. Here are some of them :

> A point-to-point in 1919 was to be a point from one point to another, and beyond the safety of the fences, there were to be no marks or signals. One may go to a great number of point-to-points now, and one really finds them nothing more than miniature steeplechase courses, and in some cases they are absolutely ridiculous. Also the condition of the horses that run. The point-to-points were made originally not so much for the best horses, but for the best man. Gradually they worked out into an amalgamation of the two, but there are some point-to-points which are perfectly ridiculous. I was at a point-to-point not very long ago where one gentleman complained that the fences were too big, and there was a ditch on the take-off side. That is only one instance. There are many other instances of things that happen at point-to-points which are very far from being in the best interests either

> of the owners or racing. You get people who keep horses solely for point-to-point races, and there have been many difficulties raised as to point-to-point meetings and a great deal of discussion as to what is and what is not proper.

Clearly, something was not only about to be done, but about to be seen to be done, and when the National Hunt Committee met in July, 1934 they approved the formation of a Joint Advisory Committee comprising three Members of the National Hunt Committee and three representatives selected by the Masters of Foxhounds Association. The three representatives selected by the M.F.H. Association to act on their behalf were Col. J. G. Lowther (Master of the Pytchley), Capt. T. Wickham-Boynton (Master of the Middleton East) and Col. R. Thompson (Master of the Rufford). And as from the July 1st, 1934, in time for the 1935 point-to-point season, point-to-point racing came directly under the jurisdiction of the National Hunt Committee, Appendix C of the National Hunt Rules being created for this purpose.

The new rules did not differ much in essentials from the old ones. The most important changes were the appointment of accredited N.H. inspectors to approve the courses and the introduction of a rule banning horses who had won three open nomination races from competing in any more such events (other than at *bona fide* hunt meetings) during the same season. There was also a stipulation that 'No horse which, since January 1st of the current hunting season has been trained by a licensed trainer, unless the horse be his own property, or by an unlicensed person (other than his owner, groom, or the proprietor of the stable from whence the horse has been hunted), shall be eligible to be entered for a point-to-point steeplechase.'

And there was a clear definition from the National Hunt Committee as to what constituted a professional rider: 'Professional Hunt servants, grooms, apprentices, stable lads, and persons who are or have been employed as paid servants in any capacity in private, hunting, racing, livery, or horse-dealers' stables, also persons who have ever received payment, directly or indirectly, for riding in a race, are regarded as having ridden for hire, and are professional riders and are not eligible to ride . . .' The same definition holds good today, except that lady riders are exempt from it.

The reactions to the new administration were, on the whole, fairly favourable, although one complainant went so far as to observe, 'The National Hunt Committee have, in my opinion, been very stupid in interfering with point-to-point racing. It is pure jealousy . . .' But mostly it was a case of congratulations all round, and there was surprising support for the new rule restricting the number of open nomination races that a horse could win in a single season. But there was one cogent criticism from a well-known rider who suggested that it would be more sensible to *confine* horses who had won three nomination races to these events, instead of driving them into the adjacent hunts' races. The same rider (clearly one based in the Midlands) suggested with some feeling that one of the worst side-effects of this rule was that it reduced the status of championship races, such as the Lady Dudley Cup at the Worcestershire, the Lady Bullough Cup at the Ledbury and the Osmaston Cup at the Meynell.

There were, of course, recurring complaints throughout the thirties that point-to-points were becoming too much like steeplechases and that the average hunter had little chance in them. The correspondence columns of *Horse & Hound* of the period are a marvellous barometer of reflected opinion, with the indicator going up and down like a yo yo. Thus one correspondent wrote (in 1939) :

> Point-to-Point races were designed for hunters carrying hunting weights and ridden by hunting men. Unfortunately they have changed considerably. A large number of ex-racehorses are now competing, and point-to-points have progressed a long way towards becoming merely bad race meetings.

And another replied :

> Where are the large number of ex-racehorses? I attend many point-to-point races, but I do not see such horses. Many winners of point-to-points can win steeplechases, but the discarded racehorse has not 'an earthly' in a present day point-to-point race.

Some of the letters published by that journal were so absurd that they achieved a kind of poetry :

> I have had a good deal of experience in the point-to-

> point races, and have often seen these races won by very bad hunters, pulling brutes and refusers with hounds. I suggest the best way out of the difficulty of not having good hunters winning these races would be to have courses for them with some very sharp turns, so sharp that the competitors had to nearly pull their mounts up. Say, two such turns.

There were various other suggestions made throughout the thirties. In fact, the Editor of the *Point-to-Point Calendar* went out of his way to solicit them, and was seldom disappointed. Among these suggestions were several about the weights carried. The Hon. Sec. of a northern meeting wanted the minimum weight in men's races to be raised from 12 st. 7 lb. to 13 st., maintaining that the extra 7 lb. would 'help to stop these thoroughbreds as compared with the genuine hunter'.

Some people, however, thought that the weight was already too much, and a 7 lb. allowance for maidens was a not infrequent suggestion. 'I am convinced that 50 per cent of the young men out hunting could not ride 12 st. racing,' said a correspondent to *Horse & Hound*, an observation which inspired the reply, 'If a man who has got himself fit cannot do 11 st. 7 lb. he should not ride in point-to-points at the pace they go nowadays, as he is too big, and will get himself hurt.'

'Reduce the scale to 11 st. 7 lb.' wrote another correspondent disgustedly, 'and it will not be long before Lady Dudley's Cup is won by a well-bred discard from Northolt Park,' which at that time was a centre of professional pony racing.

Among other suggestions made during the period were a 2s. 6d. admission charge to the paddock, the introduction of handicapping (repeated by Gregory Blaxland in *Horse & Hound* in 1970) and, from a Gloucestershire Hon. Sec. who didn't think 'that any horse winning an open nomination race in February could possibly have been "regularly and fairly hunted",' no point-to- point racing before March 1st. A Yorkshire official described the inspection of courses as 'a farce and a waste of time'; and a Gloucestershire one remarked piously that, whilst his own hunt scrupulously observed the 'rule' about not levying a charge on bookmakers for the use of pitches, others did not. In fact, it is simply a question of how one interprets this rule. Bookmakers have always been expected to make a donation to hunt funds, and most hunts have the sense to leave the collection of the cash to the leading bookmaker.

Despite the constant complaints that point-to-points were becoming more and more like miniature steeplechases, and the oft-repeated plea for 'more natural' fences, the old-style type of point-to-point course had by no means died out in the thirties, and some were even to linger on after the war. The Equitation School at Weedon used to have a different course each year and contestants were told nothing about it until the day of the race, when they were told where to meet and shown where they had to finish. This is how the *Point-to-Point Calendar* describes the course for the 1935 event:

> The race was held over a very stiff line in the Bicester country, starting in Mr. Tew's field half a mile due west of Boddington Fields Farm, near Priors Hardwicke. The course ran for two miles to Blackdown, at which there was a red and white flag which could easily be seen from the start. From Blackdown Hill a white directing flag could be seen a mile and a half away at an angle of about 75 degrees. The finish itself was in a field near the Charwelton-Byfield road, about half a mile north of Byfield. The total distance by the shortest way was 3¾ miles. The heavy-weights and light-weights were run together, the former in black coats and the latter in red.

The Puckeridge Hunt course at Brent Pelham, which was in use throughout the thirties, included posts and rails, ditches and combination obstacles; and in 1936, the High Peak meeting at Flagg Moor (where these races are still held today) ran a combined light-weight and heavy-weight members' race over a four-mile course with walls (thirty-six of them) instead of the birch fences used for the other races.

In 1937, three years after the point-to-points had come under the direct control of the National Hunt Committee, the old Masters of Hounds Point-to-point Committee was dissolved. The motion proposing dissolution was put before the Annual General Meeting of the Masters of Foxhounds Association on May 31st that year by Col. C. Spence-Colby, the chairman, in these terms:

> This Committee is of the opinion that it is not practicable

> or necessary to have two bodies dealing with point-to-point racing, and as the Advisory Committee, appointed jointly by the National Hunt Committee and the Masters of Foxhounds Association is now doing the work in a satisfactory manner, and also in view of the fact that the National Hunt Committee have expressed a desire to deal with only one authority, they recommend that the Masters Point-to-Point Committee be dissolved, with a very hearty vote of thanks for their extremely valuable services in the past.

The motion was seconded by Major Gordon Foster and carried unanimously. And, needless to say, it received the approval of the National Hunt Committee, on whose behalf Lord Stalbridge made the following statement:

> I have been authorised by the Stewards to say this, that although they cannot bind themselves or their successors in any way as to the future, still at the moment they foresee no difficulties ahead, and if difficulties did arise they think the Advisory Committee is the best possible means of thrashing out all sides of any question, and they sincerely hope that point-to-point matters will go on as smoothly and happily in the future as they have done in the past three years.

There were to be no more startling innovations until after the war.

5

The Dudley Cup

In all sports there is usually one event which takes precedence over all others, and this event in point-to-point racing is the Lady Dudley Cup at the Worcestershire, which is the point-to-point equivalent of the Cheltenham Gold Cup. When one considers that the system of prize money in point-to-points is a uniform one, and that even today the ceiling for an open nomination race is a mere £40, it is remarkable that the Dudley Cup has acquired such a reputation, especially as the Worcestershire has never been exactly a fashionable hunt. How has this come about? This is a question to which there is no simple answer, and the best explanation I can think of is that the race has a very long history and has been won over the years by some outstanding horses. But it has also been suggested to me that the excellence, and testing nature, of the original course at Crowle, near Worcester, has a lot to do with it. Mr Jervis Foulds, who, I think it is safe to say, knows more about the history of the Worcestershire point-to-point than any other living person, has described this course to me as the best he has ever seen. The distance, he says, 'measured from the centre of each fence, was 4 miles 100 yards. No fence was jumped twice. I have been told that at one time there was no fence under 5 ft. and that the tops could be walked on!' And it goes without saying that the best horse always won. Which I think was also true of the later course at Upton-on-Severn.

The Earl of Dudley was Master of the Worcestershire from 1896 to 1902; and in 1897 the Countess of Dudley presented a £50 cup for the open event, which was then known as 'The Ladies' Plate'. This was won by Mr R. Cave-Brown-Cave's Triton. But it was not until 1898 that Lady Dudley presented the first *challenge* cup (valued at £105), with the proviso that if it were won by the same owner 'twice in succession or three times in all' it became his own property. Capt. H. R. M. Porter, who won the 1898 race on his horse Rajah, also won again on the same horse in 1901 and 1902. He is now dead, but the original challenge trophy is still in the possession of his son at Birlingham, the Porters' family home.

'Of all wild, mad riders,' wrote our old friend 'Gin and Beer' in his book, 'Harry Porter took the biscuit, and was never satisfied unless he fell five times a day over the most impossible leaps.' But in later years, 'he crossed the Croome and the Worcestershire country with judgement and was hard to beat.'

Lady Dudley gave a second challenge cup, which was won in 1903 and 1904 by H. G. (Judge) Farrant on Red Hall, a horse who was never beaten in point-to-points, and after his career in these races ran third in the National Hunt Chase at Cheltenham in 1904 and was sixth to Rubio in the Grand National of 1908.

'Red Hall,' says C. P. Hawkes in *Bench and Bar in the Saddle,* 'was said to be a son of Winkfield and thus an inheritor of Barcaldine blood. He was hunted by Farrant from a five-year-old, mostly with the Ledbury and the Croome, and was probably as genuine a hunter as ever ran in a race. A chestnut, with magnificent shoulders, back and quarters, and with exceptional bone, he was a perfect performer. Fast for a hunter, he represented a combination of qualities not easy to find in an individual horse.'

And 'Gin and Beer' wrote of Red Hall's owner-rider:

> He was gifted with the best of hands, seat and brains, whether riding a race or to hounds, never losing his head, and doing damage to either fences or crops. I once saw him jump into an allotment (or to be correct, he fell into it) and he looked at me as much as to say, 'I have no right here'. There Mr. Farrant sat and as I thought expounding the law and the prophets, until on drawing a little nearer I found he was only expatiating on the merits of the finish of his chestnut horse Red Hall in the Grand National. Many good judges of horses think today that his horse Red Hall was the best hunter that ever won Lady Dudley's Cup.

In 1905 Lady Dudley gave a third challenge cup, which is the one that is competed for today. The first winner of this was Mr W. V. Beatty on his Rufus. Ned Holland, who won the Dudley

Cups of 1907 and 1909 on Potheen II, and was an uncle of Edward ('Ruby') and Thurston Holland-Martin, is another to find a place in 'Gin and Beer's' book :

> . . . Ned Holland, a gentleman who never knew how to spell fear. Had he hunted twenty years previously, he would have met Mr. Harry Porter, and then it would have been Greek meeting Greek. The bigger the country the better they liked it. I can see them now in my dreams two fields in front of hounds riding against each other. I once remarked to Mr. Holland (near to the Vernon Arms, Hanbury) 'It's no use, Sir, it can't be done.' Away he went at it, with the result that he broke his horse's back. Charles West, then first whip, went to Mr. Wilson, a farmer, who fetched a gun and shot him. Mr. Holland, never thinking, sold the horse for 10/- to a knacker man instead of letting the hounds eat him.

The first horse to win the Dudley Challenge Cup after the First World War was the 1920 winner, Liffey Bank, owned by Capt. M. W. Muir and ridden by Mr G. S. Campbell. Conjuror II, who won the following year, went on to win the National Hunt Chase at Cheltenham and finish second in the Cheltenham Gold Cup and third in the Grand National. Seti the First, the 1925 winner, won the Liverpool Foxhunters'. Minstrel Boy and Herode Bridge, the winners in 1931 and 1933, both won the Cheltenham Foxhunters'.

6

O'Dell and His Contemporaries

Although there may have been better *racehorses* running in point-to-points during the thirties, the greatest point-to-pointer of this period – and indeed one of the greatest of all time – was O'Dell, owned by Major Harold Rushton, the Master of the Worcestershire. This famous grey thoroughbred (by Book out of Scapegoat II, by Morganatic out of Madame Dreyfus, by Bird of Freedom), who got his name from his breeder in Ireland, was hunted regularly by Major Rushton riding at 15 st. O'Dell won forty races, including the Liverpool Foxhunters' two years running in the years when this race was run over the full Grand National distance. At Liverpool, O'Dell was ridden by Major Otto Prior-Palmer of the 9th Lancers, but in most of his other races Major Rushton himself had the mount.

What is it that makes a great horse? Probably it is something that cannot be analysed. But one thing I do know is that it cannot be measured in terms of the number of races won. I prefer to think of it as something that is determined in the mind by a combination of experience and instinct, and felt in the blood. Sometimes, as in the case of The Dikler, in 1969, it is recognized immediately, and sometimes it takes time. As I never myself had the privilege of seeing O'Dell, I do not know what I would have thought about him on a course. But his name is hallowed by the memory of his feats, and instinct tells me that he was a great horse; and that two other well-known horses owned and ridden by Major Rushton during the same period, Ebon Knight and Signet Ring, were simply good ones.

I did, however, see the Ledbury mare Pucka Belle, the horse I think of next to O'Dell. One of a long line of point-to-pointers who have gone on to distinguish themselves in races under N.H. Rules, this beautiful daughter of Pucka Sahib, bred, like O'Dell, in

Ireland, and ridden invariably by her owner, Mr E. W. W. Bailey, had won sixteen point-to-points by the end of the 1936 season, when she reached the peak of her career as a hunter with a win in the National Hunt Chase. The following season she was third to Royal Mail and Cooleen in the Grand National.

Can it be mere coincidence that two other outstanding point-to-pointers of the thirties, Hopeful Hero and Duty Paid, were also bred in Ireland? I have particular occasion to remember the grey Hopeful Hero, because it was through him that I had my first experience of being welshed, when I was still a schoolboy. On the day this prolific point-to-point winner won the National Hunt Chase, in April, 1937, I had half-a-crown of my pocket money on him at 12–1 with a bookmaker at the Crawley & Horsham point-to-point, which in those days was held at Littleworth, Partridge Green. No doubt some bigger bets than this were struck with the same bookmaker, thus causing him to chalk up St George II as the winner. It wasn't until I saw the evening papers some time afterwards that I discovered that Hopeful Hero, in the capable hands of Mr W. L. ('Slotty') Dawes, had beaten St George II by a length. It was a lesson well learned. But perhaps that bookmaker, whose name I haven't forgotten, although prudence tells me that this isn't the place to reveal it, should be given some credit for showing prophetic insight, since it was St George II who won the National Hunt Chase the following year, when he was ridden by Bobbie Petre.

The West Kent mare, Duty Paid, who was brought over to England after being shown in hunter classes at the Dublin Horse Show of 1935 and was ridden in all her races by Harry Freeman-Jackson, appeared first on a racecourse in 1936, when she won all three of her races. But her best season was 1938, when she won five open nomination races, an adjacent hunts' race and the Skeynes Plate over three miles at the United Hunts' Meeting at Lingfield, where Capt. Freeman-Jackson had to ride on the girth after her saddle had slipped four fences from home. In four seasons, the last of them cut short by the war, Duty Paid ran in nineteen races, won fourteen of them and was third in the Cheltenham Foxhunters'; and had it not been for the cut hocks she sustained during the 1937 season and a stumble at the last fence when she was beaten by a short head in her first race of 1938, she would probably have been unbeaten in point-to-points.

In 1949 Harry Freeman-Jackson went to live permanently in Ireland, where he was Master of the Duhallow Hounds in County Cork from 1950 to 1968, and during that period he represented his new country in the three-day event at four Olympiads. It gives me particular pleasure to write these words about Duty Paid, because when I reminded him about the mare after he had won the Burghley Horse Trials for Ireland in 1963 on St Finbarr, his reply was: 'Good Lord, I didn't think anybody would remember Duty Paid, let alone the day that I won the Skeynes Plate at Lingfield on her.' Well, some of us do, and I have since been delighted to hear that the mare produced six foals after being put to stud and that Capt. Freeman-Jackson now owns a five-year-old grand-daughter of her's who is very much like her.

The outstanding rider in the South during the thirties was Ryan Price, who was to make such a name for himself as a trainer after the war. I thought then, and still think so in retrospect, that this fine horseman, who hunted mainly with Lord Leconfield's hounds in Surrey, would have been capable of winning on a cart-horse. And he had a personality to match his ability, presenting a handsome, debonair figure as he rode round the paddock before each race smoking the inevitable cigarette. He denies this now and says he never smoked in those days, but I have the picture so firmly imprinted on my mind that it will take more than this to erase it.

Ryan Price, who had his first winner in his early 'teens, rode many horses for many owners, and on one occasion he had five winners in an afternoon. Many of his wins were in farmers' races, on such horses as Arun Lad, Swan River, Hardham Gate, Harkaway II and Mrs E. A. S. Murray's Rufus III, a horse who would have looked quite at home in front of a cart. But the two best horses he rode were probably Sir John Leigh's pair, Goldfish III and Thistle Blue. Neither of these horses had the build of weight carriers, but both were thoroughly genuine performers. Little is known of the background of Goldfish, except that he was purchased in Ireland in 1931 and was twelve years old when Ryan Price won three open nominations on him in 1936; this was the year Capt. Price won the amateur riders' hurdle race at the West Norfolk Hunt Steeplechases at Fakenham on Tom Grantham's Jap. Thistle Blue, a rather temperamental little mare, was more difficult to ride than Goldfish and frequently took her fences by the roots, but she was the better of the two. In 1937 when Ryan Price won three open nomination races on her, she put up a great performance in the Gone Away Open Hunters' Chase at Lingfield, where Bobbie Petre was riding her, giving 5 lb. to March Brown IV and St George II and beating them both.

Among other good winners in the South during those years were two horses hunted with the Crawley & Horsham, Capt. G. Hornung's Gaickster and Eric Covell's Cavalcade II. Another was Philip Kindersley's Michael, from the Whaddon Chase. Michael, whose owner is now Joint-Master with his son, Gay, of the Mid-Surrey Farmers' Draghounds, was a really splendid animal. In a career stretching from 1932 to 1939, this big bay gelding by St David won twenty-two races, including the lightweight race at the Whaddon Chase three years running. He completed the course in the Liverpool Foxhunters' of 1936 and 1937 and was fourth in this race in 1935; and in 1934, when Mr Kindersley took him over to Ireland, he was second in the Ward Union Cup at Fairyhouse.

Castle Gris, a tubed horse from the Old Surrey and Burstow, won twenty-seven races for Kenneth Urquhart, who became a Master of Harriers in Ireland after the war; and another horse to win over twenty races was Mr Snip, who stood only 15.3 hands high and was bred by his owner, Mr C. T. Nixon, in North Devon, from his Royal Sovereign mare, Queenie, whose mother T'Ould Kitty, twice won the Hunt Cup at the Stevenstone. This was a race Mr Nixon won with three generations of the same breed. Mr Snip, the outstanding banking horse at the West Country meetings, was ridden in all his races by Mr F. W. B. Smyth, whose nine winners in 1933 were only surpassed by Major Rushton's thirteen.

For many years, the point-to-point meetings of Devon and Cornwall were distinguished from those in other areas by providing opportunities for horses to run over banks and/or fly fences, and some of the West Country horses were equally proficient over both types of obstacle. One such was Duhallow Queen, owned by Mr Reginald Paltridge, a former Master of the East Cornwall. This grand-daughter of the famous Craganour (the disqualified Derby winner of 1919) came over to England from Ireland in 1934 as a four-year-old and won five races over banks in her first two seasons. In her next, 1936, she won four races over banks and the open nomination race at Mr Spooner's Harriers over fly fences. The following year she again won the nomination race at Mr Spooner's, beat that good horse Charlie Chaplin II in the ladies' race at the South Devon & Haldon Harriers, and won two races over banks in Cornwall; and in 1938 she won four more races over banks.

One of the most consistent performers in Essex, in both men's and ladies' races, Lt. Col. J. Dalton-White's Charlie Chaplin II was sixteen years old when he finally retired after recording his twentieth win, in the adjacent hunts' ladies' race at the Essex Farmers' in April 1938, when he was ridden by Col. Dalton-White's daughter Valerie. A brown gelding by Darigal out of a mare by Simon the Jester, Charlie Chaplin II was acquired as a six-year-old for £27 10s.

A bargain buy? I should say so. But Sawfish was an even bigger one. The son of a Derby winner (Spion Kop), Sawfish was bought for a fiver by Mr A. G. Anderson, a Herefordshire farmer, at an auction near Hereford in the autumn of 1937; and it appears that his new owner thought so little of him that he tried to sell him for a 10s. profit, without success, and was then given 10s. for luck by the horse's former owner. After being hunted during the winter with the South Herefordshire & Ross Harriers, Sawfish ran in the farmers' race at his local meeting ridden by Geoffrey Scudamore (the father of Michael, who became a professional jockey and now trains at Hoar Whithy, near Hereford). Sawfish won that race easily, and also his next two. He was then sold to Mr W. R. Tate, whose son Martin, himself a distinguished point-to-point rider, now trains at Chaddesley Corbett, where the Dudley Cup is run today. Mr Scudamore having broken his collar-bone, Sawfish was ridden in his last two races of 1938 by Geoffrey Hutsby, who saw to it that this six-year-old reject from a professional racing stable finished the season unbeaten. Before being put down the first year after the war, when he went lame behind, Sawfish won eight hunter chases, three of them in a week.

If one excludes Harry and Frank Atherton Brown, who virtually confined themselves to N.H. racing, I suppose the two most famous brothers riding in point-to-points during the thirties were Thurston and 'Ruby' Holland-Martin. Ruby, the younger of the two, I recall as a particularly elegant horseman who used to ride in a monocle; and when he gave up steeplechasing, he turned his attention to international show jumping with equal success. In 1935, when Ruby had ten wins with three horses, Grasshopper II, Cutty and Cheerful Marcus, the first two being bred by him from the same mare, Nancy Joycey (by Duke of Westminster), he was third on Grasshopper in the Liverpool Foxhunters' and the three hunter chases he won on the lop-eared Cheerful Marcus included the United Hunts' Cup at Cheltenham. The same year, both brothers were winners at the New College & Magdalen point-to-point and Thurston was runner-up in the National Hunt Chase on Evasio Mon and second to his brother in a hunter chase at Newbury.

Alas, Harry and Frank Atherton Brown have now both passed on. Thurston Holland-Martin died of a heart attack whilst out shooting in 1968; and Ruby was crippled in the hunting field in 1952. But at least the story of the Holland-Martin family continues in the person of Thurston and Ruby's nephew Tim, one of the leading point-to-point riders of the present day.

In Yorkshire, of course, Major Cunard, who had his first ride in a race when he was a schoolboy at Eton in 1928, and whose great grand-father on his mother's side was a Joint-Master of the York & Ainsty, was already going strong, although it wasn't until after the war that this long lean greyhound of the North had his best years. Other highly successful riders in this area during the thirties were Bobby Renton (the Ripon trainer), W. Carr (a well-known flat-race trainer), the formidable W. H. ('Gunner') Wellburn, Adrian Scrope (who came to Yorkshire from a sheep ranch in Australia), P. C. Oldfield, Capt. R. M. Fanshawe, H. Megginson and Lord Grimthorpe.

And it was Lord Grimthorpe, a man beloved by the local farmers, and whom I remember after the war standing on the hill at Whitwell surveying the Middleton course like an eagle, who gave his name to the race which is now acknowledged as the point-to-point Grand National.

The first Middleton point-to-point was held near Howsham in 1922, and it was not until 1929 that it moved to its present site at Whitwell-on-the-Hill, near Malton. Three years later, Lord Grimthorpe gave his cup for the open event, which was then run over three and a half miles (today's distance is four and a half); and the first person to win it was Lord Grimthorpe on First Venture, a horse with a fairy-tale history. I am now going to let

Harold Charlton, who rode in the farmers' race at the first Middleton point-to-point, take up the story:

> I went with my friend Eric Parke to Malton Horse Sales, which were held monthly in those days, he taking a pony to sell which made 12 guineas. In the sale was a four-year-old owned by his father's next-door neighbour, Philip Burnett, who had bred him by his own stallion, Sir Harry. This horse was First Venture, an animal with shocking bad hocks who had been fired on one of them. Eric bought him for 17 guineas, and although he had already been broken he turned out to be a rare handful (could he buck!). So I took him and hunted him that season, and the next season Eric rode him in the farmers' race, his first ride, and finished third. After that, First Venture won seven races, including five open events, without being beaten. He was then sold to Lord Grimthorpe, for whom he won numerous point-to-points and hunter chases before breaking down badly on his final gallop for the Liverpool Foxhunters'. Sir Harry was also the sire of Macmoffat, runner-up in the last two pre-war Grand Nationals. First Venture and More Honour were the two best horses I have seen win the Grimthorpe Cup.

Another fine winner of the Grimthorpe Cup in the thirties was Little Tommy Tucker, the last horse that Adrian Scrope won on before a crashing fall in the Heart of all England at Hexham ended his racing career. Although this horse used to chance his fences, he had so gentle a temperament that he was regularly hunted, in his pre-Grimthorpe Cup days, by two young teenagers, the children of his original owner, Dr H. Wynne-Davies, of Thirsk, for whom he won a number of point-to-points, including one in which he was ridden by his owner's fifteen-year-old son, a Rugby schoolboy who was having his first ride in a race. That was in 1935, the year before Little Tommy Tucker passed into the hands of Mr J. Stephenson, of Bridlington. It was whilst he was in Mr Stephenson's ownership that he won the Grimthorpe Cup, in 1936.

Further North the outstanding riders were Major Ian Straker (whose two sons, John and Clive, were to continue the good work after the war); John Eustace Smith, who became a first-class amateur under N.H. Rules after the war and was tragically killed in a bad fall at Catterick Bridge in 1951; Ted Green, an extremely tough rider who came from an old Northumbrian farming family, the Greens of Lucker; Eustace Renwick; Reg. Tweedie, who became the owner of that great horse Freddie in the post-war years; and John Marshall, who had what was perhaps the best point-to-pointer in the Border Country in those days. This was Speckled Spear, a horse who was not considered fast enough for N.H. racing but won the William Bell Gold Cup at the Tynedale twice in three years (he was second on the other occasion) and many other good point-to-point races.

And there was also Calverley Bewicke, who was to become one of the leading N.H. trainers in the post-war years and saddle a winner of the Cheltenham Gold Cup. Major Bewicke, as he now is, had his first ride in a race during his last Easter Holidays from Eton; and between 1933 and 1938 he rode twenty-four point-to-point winners and won the Territorial Army Cup at the Grand Military Meeting at Sandown on Noble Artist. His best point-to-pointer was Jugged Hare, a horse on whom his father won four races before him. Calverley Bewicke's ten wins on Jugged Hare embraced two Tynedale Gold Cups, and if he had been a little older he would probably have won hunter chases on him as well. As it was, Jugged Hare's appearances were restricted to point-to-points.

Two noted performers in the Eastern Counties were Mrs J. A. Keith's home-bred Hill Call, by London Cry out of a mare by Manxman; and Mr Walter Wales's King High, by Kingsborough out of a mare by Highlander. Hill Call was hunted with the West Norfolk, a pack which has produced a prodigious number of winners over the years, and King High with the Henham Harriers.

Mr Wales, whose fawn and white checks are still a familiar sight on the racecourses of East Anglia, though the rides have now been taken over by his elder son David, won twenty-six races on King High, who made twenty-eight winning appearances in thirty-three starts. Hill Call's record was not quite so spectacular, but then her career was shorter, as she didn't start it until two years before the war. She won five races in six appearances in her first season and fourteen altogether. Many years later the Keiths were to own one just as good – if not even better – in Mr Shanks; and

Walter Wales was to go close to winning the Cheltenham Fox-hunters' on his grand mare Salvage when past the age of fifty.

I would like to end this chapter with two stories told me by that colourful character Len Coville, who won many races on his good horse Al Capone in the thirties. The first concerns his old friend and rival, Stanley White, doyen of the Hertfordshire Hunt. Stanley was very anxious to win the open race at his local meeting on a good horse of his called Sailor Boy. Len Coville was riding a useful young horse for Sidney Banks, and this horse was going so well that after about a mile, says Mr Coville, 'I was offered the Cup, after two miles the stake, and at two and a half miles I could name my present.' At three miles, however, Basil Comerford, came up from behind and did them both.

The second story is set at Cottenham, where, on a very wet day, Len Coville was riding a young horse that he couldn't hold one side of, owing to the slippery reins. So, needing something to go in front of him, he turned to Jack Nichols, who was just behind him, and shouted to him to come on, for God's sake. Jack, being an habitual stutterer, it took him most of the race to say that his horse was incapable of coming on; although, come on, in the end it did, to such an extent that it won the race.

7

Ladies' Races in the Thirties

In the late twenties and early thirties, Miss Sylvia Spooner, the leading lady rider in England, won over thirty races, some of them against the men before the rule was altered. And if anyone tells me that this is nothing in comparison with the total of over 100 successes achieved in Ireland over roughly the same period by Mrs Masters, the Master of the Tipperary, I will agree. But Ireland has always been a law unto itself, because there are virtually no restrictions put upon women riders in that country and it is quite possible for them to have as many as three or four rides at a single meeting.

Ladies' races in England before the war were largely open races and, since most women could not hope to get more than half a dozen rides in a season, to ride anything over four winners was a fairly considerable achievement.

Two of the most famous lady riders in England were, in fact, Irishwomen, Mrs Evadne Bell and her daughter Diana, who hunted with the South & West Wilts and the Blackmore Vale. Mrs Bell was the wife of Isaac Bell, who hunted the Kilkenny hounds from 1908 to 1921 and was later Master of the South & West Wilts for nine seasons. The Bells' most prolific winner was Rattles, who was acquired from his breeder in Ireland as a five-year-old and had twenty wins, seven seconds and a third to his credit in thirty-two appearances before he retired after breaking down at the Cotswold in 1935. Mrs Bell won many races on Rattles riding side-saddle; and Diana, who was the leading lady rider of the season on three occasions between 1933 and 1939, and never rode fewer than four winners in a season during that period, had five of her six successes in 1933 on this horse, who, with Peter Payne-Gallwey in the saddle, was the first winner of the Prince of Wales Cup at the South & West Wilts.

Other notable performers owned by the Bells were Fils de Herod, who was also bought from his breeder in Ireland, and two horses bred by Mrs Bell herself, Iliad II and that charming mare Margery Daw III, by Jackdaw of Rheims. Margery Daw made her début in the year that Rattles retired. She had her first success in the ladies' open race at the Royal Air Force, Middlesex Yeomanry and 7th Hussars point-to-point at Kimble that season, and won four races in 1936, three in 1937 and four of the five races she started in in 1938.

Another rider with a fine record was the Hon. Mrs Edward Greenall (the former Joyce Laycock), who later became Lady Daresbury and died in 1966. Mrs Greenall was leading lady rider in 1934 and again in 1938; and in 1935 she was the joint leading lady with Diana Bell, Miss B. de Winton and Joyce Seaton (now Mrs Newland). Of the last-named, Len Coville says: 'I always thought her the best lady rider I ever saw. She rode all sorts well. I called her the Gerry Wilson of the ladies, and of course the two came from the same village.'

Mrs Greenall won many races on Silicon and Mimosa II, two of the horses she hunted in Leicestershire with the Belvoir. Lord Daresbury, who has been Master and Huntsman of the Limerick Foxhounds since 1947, has described Silicon to me as 'a great stayer but not too good a jumper' (this horse gave his former owner, Lady Harrington, a very nasty fall at the last fence in a race at the Blankney); but of Mimosa II, a mare bought for £400 from a dealer in Leamington, he writes: 'She was the best of jumpers and learned the art from leading three-year-olds over hurdles.' But she was apt to turn doggy when headed and could never be touched with the whip, or even shown it. The best horse the Greenalls had was the one who taught Joyce Greenall to ride, Torchlight Tattoo, 'a mean, tall horse by Spion Kop bought from Gerald Balding before he became an international polo player and set up as a public trainer.' A great hunter, Torchlight Tattoo broke his neck, and his rider's pelvis, when James Seely, of Green Carnation fame, was hunting him with the South Notts to qualify him for ladies' races.

One of the best ladies' horses of the period was Miss de Winton's Just Jane, who was hunted by her owner with the Cotswold in Gloucestershire. Before she went to stud, after the 1938 season, this little mare by Furore won twenty-one races, fourteen of them in succession; and at one time or another she beat most of the best ladies' horses in her area.

Among Just Jane's victims was Miss M. J. Parham's Another Result, from the South & West Wilts. This horse, who didn't appear on a course until he was six, once cleared an 8 ft. bullfinch which had a 6 ft. drop into a tarmac lane on the landing side. That was before Miss Parham acquired him, when he was being schooled as a five-year-old by his former owner, Mr A. G. Cowley, who used to have a number of good horses in Surrey. After Miss Parham bought him, Another Result won three races for her in 1936, beating Margery Daw III and Iliad II in two of them, and four in each of the next three seasons. Miss Parham was the leading lady rider in 1939, with seven wins, her other three being on a new horse, Fair Clune, who was still running in point-to-points after the war.

Seven wins in ladies' races in one season was mighty good going. In fact, I believe it was a record in those days. But, if so, it was shared with Miss A. M. Everitt, who was later to become Mrs Sidney Parker. In 1937, Miss Everitt won four races on her Mr Cinders III and three on Tellnell, who were hunted, respectively, with the North Warwickshire and the South Atherstone.

On Mr Cinders, a horse bred in Shropshire and obtained from Mr W. R. B. Dodgson, the Secretary of the North Warwickshire, Miss Everitt had a particularly frightening experience. It occurred in 1936, just after she had recovered from a broken jaw sustained in the Grafton Hunter Trials. Mr Cinders, a free-running horse who liked nothing better than to lead from start to finish, was favourite for the ladies' race at the South Staffordshire when the bridle broke as he rounded the first bend. With the bit out of his mouth, and his rider a helpless passenger, he went tearing on until he came to the last bend four fences out. Here there was a very sharp turn and Miss Everitt was quite unable to steer him round it. Fortunately, she managed to pull him up before any damage was done. In his other two races that season, Mr Cinders made all the running and won easily.

Few horses were kept busier in ladies' races during the thirties than Great Hope, the rather plain-looking chestnut gelding by Bachelor's Hope owned by Miss R. J. Crossman, of Bishop's Stortford, and hunted with the Essex hounds. Plain, Great Hope may have been, but he was a horse of no mean ability; and he would doubtless have won many more races if Miss Crossman had not broken her leg during the 1935 season and had a crashing fall at a ditch on the old New Forest course at Christchurch the following season. During those two seasons, when he was ridden by some half a dozen different riders, Great Hope ran in twenty races and won seven of them, with Miss Crossman up on four occasions.

One of Great Hope's chief rivals in Essex was Charlie Chaplin II, against whom he came up three times in 1936, being beaten by him at the Enfield Chace, reversing the placings at the Essex & Suffolk, and again finishing in front of him at the East Essex, where the two ran in the open nomination race and Great Hope was third to Mr W. H. Chaplin's Successful Penalty, one of the best farmers' horses in the area. In 1937, when she rode five winners and was equal second with Diana Bell to Miss Everitt in the leading lady riders' stakes. Valerie Dalton-White won three races on Charlie Chaplin II and two on his stable companion Laureate, a horse who had won several races for Miss Evelyn Bothway in East Anglia in previous seasons.

To get some idea of how difficult it was to accumulate winning rides in ladies' races in Britain during the thirties, we need look no further than the 1933 season, when the redoubtable Mrs Masters rode ten winners in Ireland. The nearest to this in England was Diana Bell, with six winners; and only three riders, Mrs W. L. Dawes in Kent, Miss B. W. Barrett in Berkshire and Wiltshire, and Mrs F. Broome with the Hampshire-hunted Volplane, rode as many as three winners. In the North, there was even less chance, because very few ladies' races were held there. The most successful riders in that area were Miss Annette Ussher, Miss Mallis Wilson, Miss E. K. Hesketh and Miss E. M. Paterson; but between 1933 and 1938, only the last-named managed to ride three winners in a single season, and these were in Derbyshire and Cheshire.

I think Mrs Dawes undoubtedly deserves the accolade south of the Thames, though a word must be put in for Mrs Dorothy Merckel, who married Derek Evatt in December 1946 and had her last ride in a race when she was over fifty. This was in April 1959, when she was second on Jack O'Donoghue's Duo in the adjacent hunts' ladies' race at the Chiddingfold & Leconfield. Mrs Evatt, who won the ladies' race at the Surrey Union five times and the corresponding event at the Old Surrey & Burstow three times, rode about twenty-five winners, post-war and pre-war. She was seldom unplaced and had several bad falls; and on one occasion I recall her being carried off on a stretcher at a meeting where her husband was giving the running commentary.

Another rider who was going strong pre-war and post-war was Miss Kit Tatham-Warter, who might be described as a late starter, since it was not until she was twenty-two that she had her first ride in a race, in Jersey, over banks. That was in 1932, when the Jersey Drag Hunt held their first point-to-point fixture and Miss Tatham-Warter rode in four races, riding two winners, a second and a third. Her mother then bought her a horse called Camrose Pride, who had been hunted in Co. Cork and placed at Punchestown. Today Kit Tatham-Warter is a successful trainer of Event horses, and she says of Camrose Pride that he taught her all she knows about the art of remaining in the plate, and that when he didn't get rid of his jockey he was always placed. At that time she was living in Dorset and therefore constantly coming up against Diana Bell, of whom she writes: 'Although very young, she was by far the best jockey of our sex and an excellent judge of pace; the best I could do was to follow her home day after day. But, whilst doing so, I was able to acquire a great deal of knowledge about pace and judgement in race-riding.' And she adds that she won on Camrose Pride on the only two occasions when Diana Bell was absent from the field.

In 1934 Kit Tatham-Warter went to ride the horses of Sir Warden Chilcott in Hampshire. One of the horses she won on for him was Wavelet, who took such a firm hold on the gallops that he was guaranteed to get anyone fit. But he was a sweet ride in a race for a rider who knew his ways, and at the Hambledon in 1935 he won two races in an afternoon. Kit Tatham-Warter's best season was 1939, when she acquired a useful horse of her own in Glen Alder II. That season she won more races than Diana Bell and her total of five winners was exceeded only by Miss Parham. There are some riders – although not all that many – who will get up on anything they are offered, and Kit Tatham-Warter was of this select number. Not even a fractured skull could keep this courageous rider out of the saddle for long.

Some ladies showed considerable enterprise. One such was the Hon. Ulrica Thynne, who is now the wife of Lt. Col. G. A.

Murray Smith, Joint Master of the Fernie. In 1934 this lady stepped out of an aeroplane on the old Chiddingfold course at Knowle, Cranleigh, just in time to ride a horse called Greenwell's Glory in the ladies' race. I remember the incident most vividly, because at that time I was living in Cranleigh and knew every blade of grass on the course. It was one of those old-fashioned courses where the horses soon disappeared into the distance and one waited interminably for them to reappear over the last few fences. It was a great moment when Greenwell's Glory hove into sight on the horizon, and a greater one still for the schoolboy who had his pocket money on him when he came home at odds of 8–1.

8

The Last Years Before the War

In the early thirties, Major Rushton and Mr E. W. W. Bailey all but monopolised the leading riders' positions; but this monopoly was broken in 1935, although Major Rushton's Signet Ring and Mr Bailey's Pucka Belle were still the leading horses of that season, along with Miss de Winton's Just Jane, who also had six wins. The leading rider, for the first time, was Gresham Wood, whose total of thirteen winners included three wins in hunter chases and a treble at the Cotswold, where he finished second in the members' race on his only other mount. Mr Bailey was his nearest rival, with twelve winners, including two hunter-chase wins on his Little Briton and a win on Pucka Belle in the open nomination race at a *bona fide* military meeting at Windmillhill; and then came Kenneth Urquhart, who pulled off doubles in three different counties and whose eleven successes included three on Rufus, a chestnut gelding by Capt. Ross who won every race he ran in (four) that season. This horse was owned by Tom Gifford, the father of Josh and Macer. 'Ruby' Holland-Martin had ten winners, the same as Capt. W. G. Carr, who achieved the feat of riding four of the five winners at the Henham Harriers; and there were nine winners that season for Guy Cunard.

Little Tommy Tucker won the open nomination race at the York & Ainsty for the third year running. Major Rushton won the Heygate Gold Cup at the North Hereford on O'Dell. Pucka Belle won her second Jim Morgan Cup at the South Herefordshire & Ross Harriers and beat O'Dell by half a length in the Dudley Cup. And one of the best ladies' races of the season was at the Wilton, where there were eight starters from amongst fifteen entries, including several top-class performers. But there was some atrocious luck for two of them. Diana Bell lost a leather at the half-way stage on Margery Daw III but carried on until the mare fell two out; and Mrs Greenall was concussed when Silicon came down.

The winner was Miss de Winton on Just Jane, who beat Joyce Seaton on Ballenvulla.

Mr E. W. W. Bailey and Ruby Holland-Martin shared the chief riding honours of 1936, with eleven winners apiece, two more than 'Slotty' Dawes, Thurston Holland-Martin, Mr W. Carr in the North, and Capt. H. C. Phillips, of the 17th Field Brigade, who won two races in two days on Bright Gem at the February military meeting at Tweseldown, two more on Herbert Lumsden's More Magic there and a fifth on the same owner's Silver Gill, on whom he also won a hunter chase at Wincanton. Five of Capt. Phillips's successes were on his own horses, Bright Gem accounting for four of them and Gold Cup winning the R.A. steeplechase at the Old Surrey & Burstow *bona fide* meeting for him.

But the most prolific winners of that season were Hopeful Hero, who won seven races, and Surgeon Major, on whom Tom Brake (who was to distinguish himself after the war in the show-jumping field) won the open nomination races at the Cattistock, the West Somerset & Quantock and the Taunton Vale, and the farmers' races at the Blackmore Vale, the Mendip Farmers and the South & West Wilts.

Down in Cornwall, the Four Burrow had a new course over fifteen banks, all of them reputed to be over 5 ft. high; and it was a West Country horse, Mr R. Glanvile's Ballykeating, ridden by Capt. J. P. A. Graham, who dead-heated with the great O'Dell in the Dudley Cup. This was O'Dell's thirty-eighth win and Ballykeating was unbeaten that season.

A record crowd of 20,000 (Can this really be true? If so it must make some present-day Clerks of the Course turn green with envy) was reported at the Barlow meeting, near Chesterfield; the Greenjacket Club had ninety-one runners for the five races at their Hampshire fixture; and the point-to-point correspondent of *The Field* was writing: 'I do not think the average point-to-point committee have any conception of the very real interest the general public are taking in these meetings today . . .' But here's what the same writer had to say of what was presumably an un-average meeting, that of the South Oxfordshire, which in those days was held at Little Milton :

> I can say unhesitatingly that I like this meeting. It is not a fashionable one, neither are the committee blest with a

> perfect course. But a thoroughly sporting atmosphere prevails, and I have a genuine admiration for the manner in which those responsible make the very most of what they have . . . Quite a few point-to-point programmes show a map of the course, but the South Oxfordshire went one better and gave a brief description of the conformation of each fence as well.

In Dorset, the Portman went so far as to print on their racecard a warning to the effect that no one who used 'foreign' oats and hay would be welcome to hunt with the Portman hounds, and all hunting folk were urged to 'feed their horses on oats and hay grown within the Hunt, and to bed their horses on straw grown by their own farmers'. If they did this today, no doubt they would be prosecuted by the Race Relations Board!

After Dick Hunt had won the open nomination race at the Mendip Farmers on Red Knight II, the tote paid out £20 to a 2s. stake. Two years later, Red Knight II was to finish second in the National Hunt Handicap Chase at Cheltenham and run sixth behind Battleship in the Grand National. The runner-up to Red Knight at the Mendip Farmers, and no doubt the favourite, was Diana Bell's Iliad II with Tom Brake up.

In the holding going at the South Herefordshire & Ross Harriers, where there were a record number of fallers, Mr E. W. W. Bailey won the Jim Morgan Cup for the third year running, this time on Vizmah, a brown gelding by The Vizier with a grey mane and tail. A certain Frank Weldon, who was to achieve post-war fame as a member of our winning three-day event team in the Olympic Games at Stockholm when he took the individual bronze medal on Kilbarry, won three races on his Golden Norris. And at the West Norfolk there was a treble for Major Eldred Wilson, one of today's point-to-point personalities and the present Hon. Secretary of that meeting. Eldred Wilson won both the lightweight race and the open race on Lt. Col. Oliver Birkbeck's Golden Sprig and then finished alone on his own Hardy Annual in the military race.

At the Pegasus Club (Bar) point-to-point at Kimble there were two dead-heats, the first in the open nominations race, between Mr R. J. Norbury's Red Hot and Mr J. S. R. Edmunds's Chatty, both ridden by their owners; and the second in the farmers' race, where two of the most consistent winners in the area, Mr P.

Franklin's Cushendun and Mr C. B. Harper's Stolen Prince, each carrying 14 lb. extra, could not be separated.

Edward Paget, a most distinguished amateur who had finished second in the Grand National of 1932 on Egremont, won the lightweight race for the Jack Russell Cup at the Stock Exchange point-to-point at Billericay on Silver Lizzie; and Mr G. H. Sheppard, the present Clerk of the Course at Stratford, finished third in this race and second in the heavyweight race.

Alec Marsh, now a Starter under N.H. Rules, brought off a notable double, winning the Cheltenham Foxhunters' on Herode Bridge (the Dudley Cup winner of 1933) and the Liverpool Foxhunters' on Don Bradman. The latter was probably the best hunter chaser of that period, though I don't think this one-time show hunter, who dead-heated with Delaneige in the Grand Sefton of 1937 and finished sixth in the Grand National after falling and being remounted, ever ran in point-to-points.

Objections galore followed the Hon. Lavinia Strutt's win on Little Tommy Tucker in the ladies' open race at the Sinnington & Derwent. But the Stewards had their own idea of how to deal with them. They disqualified the runner-up for failing to draw the correct weight and over-ruled the others. Which reminds me of a dialogue I heard outside the weighing tent at a meeting after the war.

1st Steward: 'I say, that beastly fellow ——— has objected.'

2nd Steward: 'Has he, by God! Then we'll over-rule it.'

Gresham Wood was again the leading rider in 1937, with seven winners, but this time he had to share the title with Capt. J. P. A. Graham, of the Oxford & Bucks Light Infantry, five of whose seven wins were on his own horses; and Miss Everitt, of course, had as many winners in ladies' races, a remarkable achievement with her fewer opportunities. Mr E. W. W. Bailey, Mr E. Hocking in the West Country, Ruby Holland-Martin, Mr E. G. Langford, Capt. A. G. Martyr and Major J. A. L Schreiber all rode six winners.

This was the year that Hopeful Hero won the National Hunt Chase and O'Dell had his first win in the Liverpool Foxhunters'. It was not O'Dell, however, but Ragman II who was Major Rushton's most prolific winner in 1937. With this horse, who was bred by a tenant farmer in Worcestershire from a half-bred mare mated with the premium stallion Commodore, Major Rushton won five races, in four of which Ragman was ridden by Jack Fowler, a Worcestershire farmer who was to have two post-war successes in the Dudley Cup. The only other horses to win five races that season were Hill Call (on whom Mrs Donald Steward won four ladies' races in East Anglia), Just Jane (on whom Gresham Wood won one race and Miss de Winton four), and Mr L. Whiteman's well-bred Titterstone from the Ludlow. This eight-year-old chestnut gelding, who didn't have a saddle on his back until he was six years old and won two races as a seven-year-old in his first season, traced back to Sceptre on his sire's side and was a grandson of Challacombe, the 1905 Leger winner, on his dam's side.

The outstanding military combination were W. Scott-Plummer and his March Brown IV, whose four successes included the United Hunts' Cup at Cheltenham, and two races at Sandown, the Grand Military Hunters' Chase and the R.A. Gold Cup. It seems likely that if Mr Scott-Plummer had run March Brown IV in the Grand Military Gold Cup instead of waiting for the Grand Military Hunters' Chase the next day, he would have prevented Major Roddick from recording his first success in the race on Buck Willow.

Capt. A. G. Martyr, of the Royal Scots Greys, had a highly successful season on his eight-year-old Ablington, a horse bred by Capt. Wickham-Boynton, M.F.H., and purchased from 'Gunner' Wellburn in Yorkshire. Ablington's four successes in 1937 included a hunters' race at Tweseldown and the Old Etonian Association Race, which at that time was held at the V.W.H. (Earl Bathurst's) at Siddington.

Ballykeating continued his winning vein, taking the open nomination races at the V.W.H., the Berkeley and the Mendip Farmers; and one horse who won all three of the races he started in (two open nomination races and a military hunters' chase at Windmillhill) was Mr F. H. G. Higgins's Camrose, a bay gelding by Transcendent who was bought as a replacement for another good point-to-pointer, Hiram Borlace. At Tidworth, Camrose started at odds of 20–1 and saw off such accomplished performers as More Magic and Ablington.

Mr and Mrs Dawes had a good season in Kent with Me Too, who was then in his first season of point-to-point racing and won three races with Mrs Dawes up and the Lloyd's Race at the Stock Exchange meeting with 'Slotty' Dawes in the saddle. Tom Brake won four more races with Surgeon Major in the West; and in the same area, Mr T. Pickard's Main Doctor, from the Tetcott, opened his winning account at the Fowey Harriers on Bodmin Racecourse and won four races within a fortnight.

Ryan Price, who rode five winners, had a double at the Hampshire, winning the open nomination race on Thistle Blue and the farmers' race on Mr R. Pitt's Arun Lad, a dour stayer who took a lot of beating in the mud; but his most spectacular ride, and one that says much for his horsemanship, was on Thistle Blue at the Vine. After Sir John Leigh's little mare had fallen in the open nomination race, and been remounted, she was the best part of a mile behind the field. But even a 10 lb. penalty didn't stop her making up the lost ground so fast that she passed one horse after another and was only beaten four lengths by a good horse from the Worcestershire, Mr W. R. Tate's Vestige.

Which brings me to the Dudley Cup of 1937. This was won, in a close finish, by Mrs Geoffrey Freer's Christopher Bean, thirty years before Mrs Freer won her second Dudley Cup with Tailorman. The rider of Christopher Bean was Geoffrey Shakerley, a highly promising young amateur who won several races under Rules riding against the top professionals and makes an intriguing first appearance in Frank Atherton Brown's book as a 'determined young character, in rather a loud check coat and very smart jodhpurs'.

In 1938, O'Dell won the Liverpool Foxhunters' again, Mark Roddick won the Grand Military Gold Cup at Sandown on Kilstar, Mr E. W. W. Bailey won the Cheltenham Foxhunters' on Winter Knight, and a new regulation crept into the point-to-point rules. It read: 'No horse shall be eligible to be entered or run in a point-to-point steeplechase, which since November 1st of the current hunting season has run in any race under National Hunt Rules except the National Hunt Steeplechase and steeplechases confined to horses certified by a Master of Hounds to have been hunted.' Today this regulation has been expanded to include horses which have won any non-hunter race during the current season, including the National Hunt Chase, which although frequently contested by hunters is not a race confined to them.

The leading rider of 1938 was Harry Freeman-Jackson, who rode twelve winners and finished one up on Guy Cunard. Capt. Freeman-Jackson had seven wins on Duty Paid and the rest on five other horses, none of them his own. Guy Cunard, still only a subaltern in the 4/7th Dragoon Guards, but already getting about the country a bit, won as far North as Cornhill-on-Tweed and as far South as Tweseldown, with four successes on his own horses (including two in two days on his More Cash at the Tweseldown military meeting) and seven on other people's. His most consistent winner was Mr A. W. Greenwood's Lady Billing, on whom he won the maiden race at the Badsworth, the members' race at the Rockwood Harriers and the open nomination races at the Bramham Moor and the Craven Harriers; and on Lt. Col. H. E. Joicey's Venturesome Knight, which I believe he considers the best horse he has ever ridden, he had a single success in the members' heavy-weight race at the Border Hunts'. This horse finished fifth in the Grand National two seasons later with a broken blood vessel, but that time it was not Guy Cunard who was riding him.

Stolen Prince, with seven wins (he was also second four times), was the joint-leading horse of 1938 with Duty Paid. Philip Kindersley's Michael won six races; and so did Jack of the Vale, who was hunted by his owner, Mr I. K. ('Kim') Muir with the Belvoir and the Cottesmore. This chestnut gelding by Prester John had formerly been in training with Reg. Hobbs and was bought for £60 after dead-heating in a selling hurdle at Buckfastleigh, but he was no good steeplechasing because he wouldn't jump ditches. Hunting soon cured him of that, however. Kim Muir, then a subaltern in the 10th Hussars, was killed in the war and his name is now commemorated in the title of a famous amateur riders' race at Cheltenham.

Mr and Mrs Dawes had another good season south of the Thames with Me Too, Irish Silver and Youngtown and are entitled to be regarded as the leading owners of 1938 with their eleven successes, which included the United Hunts' Plate over two miles at Lingfield won by Youngtown with Slotty Dawes up. And one race I particularly remember, for a curious reason, was the 4th Queen's Own Hussars' race at Tweseldown in April, won by Major J. L. Powell on Mr (later Lt. Col.) George Kennard's Notice Board. The runner-up was the same owner's Bayleaf III, who had started a hot favourite and was beaten a distance with his owner up. When the unfortunate Mr Kennard came in he was greeted with a storm of boos. It was the first time that I had heard booing at a military meeting.

The most consistently successful performer in military races that

Harry Dufosee on his Royal Wilts at the South & West Wilts in 1926

The adjacent hunts' ladies' race at the Wylye Valley in 1928 – Miss Helen Cross on Gossiping George leads Lady Jean Douglas-Hamilton riding side-saddle on Cavalier

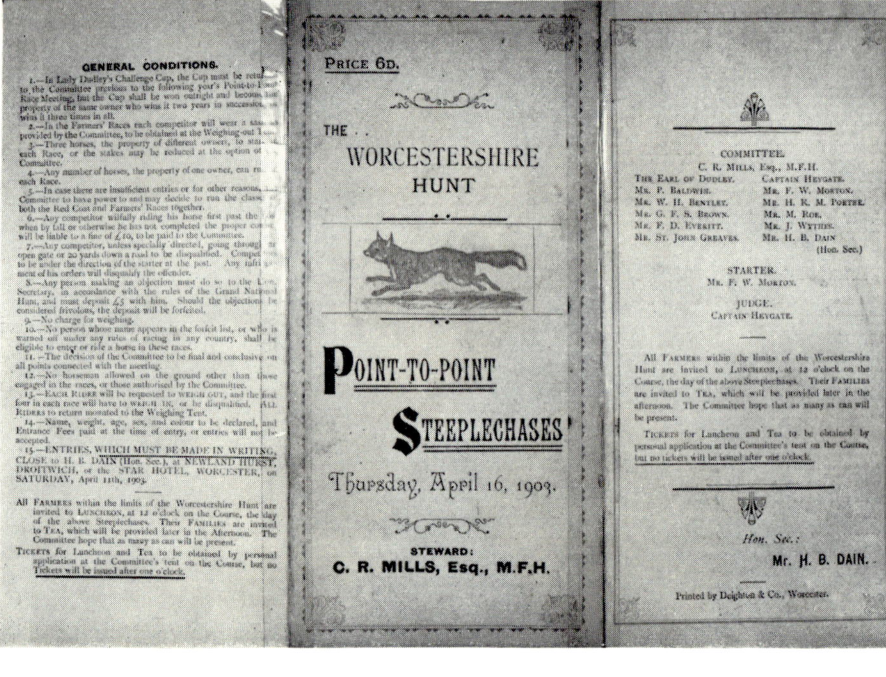

GENERAL CONDITIONS.

1.—In Lady Dudley's Challenge Cup, the Cup must be retu[illegible] to the Committee previous to the following year's Point-to-Poi[illegible] Race Meeting, but the Cup shall be won outright and becom[illegible] property of the same owner who wins it two years in successio[illegible] wins it three times in all.

2.—In the Farmers' Races each competitor will wear a sa[illegible] provided by the Committee, to be obtained at the Weighing-out T[illegible]

3.—Three horses, the property of different owners, to sta[illegible] each Race, or the stakes may be reduced at the option of [illegible] Committee.

4.—Any number of horses, the property of one owner, can r[illegible] each Race.

5.—In case there are insufficient entries or for other reasons, [illegible] Committee to have power to and may decide to run the classe[illegible] both the Red Coat and Farmers' Races together.

6.—Any competitor wilfully riding his horse first past the [illegible] when by fall or otherwise he has not completed the proper co[illegible] will be liable to a fine of £10, to be paid to the Committee.

7.—Any competitor, unless specially directed, going throug[illegible] open gate or 20 yards down a road to be disqualified. Compet[illegible] to be under the direction of the starter at the post. Any infri[illegible] ment of his orders will disqualify the offender.

8.—Any person making an objection must do so to the H[illegible] Secretary, in accordance with the rules of the Grand National Hunt, and must deposit £5 with him. Should the objection be considered frivolous, the deposit will be forfeited.

9.—No charge for weighing.

10.—No person whose name appears in the forfeit list, or who is warned off under any rules of racing in any country, shall be eligible to enter or ride a horse in these races.

11.—The decision of the Committee to be final and conclusive on all points connected with the meeting.

12.—No horseman allowed on the ground other than those engaged in the races, or those authorised by the Committee.

13.—EACH RIDER will be requested to WEIGH OUT, and the first four in each race will have to WEIGH IN, or be disqualified. ALL RIDERS to return mounted to the Weighing Tent.

14.—Name, weight, age, sex, and colour to be declared, and Entrance Fees paid at the time of entry, or entries will not be accepted.

15.—ENTRIES, WHICH MUST BE MADE IN WRITING, CLOSE to H. B. DAIN (Hon. Sec.), at NEWLAND HURST, DROITWICH, or the STAR HOTEL, WORCESTER, on SATURDAY, April 11th, 1903.

All FARMERS within the limits of the Worcestershire Hunt are invited to LUNCHEON, at 12 o'clock on the Course, the day of the above Steeplechases. Their FAMILIES are invited to TEA, which will be provided later in the Afternoon. The Committee hope that as many as can will be present.

TICKETS for Luncheon and Tea to be obtained by personal application at the Committee's tent on the Course, but no Tickets will be issued after one o'clock.

PRICE 6D.

THE WORCESTERSHIRE HUNT

POINT-TO-POINT STEEPLECHASES

Thursday, April 16, 1903.

STEWARD:
C. R. MILLS, Esq., M.F.H.

COMMITTEE.

C. R. MILLS, Esq., M.F.H.

THE EARL OF DUDLEY.	CAPTAIN HEYGATE.
MR. P. BALDWIN.	MR. F. W. MORTON.
MR. W. H. BENTLEY.	MR. H. R. M. PORTER.
MR. G. F. S. BROWN.	MR. M. ROE.
MR. F. D. EVERITT.	MR. J. WYTHES.
MR. ST. JOHN GREAVES.	MR. H. B. DAIN (Hon. Sec.)

STARTER.
MR. F. W. MORTON.

JUDGE.
CAPTAIN HEYGATE.

All FARMERS within the limits of the Worcestershire Hunt are invited to LUNCHEON, at 12 o'clock on the Course, the day of the above Steeplechases. Their FAMILIES are invited to TEA, which will be provided later in the afternoon. The Committee hope that as many as can will be present.

TICKETS for Luncheon and Tea to be obtained by personal application at the Committee's tent on the Course, but no tickets will be issued after one o'clock.

Hon. Sec.:
Mr. H. B. DAIN.

Printed by Deighton & Co., Worcester.

The Worcestershire Hunt racecard of 1903 . . . The Dudley Cup winner was No. 3 on the card

2.0 p.m.—THE RED COAT LIGHT WEIGHT RACE.

A Sweepstakes of £2 each, p.p., with £10 added money, for Horses which, since the 1st January, 1903, have been the *bonâ fide* property of Subscribers of not less than £5 before the first day of March, 1903, to the Worcestershire Hounds, and which have been in their possession and regularly and fairly hunted with those Hounds, and have never won under any rules of racing in any Country except a Point-to-Point. About 3½ miles. Weight not less than 12st. The winners of any Point-to-Point Race since the 1st January, 1902, to carry 14lbs. extra. Any horse that has been in a public training stable since January 1st, 1903, to carry 14lbs. extra. To be ridden in hunting costume, red or black coat, breeches, tall hat or hunting cap. To be ridden by subscribers to the Worcestershire Hounds of not less than £5, or sons of such subscribers, or by owners, or their sons, of land within the limits of the Worcestershire Hunt, or by members of the Worcestershire Hunt Club.

The decision of the Committee as to the qualification of any particular horse or rider to be final and conclusive.

1.	Mr. W. A. Bowen's	b. m.	*Bennicreagh*	aged.
2.	Mr. J. V. Isaac's	ch. m.	*Clonsilla*	aged.
3.	Mr. F. D. Everitt's	ch. g.	*Villafort*	6 yrs.
4.	Capt. H. A. Cheape's	ch. m.	*Avril*	aged.
5.	Capt. H. A. Cheape's	ch. m.	*Firelight*	aged.
6.	Miss Cook's	ch. g.	*Hotspur*	aged.
7.	Mr. St. John Graves'	b. g.	*Pilgrim*	aged.
8.	Major J. Chichester's	b. m.	*Lady Burghley*	aged.
9.	Mr. H. B. Dain's	ch. g.	*Knockaloe*	6 yrs.

2.45 p.m.—THE FARMERS' LIGHT WEIGHT RACE.

For Horses which, since the 1st January, 1903, have been the *bonâ fide* property of Farmers farming not less than 100 acres of land within the limits of the Worcestershire Hunt, and which have been fairly and regularly hunted with the Worcestershire Hounds, and have never run under Newmarket, National Hunt, Irish National Hunt, or Galloway Rules. About 3½ miles. Weight not less than 12st. The winner of any Point-to-Point Race since the 1st January, 1902, to carry 14lbs. extra. Any horse that has been in a public training stable since January 1st, 1903, to carry 14lbs. extra. To be ridden by gentlemen as qualified for the Red Coat Race, or by farmers or their sons, occupying not less than 100 acres of land within the limits of the Worcestershire Hunt, or by Subscribers to the Worcestershire Hounds. First horse to receive £15, second £5. Entrance fee, 2s. 6d., such entrance fees to go to the third horse.

The decision of the Committee as to the qualification of any particular horse or rider to be final and conclusive.

1.	Mr. George Pitcher's (Red).	b. g.	*Tommy Atkins*	6 yrs.
2.	Mr. George Gerrard's (White).	br. g.	*The Gift*	aged.
3.	Mr. T. L. Walker's (Dark blue).	br. g.	*Malvern*	aged.
4.	Mr. G. Baylis' (Green).	b. g.	*Bend Or*	aged.
5.	Mr. [illegible] Smith's (Black).	[illegible]	*Miser*	[illegible]
6.	Mr. W. Watkins' (Yellow).	br. m.	*Whippet*	aged.
7.	Mr. W. Grundy's (Chocolate).	b. g.	*Forrard*	6 yrs.
8.	Mr. W. Grundy's (Pink).	br. g.	*Burton*	6 yrs.
9.	Mr. W. Grundy's (Black and white).	br. g.	*Burton II.*	aged.
10.	Mr. W. S. Carless' (Light blue).	ch. g.	*Fisherman*	aged.

3.30 p.m.—LADY DUDLEY'S CHALLENGE CUP.

Open to Subscribers of not less than £5 to any recognised Pack of Foxhounds in the United Kingdom, for Horses that are *bonâ fide* the property of such Subscribers, and have been fairly and regularly hunted with their respective Packs during the season of 1902 and 1903 (Master's certificate to be sent with entry), and have never won under any rules of racing in any country. Weights not less than 12st. 7lbs. About 3½ miles. Entrance 3 sovs. Winner a Challenge Cup, value £100 (presented by Lady Dudley), two-thirds Entrance Fees, and £15 added money, such Cup to be held subject to Condition 1 of the General Conditions; second, one-third; third to save his stake. Any horse that has been in a public training stable since January 1st, 1903, to carry 14lbs. extra. The race to be ridden in colours to be declared at the time of entry.

The decision of the Committee as to the qualification of any particular horse or rider to be final and conclusive.

1.	Mr. C. A. G. Mawson's (Sir W. W. Wynn's) (Blue jacket, white sleeves, red cap).	br. g.	*Sluggard*	aged.
2.	Mr. S. F. Gilbert's (Ledbury) (Violet, primrose belt).	br. g.	*Sniper*	5 yrs.
3.	Mr. H. G. Farrant's (Ledbury) (Dark blue body, lilac sleeves and cap).	ch. g.	*Red Hall*	6 yrs.
4.	Capt. Walter Long's (Grafton) (Pale pink and green hoops).		*The Boy*	aged.
5.	Mr. P. Sherston's (Burton) (Pale blue cap and jacket).	b. g.	*Antique*	6 yrs.
6.	Mr. Frank Barbour's (Warwickshire) (French grey, crimson belt and cap).	b. m.	*Lady Eda*	aged.
7.	Mr. Frank Barbour's (Warwickshire) (Cerise, white sleeves and cap).	b. g.	*Master Harry II.*	6 yrs.
8.	Capt. Hugh A. Cheape's (Wor'shire) (Dark green).	ch. m.	*Avril*	aged.
9.	Capt. Hugh A. Cheape's (Wor'shire) (Dark green).	ch. m.	*Firelight*	aged.
10.	Mr. C. T. Garland's (Warwickshire) (Light blue, black spots, light blue cap).	b. g.	*The Tramp II.*	aged.
11.	Mr. C. S. Barratt's (Croome) (Blue and red stripes).	b. g.	*Tally Ho*	aged.
12.	Mr. R. C. B. Cave's (Ledbury) (White body, blue sleeves, black cap).	ch. g.	*Irish Light*	aged.
13.	Mr. R. C. B. Cave's (Ledbury) (White body, blue sleeves, red cap).	b. g.	*Ouzelet*	aged.
14.	Mr. Percy Whittaker's (Oakley) (Black with braid, white sleeves, black cap).	b. g.	*Nicator*	aged.
15.	Mr. Greville Clayton's (Cottesmore) (Chocolate, cardinal sleeves and cap).	ch. g.	*Lord Charles*	6 yrs.
16.	Mr. C. R. Mills' (Worcestershire) (Chocolate and gold).	br. m.	*Goldfinch*	aged.
17.	Mr. O. T. Mence's (Ledbury) (Violet jacket, black cap).	bk. g.	*The Rebel*	aged.
18.	Mr. St. J. Greaves' (Worcestershire) [illegible]	b. g.	*Pilgrim*	aged.
19.	Mr. J. G. Hill's (N'th Here'dshire) (Olive green body, light green sleeves, and quartered cap).	ch. g.	*King True*	6 yrs.
20.	Capt. R. L. Heygate's (Wor'shire) (Black, red cap).	br. g.	*Sobraon*	5 yrs.
21.	Mrs. Greswolde-Williams' (North Hereford) (Turquoise and black belt, yellow sleeves).	ch. g.	*Red Monk II.*	5 yrs.
22.	Mr. T. J. Longworth's (Cotswold) (Silver grey, black stripes, scarlet sleeves).	b. m.	*Felise*	5 yrs.

4.15 p.m.—THE RED COAT WELTER RACE.

A Sweepstakes of £2 each, p.p., with £10 added money, for Horses which, since the 1st January, 1903, have been the *bonâ fide* property of Subscribers of not less than £5 before the first day of March to the Worcestershire Hounds, and which have been in their possession and regularly and fairly hunted with those Hounds, and have never won under any rules of racing in any country, except a Point-to-Point. About 3½ miles. Weight not less than 14st. The winner of any Point-to-Point Race since the 1st January, 1902, to carry 14lbs. extra. Any Horse that has been in a public training stable since January 1st, 1903, to carry 14lbs. extra. To be ridden in hunting costume, red or black coat, breeches, tall hat or hunting cap. To be ridden by subscribers to the Worcestershire Hounds of not less than £5, or sons of such subscribers, or by owners, or their sons, of land within the limits of the Worcestershire Hunt, or by members of the Worcestershire Hunt Club.

The decision of the Committee as to the qualification of any particular horse or rider to be final and conclusive.

1.	Mr. J. F. Meakin's	br. g.	*Merlin*	aged.
2.	Mr. J. H. Cartland's	br. g.	*Trumps*	aged.
3.	Mr. G. W. Cook's	b. g.	*Brigadier*	aged.
4.	Mr. H. W. Dixon's	br. g.	*Legacy*	aged.
5.	Mr. St. John Greaves'	ch. g.	*Ecstacy*	aged.

5.0 p.m.—THE FARMERS' WELTER RACE.

For Horses which, since 1st January, 1903, have been the *bonâ fide* property of Farmers farming not less than 100 acres of land within the limits of the Worcestershire Hunt, and which have been fairly and regularly hunted with the Worcestershire Hounds, and have never run under Newmarket, National Hunt, Irish National Hunt, or Galloway Rules. About 3½ miles. Weight not less than 14st. The winner of any Point-to-Point Race since the 1st January, 1902, to carry 14lbs. extra. Any Horse that has been in a public training stable since January 1st, 1903, to carry 14lbs. extra. To be ridden by gentlemen as qualified for the Red Coat Race or by farmers or their sons, occupying not less than 100 acres of land within the limits of the Worcestershire Hunt, or by subscribers to the Worcestershire Hounds. First horse to receive £15, second £5. Entrance fee, 2s. 6d., such entrance fees to go to the third horse.

The decision of the Committee as to the qualification of any particular horse or rider to be final and conclusive.

1.	Mr. George Pitcher's (Red).	b. g.	*Tommy Atkins*	6 yrs.
2.	Mr. G. Baylis's (White).	b. g.	*Spider*	aged.
3.	Mr. G. Baylis's (Dark blue).	b. g.	*Sheppard*	
4.	Mr. G. Baylis's (Green).	b. g.	*Bend Or*	aged.
5.	Mr. Bakewell's (Black).	b. m.	*Irish Thistle*	aged.
6.	Mr. T. Pitt's (Yellow).	ch. g.	*The Cripple*	aged.
7.	Mr. John Surnett's [illegible]	b. g.	*Prince*	6 yrs.
8.	Mr. W. Grundy's (Pink).	b. g.	*Forrard*	6 yrs.
9.	Mr. W. Grundy's (Black and White).	br. g.	*Burton*	6 yrs.
10.	Mr. W. Grundy's (Light blue).	br. g.	*Burton II.*	aged.

For General Conditions—see other side.

season was Brownly, who trotted up in four regimental races with her owner aboard each time.

The Middleton was a casualty of the weather, so there was no Grimthorpe Cup in 1938. But the Dudley Cup was won by a horse from the Cottesmore, Away, the only horse running in the colours of Mr James Hanbury, of the Equitation School at Weedon. In seven appearances during the season, Away's sole defeat was in the open nomination race at the Cambridgeshire Harriers' meeting at Cottenham, where he was beaten half a length after Mr Hanbury had lost his whip as the result of a bad mistake at the final obstacle. Away's last race before the Dudley Cup was the open nomination race at the Old Berkeley, where he convincingly beat Stolen Prince. Later the same season he won two steeplechases under Rules, beating that famous horse Victor Norman over two miles at Sandown at level weights, and he was second in a three-mile handicap chase at Cheltenham carrying 12 st. 6 lb. Away was one of the vintage Dudley Cup winners.

The *Point-to-Point Calendar* for 1938 was stuffed with suggestions for the improvement of point-to-point racing, and they came from all areas. There were, of course, the customary outcries about horses not being hunted properly, and a Sussex owner went so far as to suggest that 'M.F.H.'s continue to give certificates to the most glaring cases of horses which have never been properly hunted in any sense of the word'.

A Devonshire farmer wanted to 'Stop all horses that have won a race for more than a £20 prize' (which in fact was the maximum prize money allowable for winning a point-to-point race); and a Dorset one decided that he was not going to run any horse at a point-to-point where the entry fee was more than £1.

From Hertfordshire came the cry that 'A charge should be allowed for bookmakers' stands, because by this means undesirable ones could be kept away'. I wonder what made him imagine that only undesirable bookmakers would be unable to afford paying money for pitches.

There was a suggestion from Northumberland that, except in ladies' races, all horses should carry at least 13 st.; and a Yorkshire owner-rider wanted 'the regulation distance of three and a half miles more strictly adhered to'. Nowadays, of course, the minimum allowable distance for a point-to-point race is three miles.

Best of all there was the observation that came from a Sussex owner, who remarked touchingly that 'Point-to-points get harder to win every year'. A cry from the heart, indeed, and one that is as true now as it was then.

The last season of point-to-point racing before the war was to put a stop to it for six years was the 1939 one. Point-to-point racing was then riding so high on the crest of the wave that some people considered it a serious threat to the senior sport, and a Kelso reader of *Horse and Hound* delivered himself as follows:

> One of the chief causes of the poor attendance at racing under the National Hunt Rules is that large numbers of people get quite a number of days racing at point-to-point meetings practically for nothing, and, therefore, will not pay to go to a regular steeplechase meeting. As point-to-point racing increases in popularity, regular meetings under National Hunt Rules are declining in popularity, and one meeting after another is abandoned. Is it coincidence, or cause and effect?

Needless to say, no one felt disposed to answer. But it is not difficult to see in the rigorous limitations (such as the absurdly low ceiling of prize money) that have been imposed upon point-to-point racing over the years by the National Hunt Committee, and which are now being perpetuated by the Jockey Club, a rather suspicious attitude to the sport between the flags, and a clear desire to ensure that it doesn't get too big for its boots. But what the authorities don't seem to have been able to limit, though they have made various abortive attempts to do so – the restriction on horses that had won three open races was one such – is the quality of the sport, which has increased almost yearly, so that today it is not unusual to find an ex-point-to-pointer starting favourite for the Grand National or being seriously backed for the Cheltenham Gold Cup.

In 1939, there was a new leading rider, Mr L. G. Scott, whose twelve winners in the West Country included a treble at the Tiverton. Main Doctor and Mr F. W. B. Smyth were making hay over the banking courses; and in the South West, the farming family of Dufosee, a great name in point-to-point racing over the years, were making their presence felt again, this time with Drin

Royal, who was purchased from Lord Stalbridge at a time when Harry Dufosee was managing two farms for him and Drin Royal was turned out on one of them. On Drin Royal, Harry Dufosee's son Tony won the open nomination race at the Blackmore Vale on the same day that his brother Peter won the adjacent hunts' race on Demand, who was bought off the same farm for £25. Other races won by Drin Royal in 1939 were the open nomination race at the South Dorset, the farmers' race at the Sparkford Vale and the adjacent hunts' race at the Portman. But he was beaten in the Prince of Wales Cup at the South & West Wilts by Ballykeating.

And it was Ballykeating who won the Dudley Cup, three years after his dead-heat in that race with O'Dell. This time, with Harold Payne as his pilot, he beat Mr Hugh Sumner's Shannon Boy, who was being ridden by that polished horsemaster Jack Gittins.

The Grimthorpe Cup that year was fought out by two local combinations, Major R. F. (Bob) Wormald with his good horse Putty and Guy Cunard on Coxwold Countess; and it was Putty, a horse bought for £50, who had the better of it. This horse was third in the Dudley Cup after the war, when Bob Wormald held the position of Clerk of the Course at the Middleton for twenty-two years.

Among other good open-race winners of the 1939 season were Sirocco II and No Side, who were owned by two Old Etonians, the Hon. P. M. Samuel and the Hon. M. R. Samuel. I am not quite sure which of the brothers, as I presume they were, owned which horse; but M.R. seemed to have the most mounts, and it was he who won the open nomination race at the V.W.H. (Earl Bathurst's) on No Side and the Old Etonian Association race on Sirocco II. The latter also won the old boys' race the previous year, and on that occasion I believe P.M. was riding.

Several future N.H. trainers were also amongst the winners, including Calverley Bewicke again. Arthur Stephenson won the maiden race at the Zetland on Tyros. Ken Oliver won the open nomination race at the Lauderdale on Evadne. Bobby Renton was being described in *Horse and Hound* as 'a bit of a veteran these days...'; and Ryan Price had been made to turn professional.

And some people still appreciated the correct gear, as the

Horse and Hound point-to-point correspondent made it sternly clear in his report of the Essex Union meeting:

> In the Members' Heavy-weight event the Hon. Secretary, Major V. S. Laurie, was, as usual, the only rider correctly dressed in 'hunting' costume, his top hat, however, being a bit of a liability in the high wind.

In the circumstances, it seemed a pity that the Major failed to gain a place in the field of four.

Mark Roddick won the Grand Military Gold Cup at Sandown for the third and last time. On his eight-year-old Fillip, a horse that had won on the Flat and been acquired for 620 guineas in February 1937, he beat James Hanbury on Away by six lengths. At this point, it is interesting to note that Kilstar, Major Roddick's Grand Military winner of the previous season, had since been purchased by Miss Dorothy Paget, for whom he won the National Trial Steeplechase at Gatwick and finished third to Workman (an Irish hunter) and Macmoffat (a Scottish one) in the Grand National, for which he started favourite.

Harry Llewellyn won the United Hunts' Cup at Cheltenham on his brother's Tapinette, a French-bred seven-year-old out of a winner of the French 2,000 guineas who later won the Lincoln. Duty Paid was third to the 20–1 Kilshannig in the Cheltenham Foxhunters', for which Venturesome Knight started favourite but unshipped his jockey at the fence after the water; and the Liverpool Foxhunters' was won by Capt. Peter Herbert on Mrs G. M. Lees's 11-year-old Nushirawan, a classically-bred horse for whom the Aga Khan paid 4,500 guineas as a yearling and disposed of for fifty-five after he had failed to win a race.

Six lengths behind Nushirawan and four in front of Venturesome Knight (who again started favourite) came the gallant O'Dell, aged seventeen years. It was O'Dell's last race and the end of an era.

9

The First Years After the War

Only 91 point-to-point meetings were held in 1946, the first season after the war. But this was more because of the difficulty of starting up again, owing to petrol rationing, than through any lack of enthusiasm; and when the first post-war fixture took place, at Cottenham in February, the Cambridgeshire Harriers had so many runners for their open nomination race that they had to run it in two divisions, sixteen horses going to the post for the first, won by Capt. T. Hanbury on Mrs Harry Llewellyn's five-year-old Bay Marble, and eighteen for the second, in which Mr E. J. Delfosse's Irish Bachelor beat Maltese Wanderer, the horse that was to give Major Dermot Daly his second successive win in the National Hunt Chase at Cheltenham the following season.

Bay Marble was one of four horses to win their quota of three open nomination races in 1946, the others being Main Doctor and Missed the Bus (the latter in the Ballykeating colours) in the West, and Marques in the West Midlands.

Only the West Country mare, Diana II, who won six races over banking courses and on two occasions scored twice in an afternoon, won more races than Marques that season. Many good judges considered Marques to be the best point-to-pointer of the first post-war decade. Owned by Mr Edward Turner and hunted with the North Shropshire, Marques was purchased as a foal at Newmarket December Sales in 1940. A six-year-old by Sandyman out of Blue Beauty, by Blue Ensign, he won all five of his point-to-points, ridden each time by his owner's son, R. V. (Dick) Turner, who now farms at Aston, where Marques was trained.

At the end of the 1946 season, Marques was sold to Lord Bicester and went into training with Reg Hobbs. But after easily winning a novice hurdle, something went wrong with him and he never ran again. Dick Turner, who is now Hon. Secretary of the North Shropshire Hunt Point-to-Point, writes: 'Marques was a horse with a wonderful temperament, never upset and always sleepy in the paddock but like a machine to ride – wonderful long stride and a beautiful jumper.'

For some reason, Marques did not run in the Dudley Cup of 1946, possibly because by that time the old course at Crowle had ceased to exist. That year, and for the next four, the race was run at Chaddesley Corbett, the setting to which it reverted in 1970 after nineteen years at Upton-on-Severn. The 1946 Dudley Cup was won, in a very small field, by Thurston Holland-Martin riding his brother's Hefty, who also won the members' race at the Harkaway Club (over the same course), the open nomination race at the Beaufort and the adjacent hunts' race at the Cotswold, though he was beaten by Bay Marble at the Berkeley and by Fred Hutsby's Playbill at the North Warwickshire. On his last appearance that season, Hefty was a faller in the Clifton-on-Teme open race, won by Missed the Bus from Merry Knight, the Dudley Cup runner-up.

Excluding wins in hunter chases, the leading riders of the 1946 season, with six winners apiece, were Dick Turner, Henry May and Tommy Southern (who confined themselves mainly to Kent) and Tony Grantham, who later became a top-class professional, and of whom it was once said: 'the boy's riding so short you can hardly tell his head from his arse'.

The leading lady riders, each with four winners, were Kit Tatham-Warter and Ida Croxon. The latter, one of the seven daughters of the late Fred Croxon, who used to have the Seven Sisters Riding School at Northolt and lived to the age of ninety-five, was soon to become famous for her duels with Pat Rushton, the present Mrs John Tollit.

My point-to-point going in those days was largely restricted to the area south of the Thames, where one horse I particularly remember, perhaps because his owner-rider seemed to me to personify the very spirit of point-to-point racing, was Tangerine II. This white-legged horse with a parrot mouth was one of a number brought back from Ireland by Tom Grantham, the father of Tony; and such was the reputation of this noted horsedealer that people in Surrey and Sussex were said to queue up at the station to acquire these Irish horses, much in the same way that Kent owners did in later years in the case of E. J. ('Joss') Masters, the wizard of Tenterden, who has now taken up permanent residence in Kildare.

Tangerine was purchased for 120 guineas by Mr H. L. Ireland, a neat little figure of a man who invariably rode in hunting costume. Mr Ireland was an accomplished horseman but not exactly an expert jockey, though he rode quite a few winners. In 1946 he won four races on Tangerine and would probably have made it five but for the well-laid plans of Tony Grantham and Brian Thompson before the adjacent hunts' farmers' race at the Crawley & Horsham. In this race Grantham was riding Eric Covell's Old Iron III and Thompson (who now manages the horses of Bill Shand Kydd with such expertise) was up on Wilfred How's Highland Chieftain, and they had decided beforehand that the only way to beat Tangerine was to take him on at his own game and go out in front with him from flagfall. The plan worked almost too well, with the three horses setting off at a speed more appropriate for a two-mile hurdle; and when they came to the sixth, a drop fence, where Tangerine was between the other two but fractionally behind them, Mr Ireland found himself squeezed for room and horse and rider ended up on the floor, leaving the two conspirators to reduce their pace to a nice schooling gallop and chat to each other all the way to the last fence, at which point Highland Chieftain produced the better turn of foot and went away to win by six lengths.

This wasn't quite the end of the story, because the Stewards called Grantham and Thompson up before them and required to be satisfied that they hadn't reached a gentleman's agreement regarding which of their horses should pass the post first. The next time Tony Grantham and Brian Thompson rode against each other a spectator bawled out, 'Have you got it sorted out this time, then?'

During the 1947 season (and thereafter) no horse that had run under N.H. Rules in a race other than one confined to hunters between the dates of November 1st and March 1st was eligible to run in point-to-points. And, for the first time, the regulations made mention of the prize money for places: 'The value of the prizes for second and third horses shall not exceed ten sovereigns and five sovereigns respectively.' No fourth prize was permissible, an anachronism which has persisted into the seventies.

The leading point-to-point rider of 1947 was Wilfred How, a 41-year-old farmer who hunted with the Crawley & Horsham in Sussex and won fourteen races with three good horses, Toiview, Ashurst Lad and Old Venture, the last-named coming to him via Tom Grantham, as did Highland Chieftain the previous season. Toiview and Old Venture later went into training with Ryan Price, but the former smashed a leg out at grass and the latter broke down; and the only one of the three who did any good after Mr How had sold them was Ashurst Lad, who went on to win a number of ladies' races in Kent and lived to the age of twenty-five.

No such things as lists of winning riders were published in those days, so I am not going to vouch for the strict accuracy of what is coming next; but by my calculations, after Wilfred How (who has given me his figures himself), with 11 winners, came Bertie Hill, that great West Country horseman, who was a member of our winning three-day event team at the Stockholm Olympics in 1956 and trained our gold medallists for the 1968 Olympic Games in Mexico. Guy Cunard rode nine winners that season, Arthur Stephenson, the present Bishop Auckland trainer, rode eight and shared fourth place with F. W. Ward, the Shropshire owner-rider who had six of his successes on the unbeaten Poker III. And Jack Nichols, riding Sidney Banks's nine-year-old Lucky Purchase, became the first post-war rider to win both the Liverpool Foxhunters' and the Cheltenham Foxhunters'.

At that time, very few hunts held ladies' open nomination races, because to do so meant that they had to forfeit their men's open. Consequently, these races enjoyed a status which they do not have nowadays. The ones which seemed to take most winning, and therefore had some claim to be regarded as championships, were the Warwick Vase at the Essex and the race at the Ludlow which later became known as the Corvedale Cup. The latter event, in particular, invariably attracted the cream of the ladies' horses and was usually run in two divisions. Such was the case in 1947 when Jack Cann's Wise Lad (Miss Marigold Coke) came from the West Country to win Div. 1, and Div. 2 was won by an outstanding horse from the Whaddon Chase, the late Frank Gee's Signet Ring, on whom Mrs A. G. Delahooke had previously won the Warwick Vase in a field of seventeen. This was not, of course, the same Signet Ring that Major Rushton had before the war.

With two wins on Wise Lad and three on Jack Cann's other horse, Robber, Miss Coke was joint leading lady rider of the season with a fifteen-year-old girl in Sussex, Angela Covell (now Mrs Derek Ellis), one of the three daughters of Eric Covell, who then farmed at West Grinstead and now has the Southdown Stud at Shipley, where such horses as Bleep-Bleep, River Chanter and Best Song were bred.

Angela Covell's five wins of 1947 were all on her father's Schedule, a good looking bay with plenty of quality in the blood. His sire, Trigo, was a Derby winner; and his dam, Facette, bred Seneca, who won the Champion Hurdle at Cheltenham in 1941. Who would have thought that 15 seasons after Angela Covell had proved so conclusively that young girls of tender age could sometimes teach their elders a thing or two, the Stewards of the National Hunt Committee would be bringing in legislation forbidding girls under eighteen from riding in point-to-points?

Schedule was also one of the stars of the 1948 season, when Eric Covell, who won four races with this horse and three with Texas Dan, was the leading point-to-point owner. In addition to winning two ladies' races with Angela Covell up, and successfully shouldering thirteen stone in the two races he won with Guy Lerwill riding, Schedule was the winner of a hunter chase at Wye, where his rider was George Hobbs, who subsequently became a professional jockey and then achieved fame as a show-jumping rider.

For Signet Ring it was also another good season. He started by winning in an enormous field at Cottenham, with Ronnie Holman riding; and then, with Mrs Delahooke up again, won his second Warwick Vase and the adjacent hunts' ladies' race at his home meeting; and after a walk-over at the Oakley, he won the hunt race at the Grafton. What matter if, in between, he came to grief in the Liverpool Foxhunters' and was unplaced in the National Hunt Chase? These two races were both won by Guy Cunard, then reaching the height of his powers, the former on San Michele, the Grimthorpe Cup winner of the past two seasons, and the latter on Bruno II.

Another rider to bring off a notable double that season was Harry Llewellyn, who won the United Hunts' Cup at Cheltenham on Bay Marble and, two days later, the four-mile Foxhunters' Cup on State Control, a horse who broke his back in the Liverpool Foxhunters'.

But it was a serving soldier stationed at Larkhill, Major Peter Rawlins, who had the distinction of riding the most point-to-point winners. Four of Major Rawlins's eleven wins were gained on Mr T. F. Denning's Billdare, the best horse he rode. On this eight-year-old gelding from the Mendip Farmers, Major Rawlins won the maiden race at the South & West Wilts and the open nomination races at the Sparkford Vale, Blackmore Vale and the Cotswold.

I doubt, though, if Billdare was the equal of Doughcake, whose owner, Geoffrey White, had produced an exceptional horse in the twenties called Streak, who won twenty-nine races for him. Doughcake was cast in the same mould; and this Wiltshire mare, who stood 17 hands high and was descended from two St Leger winners, was one of only three horses to win four races in 1948 and remain unbeaten. Another was the Meynell nine-year-old, Aquilo, owned and ridden by Brig. C. B. (Roscoe) Harvey, who was not permitted to run his horses under N.H. rules by virtue of his being an official of the Jockey Club (which he still is). I see that I have a letter on my files in which Roscoe Harvey says, 'I do not think there is a horse in the Midlands who would beat Aquilo this year.' But I would have liked to have seen Aquilo come up against Signet Ring.

And I would have liked to have seen both these horses opposed in a race by Rolling River, the third horse unbeaten in four races. An eleven-year-old bay gelding by Roidore, Rolling River was the best point-to-pointer seen out in Yorkshire, where his crowning achievement was his success in the Grimthorpe Cup.

Further north, in the Vale of Lune country, there was a very good point-to-pointer in Mrs E. M. Cousins's Five Letters. Ridden each time by his owner's son, this six-year-old by Dastur won four point-to-points, a hunter chase at Hexham and a steeplechase at Kelso; and he finished his season dead-heating for the Rothbury Cup.

In the Puckeridge country, Frank Harvey, over whose land at Bishop's Stortford the Puckeridge Hunt races were run for so long after the war, was winning races on his wife's Corbawn Lad, a horse bred by the Hon. Peter Beatty and so poor when the Harveys got him that he could hardly walk. This was another well-bred animal, by Sind (by Solario) out of Tetranella, a mare by the Tetrarch who produced six other winners.

But I mustn't give the impression that all the horses winning point-to-points in 1948 were bred in the pink. One of the most consistent winners in the West Midlands, an area where it has never been easy to win races, was a real commoner, Mr A. G. Hartland's Nut Gold. But this didn't prevent him from winning as many races as Signet Ring and sharing the top honours that season.

The best horse confining himself to ladies' races was probably Blue Heaven, running in the colours which were to figure so prominently in more recent years on Snowdra Queen, the McAlpine tartan of Mrs 'Jackie' Brutton. Mrs Brutton won four races on Blue Heaven, who might well have remained unbeaten but for being struck into when finishing third on three legs in his division of the ladies' open nomination race at the Ludlow. And from her stable in the Cotswolds, Mrs Brutton also produced Compton Abdale, an outstanding novice who was to make his mark at Cheltenham the following season when Mrs Brutton became the first lady to train a winner of the United Hunts' Cup there.

I now come to the achievement of Monica Birtwistle, who started race-riding at the age of twenty-three in 1947, when she had three winners in four rides. In 1948 at the Holcombe, Miss Birtwistle was riding a mare called Hill Vixen, who possessed considerable ability but usually managed to make at least one bad mistake in every race. This time she made it three fences from home when three lengths in the lead. She didn't come right down but she went clean through the fence and Miss Birtwistle came off but had the presence of mind to hold on to the reins as the whole field passed her by. The temptation to give up must have been very strong. But Hill Vixen was an odds on favourite and Monica's fiancé had had £25 on her, which was a lot more than he could afford. So she yelled to a policeman to give her a leg up and set off in hot pursuit. She rode the next fence as if it didn't exist, caught all but one of the leaders before the final obstacle and the remaining one almost on the post to win by a neck. Later that season Monica Birtwistle became Mrs Tony Dickinson, and today the Dickinsons are training N.H. horses with great success at Gisburn, near Clitheroe.

The year Monica Birtwistle won on Hill Vixen at the Holcombe was also the year Pat Rushton won at the Cheshire Forest on her father's old chaser Merry Knight. It was her first winner and she was sixteen years old.

10

1949-1951

Halloween and Teal make their point-to-point débuts, John Lawrence's future is decided, and the wrong horse wins at Cheltenham

It was in 1949 that, to quote from the *Horse and Hound Year Book,* 'point-to-point racing enjoyed its first full post-war revival'. By this time the *bona-fide* hunt meetings had disappeared from the scene; and, including the eleven fixtures which were formerly classed as *bona-fide*, 179 point-to-point meetings were held, as compared with 136 the previous season. Following the rebuilding of the fences in 1948 for the steeplechase phase of the Olympic Games, point-to-point racing was starting on Tweseldown Racecourse, where so many of the old military meetings were staged. Two point-to-point fixtures were held at Tweseldown in 1949, the Garth & Chiddingfold Farmers' in mid-March and the Staff College & R.M.A. at the end of the month.

It was the year, too, when Guy Cunard's total of twenty point-to-point winners was a record for a single season in the United Kingdom. The horses that did most to help him on his way to it were Cyril Chapman's Bramham Moor pair, Jeremy II and Finolly. These two horses shared the same dam, Lady Molly, Jeremy being by St Jerome and Finolly by Finden. Jeremy won seven races and Finolly, including a division of the Grimthorpe Cup, won six; and the thirteen races they won between them put Mr Chapman at the head of the leading owners.

Jeremy and Finolly were two very good horses. But one that neither of them could have held a candle to was the Shropshire-hunted Prince Brownie, who came from the same stable which had produced Marques. Edward Turner had bought Prince Brownie as a four-year-old in August, 1946 from Judge Wylie, who was the mainspring of the Dublin Horse Show for so many years; and Prince Brownie was a horse bred for the job. His sire, Brownie, was by Winalot; and his dam, Latonia (by My Prince), was a full sister to Red Princess, a winner of the Stanley Chase at Liverpool and many other races. In his first season, as a five-year-old, Prince Brownie won the maiden race at the Wheatland; and after winning an open event on his only other appearance that season, he came out in 1949 and wiped the board clean. He did the same thing in hunter chases the following season after he had passed into the hands of Lord Mildmay, whose brilliant career as an amateur – perhaps the finest of all – was so tragically cut short when he met his death by drowning in May 1950, just over two years after he had finished third on Cromwell in the Grand National.

The most consistent winner in the West Country during the 1949 season was Golden Morn II, a twelve-year-old gelding from the Lamerton, who was equally accomplished over banks and fly fences, winning seven races in ten appearances; while the pony races in Devon and Cornwall saw the monopoly of Brownie III and Nimrod challenged by Mr S. I. Cundy's Jolly Girl, who won all six of her races, ridden each time by the evergreen Frank Ryall, who is still going strong today with over 200 winners to his credit. It is true, Jolly Girl never met Brownie III, as the latter stuck to banking courses, but on the only two occasions when the mare met Nimrod she defeated him decisively.

In Kent, the late Willie Day's Kiltoom won all five of his point-to-points with ease. This seven-year-old by Young Buck was probably the best point-to-pointer seen out in Kent since Duty Paid and Hopeful Hero. But in his last race of 1949, at the Folkestone United Hunts' Meeting in May, he met with a fatal accident.

Signet Ring and Aquilo again displayed their brilliance, the former winning five races, including the Warwick Vase for the third year running, and the latter three; and both underwent a single defeat. Aquilo parted company with his rider at the Atherstone and Signet Ring was beaten by Sir Isumbras and Maybe II in the Dudley Cup.

Sir Isumbras, a sweet little horse, who had been troubled with red-worm in his three previous seasons, was a son of April the Fifth, the Derby winner of 1932; and, like April the Fifth, he was bred by the late Sidney MacGregor, of Leamington. Which must surely make Mr MacGregor the only man to have bred both a Derby winner and a Dudley Cup winner.

Sir Isumbras, whose four successes in 1949 included a dead-heat with Aquilo in the nomination race at the North Staffordshire, was owned and ridden by Geoffrey Hutsby, a member of that famous family of Warwickshire hunting farmers, who, like the Dufosees in Wiltshire, and others of their kind, epitomise the spirit of point-to-point racing. And surely no one cheered louder than these two families when an anti-hunting bill was defeated in the Commons that season!

Having failed in an earlier attempt to get a Combined Services meeting established at Larkhill, the Grand Military Race Committee now tried again, and this time they were successful, for the 1950 season saw the first of the United Services fixtures at Larkhill, where the Royal Artillery, the Tedworth and the Wylye Valley were already operating.

One of the advantages of writing about point-to-point racing in retrospect is that one sees things now that one didn't always see at the time. But I think most of us who saw Halloween beat Here's Edward and Johnny Pedlar II in Cowdray Park on Easter Monday, 1950, when the rain swept over the course in torrents, knew that we were seeing something out of the ordinary.

A five-year-old brown gelding by the premium stallion Court Nez, Halloween was later to make a tremendous impact on N.H. racing. At that time, he was owned and ridden by Capt. R. B. Smalley, of the Royal Marines. Capt. Smalley, now a Starter under Jockey Club Rules, purchased Halloween as an unbroken three-year-old for £90 from Gerald Barnes, who now looks after our junior international show-jumping teams. The horse was broken for him by that very able horsemaster, Bill Bundy, in whose yard at Bishop's Waltham he was stabled. Mr Bundy did the long reining and Dicky Smalley backed and rode him.

I remember as if it were yesterday Capt. Smalley saying to me, 'If all goes well with him he will be seen in hunter chases next year, when I am sure he will extend the best in this part of the world'. It was at Windsor the following February that I next saw the little horse, when he was about to run in his first hunter chase. Before the race I asked Capt. Smalley what he thought of his chances, and I recall very clearly that he said he hoped he would win but that the sticky going was not in the horse's favour and he had halved his bet. I thought he seemed rather nervous. But I didn't halve *my* bet, which was no doubt a very much smaller one. In fact, Halloween won as he liked, and repeated the performance in the four other hunter chases he contested that season, including the Cheltenham Foxhunters'. He was later sold to a patron of Ryan Price's stable, the Contessa di Sant Elia, who paid £8,000 for him; and among the twelve steeplechases he won for her were the Grand National Trial Handicap Chase at Hurst Park, the Grand Sefton at Liverpool, and the King George VI Chase at Kempton (twice). He was also runner-up for the Cheltenham Gold Cup of 1953 and third in this race the next three seasons. Not a bad record for a £90 point-to-pointer!

To return to the 1950 season, in Yorkshire someone had the bright idea of introducing a 7 lb. penalty scheme for any point-to-point rider who had ridden fifteen winners under N.H. Rules. About the only person affected by this regional imposition was Guy Cunard, against whom it was no doubt aimed. But it didn't stop him riding seventeen winners and assuming his natural position at the top of the table. Perhaps this is why the regulation only lasted for a single season. Major Cunard's two newcomers, Trianon and King of Kilcash, both purchased from Miss Dorothy Paget at the Ascot Sales in November, 1949, netted him seven of these wins, Trianon winning five races in nine appearances and King of Kilcash two of his four races.

Arthur Stephenson, another brilliant horseman, won the Grimthorpe Cup with General Ripple, a horse who started the season as a maiden and went on to win the Heart of all England at Hexham. And Terry Cartridge became the first Worcestershire farmer to win a Dudley Cup when he was successful on his Maybe II, who had the distinction of winning a hunter chase at Cheltenham in sixty-five seconds faster time than Silver Fame took to defeat Freebooter in the Cheltenham Gold Cup of 1951 over the same course.

A Sussex hunter, Greenwood, owned and ridden by John Stuart Evans, who hunted him with the Cowdray, followed a win in a big field at Larkhill by winning the Cheltenham Foxhunters'. Seventeen-year-old Hillmere, from Shropshire, won the Liverpool Foxhunters', in the first year that it ceased to be run over the full Grand National distance. (Since being reduced to two miles seven and a half furlongs – the distance of the Grand Sefton – this race has diminished in stature.) And Major Rushton's Monk's

Crest, the best hunter chaser of the season, won the United Hunts' Cup at Cheltenham.

Mr Harry Bonner's Autumn and Mr C. B. Harper's diminutive Bellock, ridden respectively by two top-class amateurs, Basil Ancil (the elder brother of Derek) and Ivor Kerwood, were outstanding in the South Midlands. The first Mrs Len Coville won four races in Surrey, Sussex and Kent on her Billy D, who had by then run in twenty-nine point-to-points and won thirteen of them. Miss Biddy Clowes won five races in the West on her Caesar IV, and had some rare duels in the process with Miss Susan Terry (now Mrs Richard Woodhouse) on Dark Tapster, who managed to get the better of Caesar at the Portman. Brownie III was unbeaten in the ponies' races, winning eight of them.

But the best horse in the West that season – and I would think one of the best anywhere – was The Mariner V, owned by Ted David and ridden by his son Ken. This eight-year-old gelding from the Taunton Vale, who had won over banks the previous season, was unbeaten in four races over fly fences.

In 1951 there was an important alteration to the point-to-point rules. Winners of three open nomination races were no longer barred from running in any more such events, with a result that Lady Dorothy won four races over the banking courses of the West Country, while Dandini, Skittles II and Tiger Tim III each won five open events in more exacting areas.

In his younger days as a hurdler, when he ran under the name of Dame Street, Dandini had acquired something of an international reputation. But he was now eleven years old, and it is comparatively rare for such horses to sweep the board when they come to point-to-point racing in the evening of their careers. Eric Cousins, who owned Dandini and hunted him with the Vale of Lune, rode fifty winners as an amateur. He now trains professionally at Tarporley, Cheshire. Skittles was produced in the South & West Wilts country by the same Geoff White who produced Streak and Doughcake.

But the best of the three was Tiger Tim III, a little chestnut gelding from the Beaufort owned and mostly ridden by Lt. Comdr. R. H. Royds. Although his bid to win the Dudley Cup was an unsuccessful one, this was Tiger Tim's only point-to-point defeat in eight appearances.

Another horse I particularly remember from the 1951 season

was Sandy Sen, perhaps because his chopped-off tail gave him such a delightfully cobby appearance. Owned by Major Charles Radclyffe, hunted with the Heythrop, and beautifully ridden by Major George Rich (whose wife won the Queen Elizabeth II Cup at the International Horse Show on Quicksilver III the following year), Sandy Sen ran only twice before being packed off to Germany, but the six-year-old by Pactolus out of a mare by Sun Yat-Sen was a winner on both occasions. At the Bullingdon Club he beat Ramright (later runner-up in the Cheltenham Foxhunters') and at Larkhill he defeated Skittles.

The Grimthorpe Cup winner that year was Archie Thomlinson's Paul Pry, on whom Arthur Stephenson went on to win the Dudley Cup, then in its first year at Upton-on-Severn. This horse, who did his hunting in Yorkshire with the Bedale, had boundless stamina but not much turn of foot. His owner was then, and still is now, one of the cleverest men with horses, and a great showman to boot. I have heard Archie Thomlinson described as a genius, and this is not far short of the truth. He could win with horses that never did much good for other people, and it has always been a mystery to me where and how he acquires them. He produces them seemingly from nowhere, like a conjuror producing rabbits from a hat. I once asked a northern sportsman where Archie got his horses from (it is not much good asking Archie himself), and received the reply, 'Oh, he just gets them from some huntsman.' But I can hardly believe that.

Another Yorkshire horse running in point-to-points in 1951 was a future Grand National winner, Mr Ridley Lamb's Teal, who was hunted by his owner with the Hurworth. This little horse, who had won the maiden race at the Cleveland and two other races the previous season, was beaten once in four outings in 1951, when he finished third to General Ripple and Paul Pry in the Heart of all England at Hexham. And in 1952, with Arthur Thompson riding, he beat Legal Joy and Wot No Sun at Aintree. John Lawrence has written of him in the *History of Steeplechasing*: 'Comparative merit between generations is impossible to measure but at his best Teal was probably at least the equal of all but a few post-war National winners and a great deal better than most.' He died of a twisted gut before he could contest his second Grand National.

It was in Teal's last year of point-to-point racing that John

Lawrence rode his first winner. This was in the lightweight race at the Pegasus Club (Bar) point-to-point at Kimble, and he has described the experience in a delightful article he wrote for *The Field*:

> The race was confined to members, or would-be members, of the legal profession (I was very much one of the would-be ones); and the horse's name, appropriate if a trifle pessimistic, was Next of Kin. She fell over backwards twice in the paddock, but the others fell over in the race itself. Next of Kin came home alone carrying a bewildered blissful burden, and in that moment, I suppose, my immediate future was settled. The distinguished judges and barristers who organized the Bar point-to-point had, quite unwittingly, deprived their profession of my services.

The hunt that turned out the most winners in 1951 was the West Norfolk, and among the many good horses produced in this area was one who was to have a most distinguished career in hunter chases, Major Eldred Wilson's River Buoy, the winner of five races with his owner up. Mr P. C. Whales's Baytiro won four, and the three wins recorded by Mr P. Gow's Flapjack included the Gone Away Open Hunters' Chase at the Folkestone United Hunts' Meeting, that highly enjoyable fixture which has taken the place of the one that was held at Lingfield before the war.

But the pride of the West Norfolk for most people's money would, I feel sure, have been Salvage, owned and ridden by the 57-year-old Walter Wales. I shall always consider this splendid combination extremely unlucky not to have won the Cheltenham Foxhunters' of 1951. After making almost all the running in this race, Salvage was beaten by Halloween and Ramright. But her bad luck lay in the fact that, as a result of flooding in March, the race had been postponed until late April and the entries re-opened; and neither the winner nor the runner-up were among the original entries.

In the ladies' races, Miss Betty Cooke's Jack Hawley was the star performer. This six-year-old from the South Berks had made his début the previous season, when he won twice in three appearances; and in 1951 he ran in six races, with his owner up each time, and won them all, finishing up, like so many good horses before him, with a success in a division of the ladies' open race at the Ludlow. And he looked every inch the thoroughbred that he was. Bred in Berkshire by his owner's father, Sir William Cooke, Jack Hawley was by Trigo out of a mare, Scusi, who shared her ancestry with Bellacose, Precipitation, Casanova and Persian Gulf.

By this time the duelling of Ida Croxon and Pat Rushton was fast getting into its stride, and it was to last into the sixties. Their two best horses at this period were Don Isle and Lucky Dip, and in the ladies' open nomination race at the North Ledbury they dead-heated with each other. Pat Rushton won nine of her ten races on Lucky Dip that year; and Ida Croxon, who won five races on Don Isle and three on Michshine, was the runner-up on four of these occasions, riding a different horse each time.

Don Isle, a grey, almost white gelding (he grew whiter and whiter the older he got) with a flowing mane, was not only one of the best ladies' horses of all time; he was also one of the most spectacular, and I am not ashamed of having once described him in action as looking like a billow of white foam. He was owned by Mrs Cecily Gaskell (who rode sixteen winners herself in the twenties and thirties) and hunted with the Warwickshire. His sire, Invershin, was a great stayer, and staying was Don Isle's forte. A winner on the Flat and over hurdles, he was bought out of a selling race at Towcester for £35 by Len Sheasby, a Warwickshire farmer and point-to-point rider. But it was not until Mrs Gaskell bought him from Mr Sheasby that he won a point-to-point.

My final memory of 1951 is of a six-year-old mare from the Puckeridge, Parasol II, who won the United Hunts' Club Race at the Cambridge University meeting at Cottenham and two hunter chases at Huntingdon and Wye. In all these races she was ridden by her owner, John Dimsdale, whose ambition it was to win the Cheltenham Foxhunters' with her. But before he could realize it, he was killed riding another horse in a race at Huntingdon, and Parasol passed into the hands of Allan Walton, a London shipping broker who hunted with the South Oxfordshire and had another good horse called Nigger Minstrel.

Allan Walton ran both of these horses in the Cheltenham Foxhunters' of 1952, with Ivor Kerwood riding Parasol and

Johnny Lombard up on Nigger Minstrel; and I have seldom felt so excited as when the two came over the last fence with little between them and Parasol strode away up the hill to win by one and a half lengths. It was, one might say, a posthumous win for John Dimsdale. But when I went to congratulate Allan Walton his face was as white as a sheet. As far as he was concerned, the wrong horse had won. He believed so implicitly that Nigger Minstrel was the better of the two that he had gone all out for him. Now all three of the principal figures in this story are dead. Parasol was killed in the Grand National of 1953. Allan Walton committed suicide a few years later.

11

1952-1953

Four Ten and Limber Hill show the shape of things to come, the four-mile races proliferate, and a compliment is returned.

The first thing to be said about the 1952 season is that it marked the point-to-point débuts of two future winners of the Cheltenham Gold Cup, Four Ten and Limber Hill; and both these horses were bred by the men who brought them out in point-to-points and still owned them when they went on to carve out successful careers under N.H. Rules.

An immense dark bay, by Blunderbuss, Four Ten stood over 17 hands high. He was six years old in 1952, when he won four of his six point-to-points, three of them with Percy Tory riding. His owner, Mr A. Strange, a Dorset farmer, bred him from Undue Praise, an unraced mare by Felicitation. It would, I think, be true to say that Four Ten flashed across the point-to-point scene like a comet, because by 1953, the year before he won the Cheltenham Gold Cup, he had already won his first race under Rules.

Jim Davey's Limber Hill (who died in 1970 at the age of twenty-three) was a chestnut gelding by Bassam out of Mindoon, a Gainsborough mare thrown out of a flat-racing stable. Hunted with the Brocklesby in Lincolnshire since his two-year-old days, Limber Hill was five years old when he made his first appearance on a racecourse, in the Brocklesby maiden race, which he won easily. The remarkable thing about this horse was that his first four successes under N.H. Rules, in the winter of 1953, after he had won three more point-to-points, were all over hurdles. It is most unusual for a point-to-pointer to reverse the normal sequence of events by graduating to hurdle racing.

It was in 1952 that the distance of the Grimthorpe Cup was extended from three and a half miles to four miles; and the winner this time was a good old horse from the York & Ainsty, Mr G. F. Fawcett's thirteen-year-old Trusty, who had been used as a lead horse in a racing stable at Malton. Both for Trusty and his rider, Harry Elliott, it was a fitting climax to a highly successful season during which they won six races in partnership.

Another good old horse that season was the Worcestershire-hunted Nylon, who suddenly took on a new lease of life at the age of twelve and won eight races in fourteen starts, an achievement which must have astonished the people who saw him racing in his earlier days when he was hunted first with the Old Surrey & Burstow and then with the Puckeridge. Running in the colours of Mr S. Turner, a Herefordshire farmer, and ridden in all his races of 1952 by Gerald Morgan, a promising young rider who was honorary huntsman to the neighbouring Clifton-on-Teme, Nylon was the winner of six open events, one of them over that exceptionally testing course at Kirtlington where (as many will remember) Frank Sheasby was killed.

But Nylon had two superiors in the West Midlands. One of them was Atlantis, a tubed nine-year-old by Davy Jones who won five races on the trot in the capable hands of Roger Guilding, then a 20-year-old amateur whipper-in to the Ledbury, with which pack Atlantis was hunted. The other was the North Warwickshire's Mythical Ray, whose five wins in open events included the gold cup at the Atherstone which now bears his name.

None of these horses ran in the 1952 Dudley Cup, which was won by George Maundrell's Right Again, who got home by half a length from one of the northern challengers, Windsor Love, on whom Mr J. R. Hindley, the Master of the Pendle Forest, was having a busman's holiday from Olympic training. A six-year-old gelding by Rondo, Right Again had been acquired as a three-year-old in Ireland, where he won the hunter championship at the Tipperary Show. After Mr Maundrell had hunted him for three seasons with the Beaufort and the Avon Vale, Right Again won three point-to-points in 1951, his first season, and four in 1952, when he was unbeaten in point-to-points and also won a hunter chase at Cheltenham; and in all these races he was ridden by Mr Maundrell's 21-year-old son David, who has since given up racing for farming.

In the East, River Buoy won three point-to-points and four hunter chases, and ended the season unbeaten in the former events, as did the hobdayed Green Frog in the Shires. And yet another good horse appeared in the Puckeridge country in the shape of Hugh Hodge's King's Rose. The winner of four of his five point-to-points, this bay six-year-old by Kingsway who came from Willy Stephenson's Royston stable, was to finish third to the dead-heaters Dunboy II and Merry in the Cheltenham Foxhunters' the following season.

Despite being handicapped by an injury towards the close of the season, Guy Cunard still managed to finish up as the leading point-to-point rider of 1952 with fifteen winners, one more than the West Country veteran, Frank Ryall. The leading lady rider was Miss G. Moore, who, in her first season of race-riding, won eight races in the West Country, six of them on Lonesome Boy, the winner of five races over banks and one over fly fences.

Eighteen hunts staged ladies' open races in 1952 as against fifteen the previous season, and those at the Wilton, the Blankney and the Ludlow were all run in two divisions. Apart from the skirmishing of Pat Rushton and Ida Croxon, the highlights on the distaff side were provided by Miss Betty Cooke with Hereford, Miss Rosemary Ransom with Corban, the two Covell sisters, Angela and Tessa, each of whom won three races on their father's thirteen-year-old Hurlement; and, in the North, by the two Bruce sisters, Patricia and Jackie, on the unbeaten Dunboy II, from the Jedforest.

Corban I remember as an especially spectacular performer, and no easy horse to hold. He was a son of Colombo and a grandson, on his dam's side, of Windsor Lad. Miss Ransom, who rode Corban so brilliantly, is now Mrs Ian Lomax, a successful trainer of flat-race horses at Baydon, Wiltshire, where one of her charges is Precipice Word. Which makes her the first lady to train a winner of the Ascot Gold Cup.

Hereford was by Felicitation, an Ascot Gold Cup winner; and when he came up against Corban in a memorable contest at the Craven, he won by a head. So there wasn't much between them. Nor between those two and Pat Rushton's little Episil, who was beaten a head by Hereford in a division of the ladies' open race at the Ludlow. Among Corban's victims was the smart Wiltshire performer, Royal Prince, who was summarily dismissed by him at the South Devon.

In 1952 Signet Ring was thirteen years old, and on April 19th, in the adjacent hunts' ladies' race at the Grafton, his home meeting, he won for the last time. In a career which stretched from 1947 to 1953, this exciting horse ran in twenty-four point-to-points, won seventeen of them and was only three times unplaced.

1953 was Coronation year, and it was celebrated in appropriate style by the inauguration of several Coronation Cup open events, notably at the United Services' meeting at Larkhill, where the race was run in two divisions and H.M. The Queen was present to see the first won by Peter Dufosee on Lucrative and the second by the young Ted Edgar in two seconds faster time on his newly-acquired Paul Pry.

Another new trophy that year was the gold challenge cup which that noted patron of the Turf, Jim Joel, presented for the open race at the Hertfordshire, where the Duke of Windsor was a surprise visitor. The first winner of this was the Warwickshire horse Hastener, a reformed character since his N.H. days when he was considered something of a rogue.

It was also the year when four more hunts, the Heythrop, the East Essex, the Ashford Valley and the Portman (then in their first year at Badbury Rings) decided to follow the example of the Middleton in the North and initiate four-mile races. The only one of these really to catch on was the race for Lord Ashton of Hyde's Cup which is still being run at the Heythrop today. Seventeen horses went to the post for the first Heythrop four-miler, and among them was Tiger Tim III, the winner of the United Hunts' Cup at Cheltenham that season. But the Heythrop winner, in a very tight finish with Hastener, was a horse who had only recently lost his maiden certificate, Len Coville's Dark Stranger.

A former inmate of Willy Stephenson's stable, this dark-brown eight-year-old by Mazarin, out of a mare by Concerto, was rather a lazy horse who had to be ridden from start to finish; and he had a brilliant pilot in Ivor Kerwood, who told Mr Coville afterwards that he was the best stayer he had ever ridden and would have a great chance in the National Hunt Chase the next season. Dark Stranger did not win at Cheltenham, but he *did* go on to win the Liverpool Foxhunters' in which he was ridden by John Bosley, who was equally complimentary about him.

The winners of the other four-mile point-to-points of 1953 were not in Dark Stranger's class; though Turkish Prince, on whom Tony Dickinson won the Grimthorpe Cup, had run fifth in the Irish Derby at the Curragh as a three-year-old. After he had won the Grimthorpe Cup, Turkish Prince was bought by Walter

Wales, for whom he won a hunter chase at Birmingham and three point-to-point races.

Humorist II, who won the Ashford Valley race in a moderate field, was then eleven years old and already past his best, but he had run up quite a string of successes in previous seasons with Jim Day riding. The Portman restricted their four-miler to the home and adjacent hunts; and this was also won by a horse who started the season as a maiden, Mrs M. Atkinson's The Baker, a chestnut son of Donatello II who proved to be a fairly consistent winner in subsequent seasons and won the Portman race three times, the last occasion when he was twelve years old.

The East Essex looked to have a success on their hands with their race, which attracted several good horses from the West Norfolk. Two of them fought out the finish, Tullaherin beating Treasurer by a short head. Treasurer, whose owner, Geoffrey Mason, was to produce a future winner of the Grand National, was a wonderful old weight carrier, virtually unbeatable in welter-weight races. His rider, Peter Mason, invariably had to put up over-weight in other races, and at the East Essex Treasurer was giving Tullaherin 4 lb. In his previous race, he had been beaten a short head in a hunter chase at Fakenham when trying to give Baytiro (one of the best point-to-pointers in the area) 16 lb; and he was to be beaten a short head in his next race when attempting another huge weight concession. Three short-head defeats in one season must almost be a record!

Tullaherin, an Irish import in his first season over English fences, was a seven-year-old bay gelding by Sandyman out of Whitethorn by Torlonia. He had a highly accomplished rider in Jeremy Everitt (the Michael Bloom of his day?) and was owned by Mr J. M. Turner, the present Master of the Suffolk.

One of the best races seen at Larkhill that season was the open event at the Tedworth, in which Alejo, a six-year-old from the Isle of Wight who had won two of his four previous races and had been second in the other two, beat Fair Epinard and Mythical Ray by half a length and a head in a field of twenty-two. This race, run in 6 mins. 13½ secs., was the fastest run over the Larkhill course for many years, a full twenty-three seconds faster than Paul Pry's time at the first Larkhill meeting and seven seconds faster than the quickest race run there the previous season.

The best horse in either Wiltshire or Dorset, however, was

probably Mr F. Crawshaw Bailey's Royal Prince, who was unbeaten in all five of his races. This horse was a son of Skoiter, an Irish St Leger winner who stood for many years as a premium stallion in Norfolk and later went to stand in Northumberland. Skoiter also sired Sunsalve, the horse on whom David Broome won the bronze medal for show jumping at the Olympic Games in 1960.

Further West, The Mariner V made light of his age by winning six more open events; and Mr H. W. Fear's Hungry Hill, a ten-year-old black mare from the Mendip Farmers, won all four of the open events she had won the previous season plus an additional one, and capped this with two wins in hunter chases.

But for another consistent performer in this area it was the end of the road. The Wicked Uncle, a horse bred by the late Mr J. V. Rank and owned by Mr L. Clapp, of Sparkford, collapsed and died after winning at the South Dorset. The Wicked Uncle, who was hunted with the Blackmore Vale and the Sparkford Vale and started his point-to-point career as a five-year-old in 1947, ran in a total of forty-six point-to-points and/or hunter chases, won twelve of them and was placed in a further fourteen.

For one of Major Cunard's best horses, gallant old Trianon, the winner of twenty-two races, never less than five in a season, it was also the end. He broke a hind fetlock at the Goathland at the comparatively early age of eleven.

Trusty, however, went marching on at the ripe old age of fourteen, winning six more open races, the same number as the year-younger Devilstone, who was unbeaten in point-to-points. Once a prize hunter in the show ring and subsequently hunted in earnest with the Tynedale and the Haydon, Devilstone was ridden in four of these races by George Milburn, who later turned professional.

Two other horses unbeaten in 1953 were Limber Hill and the Puckeridge mare Avagoli. Limber Hill was now in his last season of point-to-point racing, and two of the three races he won were ladies' races, in which he was ridden by Rosemary Ransom. Avagoli, who was owned by Mr V. H. Rowe, won five open races with Phillip Rowe riding and the Warwick Vase at the Essex, where Sybil Lambton had the mount.

For the first time in its history, the Dudley Cup was run in two divisions; and the earlier division gave George Maundrell his second Dudley Cup winner in successive years when his young horse Cottage Lace proved much too good for Hastener in a field which included Rapid River, the runner-up to Turkish Prince in the Grimthorpe Cup. The best Rapid River could do on this occasion was to finish fourth.

A six-year-old bay gelding by Interlace out of Petite Shanford by Le Prodige, Cottage Lace was undoubtedly one of the best horses to win this race in the post-war years; and he went on to win many races under N.H. Rules, including the Grand Military Gold Cup of 1956.

Flint Jack who beat Atlantis and Dark Stranger (at his laziest) in the other division, was winning for the sixth time during the season. A nine-year-old chestnut gelding by Snake Lightning, he was owned by Mr Hugh Sumner, hunted with the Worcestershire, and ridden in all his races by Jack Fowler.

The ladies' open race at the Ludlow, which in those days was the nearest equivalent to a ladies' Dudley Cup, was also run in two divisions. And what could have been more appropriate than for Pat Rushton on Episil to beat Ida Croxon on One Night in the first division, and for Ida Croxon to return the compliment by winning the second division on Franciscan from Pat Rushton on Lucky Dip?

12

1954

In which point-to-point racing achieves a post-war record, the first southern horse wins the Grimthorpe Cup, and a pony dwarfs his rivals

In 1954, the year that Four Ten won the Cheltenham Gold Cup, 200 point-to-point meetings were held, the highest number since the war; the Royal Artillery staged the first ladies' open race ever to be run at Larkhill; the Oxford University Bullingdon Club and the Bicester & Warden Hill decided that enough was enough and shifted their fixtures from the formidable course at Kirtlington to the South Oxfordshire course at Crowell; and the Middleton, combining for the first time with the Middleton East, increased the distance of their Grimthorpe Cup race to 4½ miles, thus making it the true Grand National of point-to-point racing which it has been ever since.

And the first horse to win the new-style Grimthorpe Cup was a southern one, Kitty Brook, a mare from the Vine. Although she was ten years old, Kitty Brook was in her first season of point-to-point racing. This bay daughter of Devonian from the Tolgus mare Wheal Kitty had won on the Flat and over hurdles and then been retired to stud, where she produced a foal by Auralia. She was four years at stud and, after slipping her foal to Vilmorin, was withdrawn from the Newmarket Sales and sold privately to Mrs Joan Makin, of Kingsclere, for £150. It took Mrs Makin a year to get her properly fit and to teach her to jump fences.

Before she won the Grimthorpe Cup, Kitty Brook won three other open races. The first of them was over the sharp Old Berkshire course at Lockinge, the next was the four-mile race at the East Essex; and then, a week before she went up to Yorkshire to contest the Grimthorpe Cup, she won the 3½ mile race for the Duke of Gloucester Cup at the Army meeting at Tweseldown. In all these races and the big one that was still to come, she was ridden with superb judgement of pace by Charlie Smith, the elder brother of the flat-race jockeys, Eph and Doug Smith.

There were fifteen starters for the 1954 Grimthorpe Cup; and they included two of the best hunter chasers in the North (May King and Mazawattee), a future winner of the National Hunt Chase (Kari Sou), a future Dudley Cup winner (Prospero), and those two old campaigners San Michele and Trusty, the last-named having won the open events at the Derwent, the Cleveland and the Hurworth for the third successive year. But none of these horses managed to get the Vine mare off the bit; and only May King, who was beaten by what Mrs Makin described afterwards as the longest two lengths she had ever seen, made any serious attempt to go after Kitty Brook once she had hit the front. Mazawattee finished two lengths further away third and the West Norfolk contender Tullaherin was fifth.

The four-mile race at the Heythrop took place a week before the Grimthorpe Cup and neither Kitty Brook nor Dark Stranger, the 1953 winner, were in the field for it. The going on top of the Cotswolds was rock hard, but eleven horses went to the post for the race and in an exciting finish fourteen-year-old Nylon got home by a neck and half a length from The Man in Blue and Maid of Ardgoul, and then promptly went on to win a division of the open race at the Ludlow in what proved to be his last season.

The Dudley Cup clashed with the Heythrop race and the equally hard going reduced the field to seven horses in each division. But there were two tense finishes. Mr C. S. Ireland's Blenalad, a seven-year-old from the Belvoir, on whom C. B. ('Buster') Harty had the mount, won the first division by a head from Red Idler; and Flint Jack won the second by a similar margin from Land Baby, a horse that had come to point-to-point racing after a fairly successful career as a steeplechaser.

Mr G. K. Houston's seven-year-old Rathowen, a tubed gelding from the Berwickshire, was the kingpin in the Border Country that season, being unbeaten in five races. Col. Harry Llewellyn's River Picnic, a big bay gelding by River Prince from the Monmouthshire, was the star in Wales, winning seven races in eight appearances. But even this was made to look rather pale by comparison with the record of the astonishing Lonesome Boy, who was unbeaten in his ten races in the West Country; in seven of these races he was ridden by eighteen-year-old Jennifer Renfree, who is now Mrs David Barons, wife of the Kingsbridge trainer.

Also unbeaten in the West Country that season was another pony, Mr W. B. Hookway's Gay Cashier, but whereas all his successes were in races confined to horses of his size, only two of Lonesome Boy's wins were in pony races, when Frank Ryall won on him over fly fences at Mr Spooner's Harriers and the Cury Harriers.

In the South, where Chris Nesfield was beginning a run of successes on a twelve-year-old ex-chaser called Steel Drop, there appeared an outstanding young horse in the shape of Master Cash, a six-year-old by Pylon II who had been hunted in Surrey with the Chiddingold Farmers'. Master Cash, who was bred by his owner, Mr Eric Savage, from his point-to-point mare Cash Girl, won five races in seven attempts; and in four of these races he was ridden by the lady who subsequently married his owner, Angela Marlow, then in her first season of race-riding.

At the Beaufort, in March, the Queen Mother was a distinguished visitor, a happening which may well have accounted for what I believe was the one and only point-to-point appearance of that celebrated turf adviser the late Ras Prince Monolulu, whose ostrich plumes looked particularly sorry for themselves by the end of a very wet afternoon; and in the members' race at the Aldenham Harriers, the redoubtable Stanley White, who rode his first winner way back in 1921, had the ninety-ninth success of his long and distinguished career when he steered his own horse Sunboy III first past the post. He was sixty-two years old.

At the Portman, Dick Hunt pulled off a treble, winning the maiden race on Queen's Point, the four-mile adjacent hunts' race on his thirteen-year-old Coolmuckee and the hunt race on his seventeen-year-old Playfair II, a horse that won him seventeen races.

It was also the year when Mythical Ray won the Atherstone Gold Cup outright; Royal Prince and Gay Walker won the ladies' open race at the Minehead Harriers for the fourth time; Mrs Jessop (the former Sybil Lambton) won the Warwick Vase at the Essex for the second year running on Avagoli; Monica Dickinson failed by inches to supplement her success on Mazawattee in the first division of the ladies' open race at the Blankney with a win on Ray Westwood in the second; and up in the Border Country a horse called The Callant made his first appearance on a point-to-point course and won three races.

13

The Callant and Colledge Master

The Callant was unquestionably one of the really great point-to-pointers and hunter chasers of the post-war years, 'the kind of horse', as his owner put it so well, 'that a farmer breeds once in a life-time'. A flea-bitten grey, The Callant was foaled in 1948 on the farm of Mr C. D. (Charlie) Scott at Mossburnford, Jedburgh. His sire was the premium stallion St Michael and his dam, Windywalls (by Shining Tor), was a thoroughbred mare who escaped being put down as a war-time measure through being given to Mr Scott as a present when she was three years old.

The Callant was Windywalls's third foal and, until he went into training in later years with Stewart Wight at Grantshouse, he spent all his life on his owner's farm in the Jedforest Country, where at that time Mr Scott was Assistant Whip and general factotum with the hounds. And it goes without saying that The Callant was hunted from morn to nightfall, often doing as much as twenty-five full days' hunting in a single season. At one time or another, I believe all Mr Scott's friends had a day's hunting on this splendid animal; and I know that one season The Callant carried a grandfather, a grandmother, a father, mother and a young girl, as well as his owner, who at that time was still a bachelor but is now married to a lady who was herself a noted point-to-point rider, Rosemary Bird. And when he wasn't hunting or racing, The Callant carried Mr Scott around the farm, and grazed with the cattle in the winter.

In 1955, his second season, The Callant won five point-to-points and three hunter chases, including the Heart of all England at Hexham; and in all these races, and the three that he won in his first season, he was ridden by J. Scott-Aiton, a quiet and confident rider who knew how to get the best out of him. In his

Major Harold Rushton on his famous O'Dell at the Warwickshire in 1935, when this fixture was held at Chesterton, near Leamington

Miss Diana Bell on Iliad II (nearer camera) at the South & West Wilts in 1931

Miss Pat Rushton, who is now Mrs John Tollit. Miss Ida Croxon, who later became Mrs Philip Marshall. These two riders competed against each other on no fewer than 60 occasions and were either first or second on 31 of them

Ida Croxon on the grey Don Isle and Pat Rushton on Episil

third season, The Callant won six more hunter chases, including the Cheltenham Foxhunters', which he won again the following year, when he beat Colledge Master. His admirers fully expected him to win the Whitbread Gold Cup at Sandown that season, but unfortunately he fell at the eighth fence.

By this time The Callant was established as an inmate of the professional stable at Grantshouse; and in the 1957–58 N.H. season he demonstrated conclusively that the transition from hunters' races to handicap steeplechases was something he could take in his stride, winning three races in the hands of the stable professional, Micky Batchelor.

It is probable that The Callant would have won a lot more races, perhaps even some in the highest class, if he hadn't made periodical returns to the hunting field. I well recall Lawrence Morgan, the Australian Olympic rider who owned and rode Colledge Master, giving voice to the opinion that if The Callant had run in the Cheltenham Gold Cup of 1957 he would have won it. Curiously enough, in January of that year the writer of a letter to *The Sporting Life* had the same idea about Colledge Master. 'It would appear', he wrote, 'that if Mr L. R. Morgan had entered his grand hunter chaser Colledge Master for the Cheltenham Gold Cup he would have a favourite's chance to emulate Four Ten and Limber Hill.' In fact, the race was won that year by another horse who had come up from the point-to-point ranks, Mr David Brown's Linwell.

Colledge Master came on the scene a little later than The Callant, but as he was the grey's rival, in reputation if not always on the course, it is appropriate to consider him in the same chapter, even if it means jumping a few years in time.

A chestnut gelding by Grandmaster out of a Columcille mare, Colledge Master had never appeared on a racecourse when Mr Morgan (who had just arrived in England from Australia) bought him for 300 guineas at the Ascot Sales in February, 1955 as a five-year-old. The same year he rode Colledge Master in several one-day horse trials, and in the winter the horse was hunted with the V.W.H. (Earl Bathurst's) and the Beaufort preparatory to starting in point-to-points. He had his first race in a division of the open race at the Oxford University meeting at Lockinge in March, 1956 and, with his owner up, finished second. He then won the maiden race at the V.W.H. (Earl Bathurst's), and this was followed by a success in the open event at the V.W.H. (Cricklade) the day after his owner-rider had finished third on another horse in the Badminton Horse Trials. His next two races were the open event at the Tedworth and a hunter chase at Taunton, and he won these well.

The following season, the sheep farmer from New South Wales who was to win an Olympic gold medal on Salad Days in the three-day event at Rome in 1960 at the age of forty-five, achieved the second of two life-time ambitions which had nothing to do with the Olympics. The first was to breed a Derby winner, and this he had accomplished when a horse that he bred himself won the Australian Derby of 1947. The second was to ride over Cheltenham and Aintree. He did more than this. After being beaten by The Callant at Cheltenham, Colledge Master won the Liverpool Foxhunters'.

Colledge Master was a true stayer who raced, as so many of them do, with a low head carriage. And his rider was a very great horseman and no mean jockey. The riding style of Lawrence Morgan was frequently criticised in the British press for its 'roughness'; and not everybody appreciated the triumphant grin with which he favoured his opponents as he left them standing. The fact remains that Colledge Master went better for Lawrence Morgan than for anyone else. Perhaps, though, the really amazing thing is that when Mr Morgan offered Colledge Master to the Australian Olympic team the offer was turned down.

14

1955

In which a coup comes unstuck and a cure is effected

This was the year when Reverend Prince, owned by a Dufosee and ridden by a Dufosee, won the National Hunt Chase; when the Bicester & Warden Hill shifted their fixture from Crowell to Kimble; when trophies were introduced for two of the premier ladies' races, the Corvedale Cup at the Ludlow and the Blankney Vase at the Blankney; and when that brave rider Gay Kindersley had his worst accident. In the Final Hunter Chase at Stratford he broke both his back and his neck. But this was not going to stop him becoming the leading amateur under N.H. Rules four years later.

It was also the year when Kitty Brook made her last appearance on a course. The mare from the Vine lamed herself so badly beating Highland Ballad and Mythical Ray in the open race at the Old Berkshire that she was retired permanently to stud, where she had five more foals; and Mrs Makin, who now lives in Ireland, has been kind enough to give me details of them. Peter Brook (by Vilmorin) went hunting after an abortive attempt to become a show jumper. Stella Brook (by Star Signal) was exported to Columbia, where she won several races on the Flat. Military Secret (by March Past) was a winner over hurdles. Honeybrook (by Heswall Honey) and Aquilino (by Quorum) went point-to-pointing, and about the former I shall have more to say later. Kitty Brook herself was put down at the age of twenty shortly before Mrs Makin went to live in Ireland.

Ever since 1946 *Raceform* had been performing the valuable service of printing an annual point-to-point formbook; and in 1955 they delighted their customers by producing a weekly one. Unfortunately, it only lasted for two seasons, after which it was presumably no longer considered an economic proposition, and at the same time the annual formbook fell by the wayside. Fortunately, the point-to-point results still continued to appear in the *Horse and Hound Yearbook*; but for the appearance of another weekly formbook we were going to have to wait until *Hunterform* came on the scene eleven years later.

The leading point-to-point riders of the 1955 season were Jeremy Everitt and Jennifer Renfree, the former with fifteen winners (plus three in hunter chases) and the latter with thirteen. Miss Renfree, the Sue Aston of her day, had nine of her successes on the East Cornwall pony Lonesome Boy, who went one better than in the previous season and won eleven races without conceding defeat.

Jeremy Everitt won five races (including two hunter chases) on Mr Shanks, four on Joe Turner's Tullaherin and four on his own Rosana III, all three horses being hunted with the West Norfolk, the hunt that had produced River Buoy and Treasurer, both of whom continued to win races. The star of this hunt was Mr J. A. Keith's Mr Shanks, a lop-eared gelding by Long Walk, who was a son of Double Walk, the dam of Meld, the winner of the 1,000 Guineas and the Oaks that year. Mr Shanks's sole defeat of 1955 was in the John Peel Cup at Manchester, where he went under to Happymint and May King, two horses that had been in the top rank of the hunter chasers for several seasons. The following season Mr Shanks was to get into this class himself with a win in the Liverpool Foxhunters'.

The six-year-old Rosana III, who was also destined to distinguish herself on the racecourse proper, had been acquired by Jeremy Everitt as an unbroken four-year-old. A daughter of Skoiter, she was bred by Mr T. Mitchell, of Fakenham, from All-a-Fire, a mare bred by King George V at Sandringham.

Another horse with a major success ahead of her was Sydney Maundrell's wonderfully game mare Solbay, from the V.W.H. (Cricklade), the winner of open races at the Oxford University Bullingdon Club and the Cotswold, and of a hunter chase at Fontwell. Solbay, who won her first race in 1952 as a five-year-old, was a lop-eared mare by Baman out of Soldeneeze, and thus a half-sister to Prince Deneeze, a good winner under Rules. Unable to run in 1953, Solbay came out again in 1954, after being fired, and won four races; and in 1955 the only horse to beat her in point-to-points was Charlie Nixon's Creeola II.

Creeola was a really hard-pulling horse who needed an exceptionally strong rider. So, after he had won three races, and been beaten in three others, 'Buster' Harty was flown over from Ireland to ride him in a division of the Dudley Cup. It was, in fact, from Buster's father that Mr Nixon had bought Creeola in Dublin, for £200 in 1953. The horse had subsequently been hunted with the Croome by Mrs Fred Rimell riding side-saddle. How Mrs Rimell managed to hold this tearaway horse in the hunting field, I have no idea; but perhaps he settled down there better than on the racecourse, where he was away like the wind as soon as he sniffed the first fence. Needless to say, nothing else got a look-in with this son of King's Approach in his division of the Dudley Cup. The following season he went into training with Fred Rimell, for whom he won several steeplechases, including the Welsh Grand National.

Cash Account, on whom Martin Tate won the other division of the Dudley Cup for Mr H. M. ('Joe') Ballard, was even more impressive than Creeola as a point-to-pointer; and although he won two other races that season his best was yet to come.

In the meantime, there was Gelderland, a horse many people in the West Midlands would have backed to beat either Creeola or Cash Account had he run in the Dudley Cup of 1955, for Gelderland was unbeaten that season in point-to-points; and he had two defeats of Creeola to his credit, one of them in the Charles Coventry Cup at the Croome over the Dudley Cup course. Owned by Mr W. R. Yardley, a Worcestershire farmer who is a familiar and jovial figure on the point-to-point courses of the West Midlands today, Gelderland was ridden in all his races by Mr Yardley's eldest son George, and looked after exclusively by George's young brother Bill, who was sixteen in 1955. In the course of his career, Gelderland won seventeen races, all but one of which were open events.

The Grimthorpe Cup attracted twenty-three starters, the highest number since the war. It was won, for the third time in six years by Arthur Stephenson, this time riding a horse he had purchased only ten days beforehand, the 17-hands-high Mr Gay, in a time that was considerably faster than Kitty Brook's the previous year. It was Mr Gay's first season in point-to-points, and he soon went on to make a name for himself under Rules, winning, among other races, the four-mile Withington Handicap Chase at Birmingham and the National Trial Handicap Chase at

Hurst Park; and he was third to Oscar Wilde and Crudwell in the Welsh Grand National of 1958.

Notwithstanding the fact that Pat Rushton won seven races on her little Episil, the only horse to win on the first and last day of the season, it must have been a toss-up between Mr J. M. Spurrier's seven-year-old Joyess, from the Meynell, and Mr Gilly Guilding's six-year-old Tweedledee, from the Ledbury, which was the best ladies' horse of the season. Pat Wint won four races on Joyess, including three ladies' opens; and Diana Guilding won five on Tweedledee, who won a sixth with her brother up and finished the season unbeaten. The two horses did meet once, in the ladies' open race at the South Shropshire, but on that occasion Joyess came down at the second fence.

Had Gay Roger been kept to ladies' races, however, Joyess and Tweedledee would certainly have had a close rival. This horse won three ladies' races, two men's open events and a hunter chase at Newton Abbot, to give a taste of the impact that was to be made by that clever establishment in the Mendips run by Miss Lucy Jones and her stable of girls.

In Surrey, Eric Savage produced a full brother to Master Cash. This was the five-year-old Newlands Prince, who proceeded to make an even bigger impression in his first season. With Mrs Savage riding, Newlands Prince won six ladies' races, winding up with a success in a division of the Corvedale Cup. The only horse to beat Newlands Prince was Episil, who got the better of him in the Gibbon Bowl at Larkhill, a success that owed much to Pat Rushton's superb riding.

It was during this time that Sheilagh French began to make the mark that has grown bigger and bigger as the years have gone by. She was riding a horse that most people hadn't heard of in the ladies' open race at the Wilton, and in that part of the country there weren't so many people who had heard of Sheilagh French either. The horse was Belsen Baby, an eight-year-old black gelding by Court Nez, the sire of Halloween; and in a field which included Episil and Gay Roger (both of whom came to grief) Mrs French got up in the run-in to beat the experienced Ida Croxon on Commando Assault. It was a remarkable performance, over a particularly testing course, especially when one considers that Belsen Baby, who had been hunted for two seasons with the West Kent, was making his first appearance of the season and that in his four outings the previous season he had never even been placed.

Since those days, Sheilagh and John French, have produced a whole string of winners from their stables at Cobham, near Gravesend, and I would be surprised if they have paid very much for any of them. Nevertheless they have now ridden some seventy winners apiece and won a Dudley Cup.

It was in 1948 that Sheilagh Desborough, as she then was, had her first ride in a race, on Rare Commotion at the Romney Marsh. She had borrowed a 30 lb. saddle for the occasion and before the race she downed a couple of large whiskies, which possibly explains the fact that when she was hoisted up on the horse she went straight over the other side. Put up again, she started off last, and was still last when she got to the second fence and came upon a horse that had refused. Her horse tried to do the same. So she gave him a kick and he jumped the obstacle from a standstill and shot her over his head. It was because of this appalling start, she says, that she never has a drink before a race nowadays, although she was once offered one when riding on the Flat in Italy; and when she declined it, her host said, 'Oh, but all the gentlemen riders always have a drink before a race and wouldn't think of starting without one.'

There are other ways of preparing for a race, of course; and in 1955 one of them concerned a coup that came unstuck. I regret to say that I was partially responsible for this coup being launched. An old friend of mine, Lionel Ensten, had a horse called Peeper who was doing very nicely in the precincts of the Puckeridge country, and I was rash enough to assure him that if he brought the horse to Cowdray Park on Easter Monday he could back himself to win the open race for the Pearson Cup for pounds, shillings and pence. Unfortunately for Peeper (and also for his supporters, of whom I was naturally one), the Cowdray course proved a trifle sharper than those he was used to and Peeper got done by a horse from the Chiddingfold Farmers, Harold Flux's Peerflex.

This horse Peerflex, who was purchased by Mr Flux for £100 as a four-year-old, had what might be called a chequered career. Later that same season he slipped up on the flat rounding a bend in a race at the Old Surrey and Burstow and the after-effects of this injury were such that it was thought he would have to be destroyed. His shoulder muscles rapidly deteriorated and he was found to be suffering from brachial paralysis. Mr Flux, however, had a very good friend in the Bramley veterinary surgeon, Donald Underwood, to whom Peerflex was sent; and when Mr Underwood's skill and patience were at last rewarded, the horse was able to return to his owner's farm in Surrey. After nursing Peerflex for the best part of a year, and walking him out each night, Mr Flux took him down to Hayling Island on the Hampshire coast and let him swim in the sea. The sea water treatment completed the cure that Donald Underwood had initiated and when the hunting season came round Peerflex was able to go out once more with the Chiddingfold Farmers. He had his first race for two years in an open event at Larkhill in February, 1957 and finished just behind the placed horses. That year he won three races, including the Duke of Gloucester Cup over 3½ miles at Tweseldown, a race he won again two years later. And in 1962, when he was thirteen years old, he won the hunt race at his home meeting.

Mrs Rosemary Lomax (née Ransom)

Mrs Sheilagh French

The scene in the paddock before the first division of the open race at the Golden Valley in 1953. Mythical Ray, who won this race, is No. 21. The figure in the foreground wearing plus-fours is Major Rushton

Roger Guilding on Atlantis in 1952

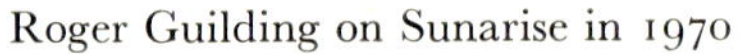

Roger Guilding on Sunarise in 1970

15
1956

In which a Kent horse wins the Dudley Cup and a Yorkshire one breaks a record in the Grimthorpe Cup

Many derogatory things have been written about point-to-pointers in the Press over the years; and there are some regular race-goers for whom a point-to-pointer is still in the same class as a donkey on Margate sands. But in 1956 a well-known racing journalist was writing: 'A horse I remember selecting for the Cambridgeshire some years ago was winning point-to-points almost before I had finished making excuses for its failure.'

This was the year the Melton Hunt Club was re-formed and the first of their memorable fixtures was held at Garthorpe, Leicestershire, on the permanent course already in use by the Belvoir; and, appropriately enough, there was a treble for two of the principals, Lance and Ursula Newton, who won the club members' race with Misty Nook, the farmers' race with Mr Speaker and the maiden race with Royal Demand, all of them ridden by R. L. ('Dicky') Black.

But for another kind of principal, Mr G. F. Fawcett's Trusty, the time had come for retirement, after a single unsuccessful appearance at the Hurworth. He was then seventeen years old and, in a career which spanned a complete decade, had run in thirty-six races, winning twenty of them, with Harry Elliott up on all but three occasions.

Owing to the prolonged frosts, there was no point-to-point racing until March. So the West Norfolk mare Rosana III had to go to Cheltenham without a preliminary race under her belt. But she still managed to win the National Hunt Chase, an achievement which reflected great credit on Jeremy Everitt.

Solbay, who was able to get in a couple of early races in hunter chases, gave Sydney Maundrell a fine ride in the United Hunts' Challenge Cup, beating Creeola II and Gay Roger; and before the season was out, the V.W.H. mare had won five more hunter chases, with her owner-rider putting up several lbs. overweight each time. Like Kitty Brook, she has since perpetuated the species; and one of her sons, Solboy, is now in training with Bryan Marshall, for whom he won a two-mile chase at Wincanton in November, 1969.

There were two joint leading riders in 1956, each with 12 point-to-point winners. One of them was a 23-year-old Welshman, Fred Mathias, who achieved the feat of riding four of the five winners at the South Pembrokeshire, and but for being beaten into second place in the hunt race would have made it five out of five. The other was Ted Greenway, the Lancashire veterinary surgeon who had been second in the list of leading amateurs under both sets of Rules, to Lord Mildmay under N.H. Rules and John Hislop on the Flat.

Thanks largely to the machine-like precision of Lonesome Boy, who remained unbeaten, Jennifer Renfree was again the leading lady rider with eleven wins, nine of them over banking courses, on Lonesome Boy, who also won over birch fences with Frank Ryall up.

Treasurer performed yet another weight-carrying feat in the Eastern Counties, at the ripe old age of fifteen. Mythical Ray, also aged fifteen, showed them all the way home in four more open events but got beaten in his own cup race at the Atherstone by the locally-trained Green Linnet; and Gillian Pearce, who had yet to reach her twentieth birthday, had two shining wins on Boroford, a spectacular little character who liked nothing better than to bowl along in front and invariably frightened the life out of those behind him by persistently jumping to one side.

But the best ladies' horses (though I hardly expect my West Country readers to concede that Lonesome Boy had any superiors in this department) were Newlands Prince and Archie Thomlinson's Kari Sou. Newlands Prince, who was to make the grade in N.H. racing the following season, started with a decisive defeat of Royal Prince in the Gibbon Bowl at Larkhill, where he knocked several seconds off the course record, and then proceeded to win his six remaining races, which included a division of the Corvedale Cup again on his final appearance of the season. Kari Sou, a son of Souverain, the Ascot Gold Cup winner of 1947, also ended up at the Ludlow, recording his fifth success of the season in the other division of the Corvedale Cup. This division was run in much faster time; so fast, in fact, that even the front-running Boroford could not go the pace. Archie Thomlinson has never put a mug up on any of his horses, and he certainly knew what he was doing when he engaged Molly Ratcliffe to ride Kari Sou.

Only two horses managed to win as many as five open point-to-points; and one of them, Mr E. Forshaw's Sleigh Run, from the Vale of Lune, would have made it six but for a disqualification for crossing at the Pendle Forest. The other was Cash Account, who won his second Dudley Cup and, before that, the four-mile race at the Heythrop. But in between these two races, he was beaten by Creeola II at the Wheatland and then, when sent up to Yorkshire to contest the Grimthorpe Cup, was unlucky enough to come up against More Honour.

And More Honour, who was at one time in training with Calverley Bewicke, was some horse! His time of 8 mins. 43½ secs. still stands as a record for this 4½ mile race. He was unbeaten that season; and had it not been for the fact that he was kept at livery, and was therefore ineligible to run under N.H. Rules, I am convinced that he would have walked away with the National Hunt Chase of 1957. This, in fact, was won by Kari Sou, who had finished sixth to More Honour in the Grimthorpe. Owned and ridden by Sidney Webster, a farmer in the East Riding of Yorkshire, More Honour was purchased at the Stockton Sales in 1953; and after being hunted by his owner with the Middleton and the Derwent he had his first success in the maiden race at the Middleton in 1955 at the age of eight. A bay gelding by Honor's Choice out of Kilmore Lass, he was closely related to Kerstin, the mare Major Bewicke trained to win the Cheltenham Gold Cup of 1958.

The Dudley Cup was run ten days after the Grimthorpe Cup; and Cash Account had no trouble at all accounting for Arthur Stephenson's Livery Man in the first division. In this race, and in all his others that season, he was ridden by Bill Foulkes, who has been associated with a number of good horses since then.

The other division was won by Galloping Gold, a horse I can safely claim to have needled Chris Nesfield into bringing up from Kent by telling him that it was all very well Galloping Gold sparkling away in his own area but the only way to see whether he was any good or not was to test him out in the Dudley Cup against the crack performers of the West Midlands. In his own area, Galloping Gold was so renowned for his finishing speed that a local newspaper correspondent had been inspired to describe him as 'the fastest horse ever seen on a course'; and at the Worcestershire this correspondent had the last laugh. Brilliantly handled by Chris Nesfield himself, Galloping Gold landed over the last fence on the heels of Gay Roger and Bob McCreery and sprinted away on the flat to win by a length, with Hyhal, a horse who had broken the course record at Crowell that season, eight lengths away in third place, followed by two of the best horses in the West Midlands, Danny Boy II and Gelderland. It was the first time that a Kent horse had won a Dudley Cup.

This was Chris Nesfield's last season before he became a professional trainer, and it was a particularly good one for him. Besides winning three races on Galloping Gold (who won a fourth with Bob Hacking up), he also saddled his ancient Steel Drop to win five races, four of them with his sister Pam riding.

But there was one horse in Kent who managed to beat both Galloping Gold and Steel Drop. This was Mrs W. N. McGaughey's eight-year-old bay gelding The Mhor, the winner of five races. The Mhor beat Steel Drop in the ladies' race at the East Kent and Galloping Gold in a division of the open race for the Harewoods Cup at the Old Surrey & Burstow.

And if I may add a postscript about Galloping Gold, he was never quite the same horse after his Dudley Cup win; so in one sense he paid rather dearly for it.

16

1957

In which Joe Ballard makes hay and Tim Forster looks over his shoulder

The 1957 season saw one notable relaxation in the regulations governing point-to-point races. Girls employed in a professional capacity were now permitted to ride in races. This was so sensible a move that the only curious thing about it was why it hadn't been initiated before. In future years it was to have a noticeably beneficial effect on the standard of riding in these races.

We also had the first ladies' race to be run officially over four miles. The experiment was inaugurated by the North Warwickshire over their course at Alcester Heath, and Lady Leigh, whose husband was Chairman of the Hunt and a Joint-Master, put up a handsome trophy for it. The experiment proved a great success and there were so many entries for the race that it had to be run in two divisions. A side-effect of this splendid enterprise was that it enabled Midlands racegoers to get their first sight of one of Scotland's star combinations, Barbara Paterson and her grey Corporal Major, a horse who had become known, in deference to his distinguished compatriot The Callant, as 'the other grey'.

It would be nice, after this, to say that Corporal Major, who came to Alcester with four wins behind him, was successful in his bid; but a fall at the last fence (his first in twenty-seven appearances), where he was being challenged by Coo, left the latter in complete command. It was the Dartmoor mare's sixth successive win in partnership with her owner, Mrs Gillian Chamberlain.

The other division was won by a horse from the Meynell, Mr John Spurrier's Joyess, who was just about the best ladies' horse of the season. A consistent winner for several years, Joyess was unbeaten in 1957, when he won five races. He was a good-looking, class horse, a grandson of April the Fifth, and he had two other Derby winners in his pedigree, Grand Parade (1919) and Sunstar (1911).

Pat Wint, who rode Joyess in all his races, was one of the best lady riders in the Shires for many years. She learned to ride from her uncle, Frank Wint, who used to train under N.H. Rules and rode many point-to-point winners himself. She had her first winning ride in 1950 at the age of twenty-two. But although she won a number of races on other good horses of Mr Spurrier's, notably Tartine and Icy Steel, I think she would probably agree that Joyess was the best horse she ever rode. At any rate, she won sixteen races in eighteen starts on him.

It goes almost without saying that in 1957 the West Country pony Lonesome Boy was still dominating the situation in his area, without a taste of defeat; and Jennifer Renfree was at the head of the ladies again, although this time she had to share her title with Sheilagh French, who won five races on Belsen Baby (unbeaten that season in point-to-points) and three on Poor Tips. Pat Newton, a leading lady rider of the future, won four races on Brown Adam and two on Clear Profit. Diana Guilding won six confined races on the Ledbury horse Singing Spider; and up in the far North, Mrs T. D. C. Dun was riding a future winner of the National Hunt Chase, Spud Tamson, the runner-up to the Tynedale mare Surprise Packet in the Heart of all England at Hexham that season.

The leading gentleman rider was Major R. W. Ingall, who had fourteen winners in the West Country. But whether he would still have been so had not three of Guy Cunard's horses Manar, Provident and fifteen-year-old Nigger Minstrel (the same Nigger Minstrel who had formerly belonged to the unfortunate Allan Walton) rendered themselves ineligible for point-to-point racing by winning modest races under Rules, is a matter for conjecture. I have always thought that this rule, whereby a horse who wins any kind of race under Rules during the current season – and it is one that still applies – is an unfair one, since it is very often much easier to win a selling chase in the autumn than an open point-to-point in the spring. It would be more sensible, I feel, if the amount of prize money were made the criterion.

Despite this, however, and the additional burden of a crippled arm, it was a fairly good season for Major Cunard, who won nine races, four of them in a row, including the new Henry Waterford Cup for the open race at the Melton Hunt Club, on Calypso Mio, perhaps the best horse he has ever had in his stable.

The leading owners must surely have been Mr and Mrs Lance Newton, who won seventeen races with their horses hunted in the Shires with the Belvoir and the Cottesmore. Another successful owner in this area was Mr J. T. Emerson, whose three horses won him eight races. The best of them was Treacle Tart, a horse that changed hands for 1,800 guineas after an inglorious career on the Flat. With Lord Patrick Beresford riding, this horse won five point-to-points and would have beaten two of the top hunter chasers, Happy Morn II and Solbay, in a hunter chase at Stratford but for ducking out at the last fence when in a clear lead.

In the East, the fawn and white checks of Mr Walter Wales were carried with prominence by his son David on the Irish mare Highland Trout, who won five open point-to-points and a hunter chase at Fakenham. But the coming star in these parts was Mr Geoffrey Mason's six-year-old Oxo, a more than satisfactory replacement for gallant old Treasurer, who collapsed and died at the Newmarket and Thurlow. At the close of the season, Oxo was sold at the Newmarket Sales to a patron of Willy Stephenson's Royston stable; and two years later he won the Grand National.

Ever since 1896, the Barclay family have enjoyed uninterrupted mastership of the Puckeridge, which is surely some record. The Joint-Masters today are Capt. C. G. E. Barclay and his wife; and in 1957, when the hunt's point-to-point jubilee was celebrated by the introduction of the Maltsters' Cup for the open event, Capt. Barclay was Joint-Master with his father.

Although the first Maltsters' Cup was not won by a member of the Barclay family, it was won by a member of another family which had a long connection with the hunt, the Harveys of Bishop's Stortford who farmed the land where these races were run for a quarter of a century.

And it was won in most spectacular style by the young Ted Harvey, who had broken his back in 1949 when having his first ride in a race at the age of fourteen. Landing clear over the last fence on his mother's Charles Ross, he was virtually put on the floor when his horse buckled at the knees and went down; but he was back in the saddle with such speed that he still managed to get Charles Ross home in time.

For Cash Account, it was a remarkable season even though he had four failures. One of these was when he made a bid for a repeat success in the four-mile race at the Heythrop, where he was well beaten this time by Star Bar, on whose dam Sydney Maundrell had had his first winning ride.

But I doubt if this setback to the apple of his eye worried Joe Ballard overmuch, because on his next appearance Cash Account, who was now being ridden by Billy Wynn, the 47-year-old Shropshire farmer he was thought to go best for, won the Charles Coventry Cup at the Croome, then beat Brown Sugar in the Grimthorpe Cup and wound up the season by becoming the first horse (and indeed the only one so far) to win the Dudley Cup three times. This last performance was the most satisfying of all for Joe Ballard, that indefatigable point-to-point enthusiast for whom the winning of a Dudley Cup was much more important than winning the Cheltenham Gold Cup. Besides, he had now gone one better than his brother George, who won the Dudley Cups of 1927 and 1928 on Merrivale II.

It was a particularly hot division this time because Flippant Lad, the runner-up, had already won seven races that season, and one of the other horses murdered by Cash Account was the Hutsby horse Gin and Sherry, an animal of high promise who had won hunter chases and was to go on to win many more (by the end of the 1959 season he had won ten in a row).

When I think of Gin and Sherry I am immediately reminded of The Dikler, that exceptional novice of the 1969 season. Like The Dikler, Gin and Sherry was a majestic personality who pulled like a train; but although he was bred for both speed and stamina, being by the Guineas winner Happy Knight out of a mare by Salmon Leap, in a true-run race he only just got three miles. Fred Hutsby, who bought him as a five-year-old and gave him to his son Henry, was an old rival of Joe Ballard on the racecourse in the early twenties, and he once told me that he had a cup dated 1922 for the farmers' race (owners up) at the Harkaway Club in which Joe Ballard was the runner-up. But now these two splendid representatives of the breed that is the very life-blood of point-to-point racing have both moved on and are no doubt racing against each other in the Elysian Fields.

The other division of the 1957 Dudley Cup was won by Reg Hindley's Prospero, a one-time show hunter who, with Peter Brookshaw up, achieved the rare distinction of making all the running over the Upton-on-Severn course. Prospero was winning his fourth race in a row, and in doing so he beat a red-hot favourite, Miss Lucy Jones's Gay Roger, the winner that season of six point-to-points and three hunter chases, including the United Hunts' Cup at Cheltenham. So for Miss Jones, and her jockey John Daniell, it was a case of two runners-up in the race they most wanted to win.

As a tailpiece to the 1957 season I shall now tell the story of the 11th Hussars. The regiment had not long returned from Malaya and were stationed at Carlisle, from which base they went hunting in Scotland with the Dumfriesshire. They brought six of their horses down from Carlisle in an elephant truck to run at the V.W.H. (Earl Bathurst's), where they won both divisions of the open event. Mr G. D. H. Wiggin won the first on his Jack's Crest; and another Hussar, Philip Payne-Gallwey, whose father was one of the distinguished soldier riders between the wars, was the runner-up on Unpredictable. The second division was won by Capt. Tim Forster, who now trains so successfully at Letcombe Bassett. Capt. Forster was riding his eight-year-old Struell Well, who gave him such an arm-chair ride that before the penultimate fence he was doing something that I am sure he would not tolerate from any of his jockeys today– looking over his shoulder!

17

1958

In which a Scottish hunter makes his mark and a classic rogue is saluted

The retirement of an old warrior is always rather a sad occasion. But when it is celebrated with a win it can also be an exhilarating one; and this is what happened in the case of Mythical Ray when he won the hunt race at the N. Warwickshire in May 1958 at the age of seventeen for Mr Jack Jones, a farmer at Preston Bagot who hunted with the N. Warwickshire for fifty seasons and died in 1970. Starting in 1951, Mythical Ray ran in sixty-one races, won twenty-eight of them and finished either second or third in a further nineteen. And in the vast majority of these races the man on top was Tony Rogers, who started his racing career the same year as Mythical Ray, as a very young man on an old scrubber.

There is not much doubt what the best horse to run in point-to-points during 1958 was, for that was the year when Merryman II won two ladies' races in the hands of his owner, Miss W. H. Wallace, who had bought him as a five-year-old two years beforehand for the proverbial song and hunted him with the Buccleuch. This was yet another point-to-pointer who was to attain the highest honours; after winning the Liverpool Foxhunters' and the Scottish Grand National in 1959, Merryman went on to become the first Scottish-bred horse to win the Grand National. That was in 1960, and he was runner-up to Nicolaus Silver in the 1961 race. Merryman was a horse with a romantic history. A son of the premium stallion Carnival Boy, he was bred by the late Lord Linlithgow and was the first foal of Maid Marion, a mare by Bold Archer who was acquired by Lord Linlithgow with the express intention of breeding a National winner from her.

It seems a pity, looking back, that Merryman was never given a chance to win the point-to-point Grand National, as he must surely have accounted for the 1958 Grimthorpe Cup winner,

Brown Sugar; although a prodigious stayer (he also won the 4½ mile Melton Hunt Club Cross Country Ride), this horse was not in the same class as More Honour or Cash Account.

For the first time in its history, the Dudley Cup was run in three divisions; and in the first of them Brown Sugar was well and truly put in his place by a young horse from Wales, Master Copper, who rewarded his supporters on the tote with a pay-out of over £9 for a 4/– stake. But at that time, of course, one could hardly have suspected that the owner-rider of this horse would later become a leading trainer under N.H. Rules. His name was Colin Davies, the future trainer of Persian War. In those days, Colin Davies was rather more interested in racing motor-cars than he was in point-to-point riding, and his profession was that of a chartered secretary in a family estate business. But besides racing cars and riding in the odd race, he was Hon. Sec. of the Pentyrch Foxhounds. Master Copper proved a most useful servant to him, and among the races he won was the United Hunts' Cup at Cheltenham in 1960.

The second division of the Dudley Cup was won very comfortably by John French on what was probably the best horse he and Sheilagh have ever had, their chestnut mare Domabelle, who was acquired from her breeder, Gerry Langford, the Lingfield veterinary surgeon, one of the star point-to-point riders in the South before the war. It was Domabelle's first season of point-to-point racing and she had won her six previous races with Sheilagh on top. Although this chestnut mare was a consistent winner for the Frenches, she can't have been an easy ride, for she went clean through the middle of most of her fences. Fortunately, she had a front on her like the prow of a battleship. Atom Bomb, the fourteen-year-old grey from the Devon and Somerset Staghounds who finished third to Domabelle in the Dudley Cup, won ten of his twelve races that season; and N. H. Williams, who rode this horse, was joint leading rider with another West countryman, R. J. Edwards, each riding 12 winners.

The favourite for the third division was Sydney Maundrell's six-year-old Kolpham, the winner of the four-mile race at the Heythrop and runner-up to Spud Tamson in the National Hunt Chase. But they went too fast for him and he was beaten into fourth place behind the Warwickshire horse Some Baby, who was ridden by that very skilful rider John Thorne. This horse virtually had the Cheltenham Foxhunters' presented to him on a plate the following season when the northern hunter chaser Whinstone Hill fell at the last fence and left him in a clear lead.

The Scottish horse Corporal Major again made a raid on the Lady Leigh Cup at the N. Warwickshire, only to come up against a real cracker in the Blankney mare Oh! Mavis, who duelled with him most of the way and then sprinted ahead from the last fence to win by four lengths, with little Boroford ten lengths away third. There was not much of this mare, but what there was was wonderfully game, and she had a splendid partner in Sybil Jessop, who won four races on her that season, including a division of the Corvedale Cup at the Ludlow.

If I were to be asked what was the best horse to run in Kent during the fifties, I should be stumped. But I have no doubt at all what was the biggest 'rogue' in that part of the country. The answer is Hymettus, the chestnut son of Hyperion who for five years, between 1957 and 1961, waged war with his incredibly patient and good-humoured owner-rider, Mike French, a brother of John. Why then do I bother to mention Hymettus in this book? Because he was not only a very great rogue but a very great character who contributed greatly to the enjoyment of point-to-point-goers in Kent. Especially if they hadn't backed him. This horse was a genuine equine eccentric and no one knew it better than his owner, who loved him for it, and bought him the most magnificent pair of blue blinkers I have ever seen.

But if Hymettus was a rogue, he was also a brilliant rogue, and on those occasions when Mike French kidded him into completing the course there was nothing to touch him. 'The heyday of Hymettus', and I am now quoting from an article on 'The Poetry of Rogues' that I wrote for *The Light Horse*, 'was 1958, when he was kidded into winning three open point-to-points and two hunter chases, but retaliated by putting Mike French in his place on three other occasions. After that, not even the famous blinkers worked any more; and after he had failed seven times in 1959 to persuade Hymettus to complete the course, once more in 1960 and twice more in 1961, Mike French finally gave up the unequal struggle and acknowledged the horse as his Master'.

Hymettus, I salute you, on behalf of all other rogues.

18

1959

In which Spinning Coin II shows her class, the Novices' Championship commences at Melton and a race is lost in the Objection Room

1959 was a season at once sad and inspiring. It was the year that a seventeen-year-old girl, Sally Haynes, won her first race in her first ride, on Allan Walton's Problem Boy at the Oxford University meeting at Lockinge; and then, two months later, broke her back riding another horse at the Grafton. Today Sally Haynes is confined to a wheel-chair; but she has won a gold medal for fencing at the Paralympics (Israel 1968) and is the very active Chairman of the Finmere Jumping Show in aid of the Stoke Mandeville Games – the Sports Movement of the Paralysed.

It was also the year that Arthur Stephenson became a professional trainer; the year when the Old Etonian Association Race, which had last been run at the V.W.H. (Earl Bathurst's) in 1947, was revived at the Heythrop, and won by twenty-two-year-old Tim Holland-Martin on his Hilly Wood; the year that Dicky Black had his 100th win, on Not a Link at the Belvoir; the year that Bantry Bay and Hard Frost made their point-to-point débuts and Lonesome Boy retired.

The East Cornwall pony was now fourteen years old and he departed from the scene in a trail of glory, winning seven races and preserving intact the sequence of wins which extended over six seasons. There has never been another animal of his size (he was no more than fifteen hands) to touch him. Beginning in 1950 as a five-year-old, Lonesome Boy won sixty-five races, fifty-three of them in succession, and he was equally proficient over banks and fly fences. His owner, Mr W. J. Rogers, a Bodmin farmer, bought him ungelded as a two-year-old and put him to a mare of his called Lazy Bones, who produced a colt which he named Lazy Boy; and on March 27th, 1954, when he was five years old, Lazy Boy won the maiden race at the Silverton and Lonesome Boy won the ladies' race there. I think this is probably the only occasion when a father and a son have won at the same fixture.

Hard Frost, a rather narrowly-built gelding by Winter's Tale out of a mare by Spearmint, was certainly the most prolific winner produced in Essex since the war, and he had won a couple of two-mile chases before he came to point-to-point racing at the age of nine and carried the colours of the Purleigh farmer George Barber so successfully. Mr Barber, a refreshingly forthright character, who was never slow to take up the cudgels when anyone dared to cast doubts on the ability of his champion to thrash everything in sight, had won a fair number of races in his time on a good old horse called Rumplestiltskin II; but by 1958, when Hard Frost won five races, he had handed over the reins to his two sons, Mick and Roy, and it was the twenty-two-year-old Mick who assumed the partnership with Hard Frost that was to draw the crowds like a magnet.

The Dufosee horse Bantry Bay, another son of April the Fifth, had been in training with Frank Cundell, for whom he was placed several times over hurdles, before he started in point-to-points at the age of eight. He won only a single point-to-point in his first season, but he was also successful in two hunter chases, the events in which he was really to make his name. Like so many of the Dufosee horses, this own brother to Spring Corn was bred at Harry Dufosee's Stalbridge Park Stud in Dorset and traced back to Maybush, the foundation mare that Harry Dufosee received as a gift from Lord Stalbridge. Harry Dufosee, who had his first ride in a race in 1913 and rode numerous winners after the First World War, had long since given up race-riding by this time, and Bantry Bay was being ridden in 1959 by his son Tony, who was then aged forty.

As a point-to-pointer (she was a comparative failure when tried in hunter chases), the Taunton Vale mare Spinning Coin II (by Artist's Son) was the superior of Bantry Bay and all the others in the South West. In fact, she was almost in a class of her own. Owned by Tim Handel, a Somerset farmer, she won two races as a five-year-old in 1958 and was unbeaten in 1959, when she won eight open events and numbered amongst her victims the eventual winner of a division of the Dudley Cup, Miss Lucy Jones's Flippant Lad. I would put Spinning Coin II among the very best that I have seen in point-to-points and it was a great tragedy that she always seemed to find N.H. fences too much for her. But she has left her mark on the N.H. scene in another way. One of her sons, Royal Toss, won the Whitbread Gold Cup at Sandown in 1970.

The leading rider of the 1959 season was the long-legged David Wales, a quietly efficient horseman, very strong in a finish. He rode sixteen point-to-point winners and also had a win in a hunter chase. Seven of these wins were on his father's Pearly Glint, a seven-year-old gelding in his first season of point-to-point racing; three were on Highland Trout, a horse just about to go out of the King's Lynn stable; and three were on Master Fifty, a horse about to come into it. At the end of the season, Mr Wales, Snr. engaged in a swap with Master Fifty's owner, who had his eye on Highland Trout for breeding purposes, while Mr Wales saw the potential of Master Fifty as a racehorse, possibly because he was by Grandmaster, the sire of Colledge Master.

A word is not out of place here for another West Norfolk stalwart, Eldred Wilson. Although he had now left his fiftieth birthday behind him, Major Wilson won two point-to-points and three hunter chases on his young horse Essandem, who was proving a worthy successor to River Buoy.

There was a remarkable riding performance that season in the West Midlands, where Bill Yardley (the same who looked after Gelderland so tenderly) won the adjacent hunts' race at the Albrighton Woodland on Merry Courier after losing a stirrup iron at the start and riding over the entire course without any irons at all. Old man Yardley, standing on the touchline, almost died of pride.

The Dudley Cup was chiefly notable for the fact that Miss Lucy Jones and John Daniell, were at last rewarded for their persistence when Flippant Lad got the better of Hilly Wood in a rather sub-standard division. The other division was won by the South Pembrokeshire mare Clover Bud, who subsequently became an accomplished steeplechaser, winning the Welsh Grand National among other races.

As for the Grimthorpe Cup, with More Honour once again in the field, the result was a foregone conclusion. The Yorkshire horse had no trouble disposing of Livery Man and Scotland's Clydebrook (in the Corporal Major ownership), thus becoming the only horse to win this endurance test twice since the distance was increased to 4½ miles.

Corporal Major, who had won four ladies' races in the Border country that season, was in the field once more for the Lady Leigh Cup at the N. Warwickshire, but again it was a case of returning home with the minor spoils. The race was run in underfoot conditions that were little short of a morass. But there were twelve starters for it, only two of whom were able to act properly in the going. The 'other grey' was one of them, and he and Tartine went right away from the others and were together until they got to the last fence, where Tartine's superior turn of foot proved the deciding factor. This eight-year-old mare was in the same stable as Joyess, and she was very nearly as good. She had won her only race the previous season and was unbeaten in her three races of 1959, with Pat Wint riding each time. After the season was over, Mr Spurrier sold both Tartine and his other good mare Icy Steel at the Ascot Sales, where the former fetched 1,600 guineas and the latter 1,250 guineas. Tartine subsequently won a couple of chases from Calverley Bewicke's Alnwick stable, while Icy Steel went on to win many more ladies' races for 'Fizz' Robarts, the present Mrs David Chown.

Joyess having now graduated to handicap chases (he won four of these between October, 1958 and April, 1960), the best ladies' horse of 1959, apart from Tartine, was almost certainly the Blankney mare Oh! Mavis, who gave Mrs Jessop five wins in a row and captured three major trophies, the Blankney Vase, the Corvedale Cup and Lord Astor's Cup at the Melton Hunt Club.

The Novices' Championship, for horses that hadn't won a race before the start of the season, was now in its first year at Melton; and this race, which has grown in stature over the years and produced some highly promising horses, was won in 1959 by Archie Thomlinson's Croizet, an extraordinary customer who cost his owner thirty guineas as a yearling and had a nasty habit of diving right into his fences. A brilliant horse when he had a strong jockey, Croizet got one at Melton in the shape of Guy Cunard, who wrapped his long legs round his flanks and stuck to his back like a limpet. At the end of the season Croizet was bought by a patron of Peter Cazalet's stable, but he never won a race for the Fairlawne stable (he had to wait until he was back with Archie Thomlinson for that) though he was third to Kerstin in the Hennessy Gold Cup.

Although 1959 wasn't a conspicuously successful point-to-point

Lawrence Morgan and Colledge Master at the Tedworth in 1956

Cash Account (Bill Foulkes) returning to the paddock after he had won his second Dudley Cup, in 1956. Behind him is his owner, Joe Ballard; and behind Joe Ballard is Arthur Stephenson on Livery Man, the runner-up

Miss Lucy Jones leading in her Gay Roger after he had finished second to Prospero in a division of the 1957 Dudley Cup with John Daniell up

More Honour, ridden by his owner, Sidney Webster, jumping the last fence at Whitwell-on-the-Hill in 1959 to win his second Grimthorpe Cup

Lord Grimthorpe presenting his cup to Mr Webster. In the centre of the picture is John Russell, who did sterling work as Hon. Sec. of the Middleton point-to-point for many years

season for Major Cunard, who was even without a mount in the Grimthorpe Cup, he won five hunter chases on the ten-year-old Calypso Mio, including the Past and Present Hunters' Chase at Sandown. In this race, John Thorne, riding that good horse Mr Teddy, had the temerity to squeeze through an opening on the rails that promptly closed as soon as the Major tumbled to what was happening. The two horses gave each other an almighty bump from which Calypso Mio emerged much the worse for wear, and Mr Teddy went by the post first. Well, one doesn't do that sort of thing to the Major and get away with it. Not only did Mr Teddy lose the race in the objection room but the Warwickshire rider was fined by the Stewards and cautioned for 'injudicious riding'.

19

1960

In which a point-to-point Bible is born, Scotland is dispossessed and Sue Aston follows in the footsteps of Pat Tollit

For the point-to-point punting fraternity – and it is larger than most people imagine, though its betting boots have sadly decreased in size – the most momentous event in 1960 was the first appearance of Geoffrey Sale's *Annual of Hunter Chasers and Point-to-Pointers*, which dropped like manna from Heaven and might now be justifiably described as the point-to-point Bible. Certainly it is a book which no regular point-to-point-goer in his right senses would be without.

For some years Geoffrey Sale had been demonstrating his talents as a human calculating machine in the correspondence columns of *The Sporting Life*, where his pre-season letters were eagerly awaited by an ever-growing body of readers, some of whom even had the temerity to dispute his handicap marks and produce their own. His first annual, printed in roneo-type and published in paper-back form (it is a hardback these days and the roneo-type has given way to the real thing), listed every animal that had run in hunter chases or point-to-points during the 1959 season. There were descriptions of each horse, varying in length from the best part of a page to a few lines, and some 900 horses were awarded handicap marks ranging from 12–7 to 7–4. Not unnaturally, the top of the handicap was dominated by the hunter-chasing brigade. At the top of the list was Whinstone Hill (12–7), who subsequently won the Cheltenham Foxhunters', and after him came five others of similar calibre, R.U.C.D. (12–4), Gin and Sherry, Happy Morn II, J'Arrive and Speylove, all on the 12–2 mark, followed by three more hunter chasers, Mighty's Niece, Felhampton, Sabaria and the top-listed point-to-pointer, Spinning Coin II, all at 11–13. Lonesome Boy, it is interesting to note, was awarded 11–1.

There was one race in 1960 that I shall never forget, and that was the Grimthorpe Cup. There was a determined Scottish bid to win the race that year, and when Mr William Hamilton's grey Earlshaugh, from the Jedforest, who had previously won the four-mile race at the Percy, appeared to go past the post with a good half length in hand of the Northumberland horse Gay William a great Scottish roar went up. But it was short-lived because the judge had other ideas and declared Gay William the winner by a neck. I am bound to say that the Scottish contingent (particularly the connections of the unfortunate runner-up) took their defeat in a most sporting manner and no whisky bottles were thrown, although after I had written a fairly discreet report on the race in *The Sporting Life* I did receive an anonymous letter from Scotland signed 'We Wus Robbbed'. The judge, a distinguished soldier, is now dead, so I feel free to tell the following story with impunity. I was once given a lift off the course by him and was much amused to hear him deliver himself as follows: 'What I say is, when two good horses run a genuine race over three miles and finish within a length of each other they deserve to be given a dead-heat, what!' I am still wondering why he didn't settle for a dead-heat in the case of Gay William and Earlshaugh.

In that other great test of endurance, Lord Ashton of Hyde's Cup at the Heythrop, Mr Raymond Johnson's Mascot III, an eleven-year-old gelding from the North Warwickshire, made every inch of the running to beat two former winners of the race, Kolpham and Andy Pandy. The rider of this winner, Bob Woolley, a twenty-year-old coalminer, had had his first ride in a race three weeks beforehand when he won the open race at the Albrighton on the same horse. Needless to say, his background was far from being a horsy one, and he had never had a riding lesson in his life so far as I know. But he had been observed by Mr Johnson running after riderless horses, catching them, and riding them back to the paddock. So the shrewd Mr Johnson decided to offer him the ride on Mascot. Bob Woolley, whose riding style that season was described by one unkind critic as 'like Scobie Breasley in a five furlong sprint', is no longer a coalminer; but he *is* one of the most talented riders in point-to-point racing today, a natural-born horseman if ever there was one; and in recent years he has frequently turned what has looked liked certain disaster into a breathtaking win.

It was Mascot, too, who won the four-mile ladies' race at

the North Warwickshire, and on this occasion he was ridden by Pat Rushton, who by this time had become Mrs John Tollit and was generally acknowledged to be the finest lady point-to-point rider of all time. The Guy Cunard of the distaff side, in fact. Yet strangely enough this was only the second time in 10 years that Mrs Tollit had actually been the leading lady rider. The first was in 1951, when she rode nine winners; and in 1960 she also had nine wins, six of them on her father's Rosie's Cousin, a winner at Melton. Rosie's Cousin, then six years old, later made a considerable reputation as a hunter chaser, and though his best distance was under three miles, Pat Tollit was never beaten on him in a point-to-point. But he was by no means her most prolific winner. Episil, on whom she won 24 races, had this distinction, and Lucky Dip was close behind with 20 wins.

It was in 1960 that the Wiltshire-born Sue Aston had her first win, on My Milly, at the Mid-Devon. She was then fourteen years old and she rode five winners that season. This superlative rider, who sits a horse like a professional flat-race jockey, is Pat Tollit's natural successor and today she is unexcelled in the art of riding a finish. In recent years she has learned a great deal from the experience she has had of riding on the Flat in France, where she rides out regularly for professional trainers during the summer. In that enlightened country she has won a number of races against top-class opposition. Her greatest ambition is to ride in a ladies' hunter chase in England. But as the very idea of such a race is enough to give the Jockey Club a heart attack, it seems she will have some time to wait.

Bantry Bay and Spinning Coin II were now confining themselves mainly to hunter chases; but both made winning appearances at Larkhill, where Bantry Bay broke the course record with a time of six minutes ten seconds when winning at the Tedworth in May, the previous best being the six minutes eleven seconds recorded by Newlands Prince in 1956 with a stone less weight. Bantry Bay's record was to stand for the next five years.

The four wins in hunter chases registered by Bantry Bay during 1960 included one in the Final Champion Hunters' Chase at Stratford for the *Horse and Hound* Cup, a race he was to win again the following year, ridden on both occasions by Michael Tory. But he was beaten at Wincanton by Spinning Coin II. The Taunton Vale mare also won at Newton Abbot, but she was a faller in her three other races, and these included the National Hunt Chase at Cheltenham, where she started favourite.

Neither Spinning Coin nor Bantry Bay essayed the Dudley Cup, the two divisions of which were both won by West Country horses, though neither was ridden by either of the two West Countrymen, Frank Ryall and R. J. Edwards, who were the joint leading riders of the season, with fourteen winners apiece. George Small won the first division on the Blackmore Vale ten-year-old Precious Gem, who beat Lucy Jones's Flippant Lad; and John Daniell won the second on Miss Jones's Culleenpark. But it was not a vintage year for the race.

But one race it was a vintage year for, at least in a manner of speaking, was the Old Etonian Association Race at the Heythrop, even if the winner was barely heard of again. Guy Cunard on John Lawrence's Newbridge Lad and Capt. Ramsey on The Boss Man were approaching the last fence a street in front of the others when Newbridge Lad hit the fence hard and came down; and Capt. Ramsey, looking over his shoulder to see what had happened, was evidently so astonished by what he saw that he promptly fell off, leaving Sir Mark Palmer to come up from nowhere and win the race on his appropriately named Hopeful Charlie.

In the Lutwyche Hunters' Cup at Hereford the Monmouthshire mare Mariji, a wonderfully consistent performer in ladies' races, won for the last time. She was eleven years old and had won 23 races, 22 of them with Miss Isobelle Lewis in the saddle.

And in the adjacent hunts' ladies' race at the Lauderdale, The Callant appeared for the last time on a racecourse. He was ridden by Mrs Rosemary Bird, the lady who subsequently married his owner, and the horse that he beat was his Scottish compatriot Corporal Major.

20

1961

In which the prize money is increased, Lucy Jones has a notable double, Baulking Green makes his appearance, Hymettus has a successor

For years a campaign for increased prize money for point-to-point racing had been waged; and at last, in time for the 1961 season, a tiny step forward was taken. The National Hunt Committee raised the ceiling from £20 to £40 in the case of a winner of an open event and to £30 for the winner of any other event. But the place money remained miserably the same, £10 for the second, £5 for the third, and sweet Fanny Adams for the fourth.

And what they gave with one hand they took away with the other, for it was also stipulated that 'No further prize from any source whatsoever may be given,' apart from the customary challenge cups and mementoes, the latter not exceeding £10 in value. This anachronistic regulation, which still persists today (as does the same level of prize money) effectively put a stop to the handsome subsidiary prizes in kind (cocktail cabinets, etc.) that some meetings were giving, notably the Melton Hunt Club. works of art were also taboo, and those meetings which had been in the habit of commissioning that noted horse painter Peter Biegel to execute paintings for presentation to the winners of their open races (the Grimthorpe Cup race was the first in the field in this department) were no longer able to do so.

The increased prize money was thankfully received by the point-to-point fraternity, though enthusiasm for the concession was tempered by regret for its niggardliness; and John Tilling, the forward-looking Hon. Sec. of the Old Surrey and Burstow meeting, pointed out acidly that the prize money for point-to-point racing, even with this increase, was now actually less than it was in 1884; while Guy Cunard, who has never been slow to castigate the N.H. Committee when he thought they deserved it – which was quite often – described the increase as 'hopelessly inadequate' and was all for the sky being the limit, with point-to-points left to find their own economic level. He had no time at all, he said, for the argument that any substantial increase in prize money would put the smaller meetings at a disadvantage. It was like saying that 'Cheltenham must not put on a big race because Buckfastleigh can't match it.'

There was a human tragedy during this season. That fine rider Sybil Jessop died as the result of a fall at the Brocklesby at the untimely age of forty-one. And I regret to say that this was seized upon by a correspondent to *Horse & Hound* as an excuse for making the most outrageous suggestion of the year, namely that ladies' races should be abolished. It was a suggestion that Mrs Jessop herself would have dismissed with contempt.

Although it can hardly have been considered significant at the time, it is interesting to recall now that a fourteen-year-old boy namely that ladies' races should be abolished. It was a sugges- event at the South Shropshire on April 29th 1961, and won on Green Turban. This was the same Bob Davies who was to turn professional six years later, after finishing at Wye College; and who was joint leading jockey under N.H. Rules with Terry Biddlecombe in the 1968–69 season and champion in his own right the the following season.

Two good old point-to-pointers had the last wins of their careers in 1961, the West Country banking pony Delilah (who, if not so spectacular as Lonesome Boy, was almost as consistent) and Scotland's Corporal Major. Starting in 1954 as a five-year-old, Delilah won forty-eight races and was rarely beaten after her first season. Corporal Major, facing tougher opposition, was the winner of twenty-two races in forty-four appearances, and only on four occasions was he unplaced. He won the ladies' race at the Lanarkshire and Renfrewshire six times in succession, and the ladies' race at the Dumfriesshire, his home meeting, six times in seven years; and on every occasion this grey son of The Grey Abbot out of an Arab mare was ridden by his owner, Miss Barbara Paterson, of Langholm.

'When the grandchildren of those of us who attended the Cambridge University point-to-point at Marks Tey invite us to enthuse over the exploits of some equine hero of the future,' wrote the point-to-point correspondent of the *East Anglian Daily*

Times that season, 'they will be met with a patronising air and the words : "You never saw Hard Frost".'

I have no doubt this is true. By this time the name of Mr George Barber's Essex champion was almost sacred in the Eastern half of the country, and the idea of his defeat was practically blasphemy. In 1961, when he won six open point-to-points and a hunter chase at Market Rasen, his only defeat in point-to-points was when he ran off course in the open race at the Essex and Suffolk, lost the best part of two furlongs and came back again to finish within five lengths of the winner.

Although, like so many others, I had a great admiration for Hard Frost, I often wondered how he would have fared against the crack point-to-pointers of the West Midlands, and it was a source of considerable regret to me that he was never sent to contest the Dudley Cup.

One horse Hard Frost might have found very difficult to beat that season was Young Rajah, a lop-eared six-year-old from the Beaufort, owned by Mr R. J. Horton and ridden by his son David. After he had won three open events and beaten Flippant Lad twice, many people had their eye on Young Rajah as a potential Dudley Cup winner. But they were disappointed. Before this race was run he had passed into the hands of the Queen Mother and was soon in training with Peter Cazalet. But although he managed to win a novices' chase, he was not a conspicuous success under Rules; nor when, in later years, he appeared in point-to-points in the Surrey area. One might say of him that he lit up the point-to-point scene for a single season and then disappeared into obscurity.

The Dudley Cup continued to be run in two divisions, and in 1961 Miss Lucy Jones and John Daniell achieved the unparalleled feat of winning both of them, the first with Flippant Lad (for the second time in three years) and the second with Corn Star.

The remarkable thing about Flippant Lad was that he went very lame in the summer of 1959 and the X-rays showed that he had pedalositis. Since there was no cure for this, Miss Jones had him de-nerved, an operation which was performed by Peter Scott-Dunn, the veterinary surgeon to our Olympic three-day event team. The horse rarely put a foot wrong afterwards.

Corn Star was a son of Cacador, who stood at the Clonmult Stud in Dungourney, Co. Cork, and whose progeny won nineteen

The Callant and his owner, Mr C. D. (Charlie) Scott, taking part in the Parade of Horse Personalities at the Horse of the Year Show at Harringay Arena in 1958

Another of the point-to-pointers who made a great impact on the N.H. scene – Merryman II, ridden by Charlie Scott, going down to the post for the *Horse & Hound* Cup at Stratford in 1959

Mr George Barber's Hard Frost, the pride of the Eastern Counties for so many years, seen here at the Hertfordshire in 1962 with Mick Barber up

Major Guy Cunard winning the hunt race at the Middleton on Puddle Jumper in 1962

races worth a total of £3,743 during the 1959–60 season. He was bought unbroken from Mr Corny Barry, of the Leadington Stud in Co. Cork, the source from which Miss Jones also got Culleenpark and Flippant Lad; and the man who broke Corn Star, and hunted him with the Mendip Farmers', was Maurice Ffitch, one of the grooms who went with the British three-day event team to Helsinki in 1952.

A brilliant point-to-pointer, Corn Star, like Spinning Coin II, was not really a success over regulation fences; and in 1962, when he was tried in hunter chases, he never managed to win any of them, though he was runner-up to Bantry Bay at Wincanton and to Mr Teddy in the United Hunts' Cup at Cheltenham, where he came over the last fence in front.

The star hunter chaser of the 1961 season, if one excludes Colledge Master, who won the Cheltenham Foxhunters' at the age of twelve, was Pride of Ivanhoe, owned by Mr S. T. Hewitt, of Ashby-de-la-Zouch, and hunted in the Shires with the Atherstone and the Quorn by his owner's sixteen-year-old son, Philip. This horse, who had won two point-to-points in 1960 as a five-year-old, was unbeaten in hunter 'chases during 1961; and when he won the first of them at Stratford, with Norman Swinnerton up, he started at odds of 33–1 (nearly 90–1 on the tote). In his six remaining races, all of which he won, he was ridden by Philip Hewitt. It was thought at the time that Pride of Ivanhoe would make a Gold Cup horse but he never quite attained that eminence, though he won a couple of good handicap chases.

But there was an even greater hunter chaser than Pride of Ivanhoe coming up from the ranks in 1961. One of the greatest ever, in fact, a horse who can certainly be ranked with Colledge Master and The Callant. The horse was Baulking Green, the winner of the maiden race at the Craven Farmers. This big raking chestnut by Coup de Myth was out of a mare by Irish Trout called Nicotine Nellie, of whom John Lawrence has written : 'she was so wicked as to be almost unridable. A particularly brave man did once persuade her to go out hunting – but got no further than the meet before he was begged for his own and everyone else's safety to go home!'

But there was nothing ungenerous about Baulking Green. All that he could be faulted for were his sore shins, which necessitated his being given a fortnight's rest after every race; and when early in 1963, Mr Jim Reade, the sporting Berkshire farmer who owned and bred this great horse, sent him to Tim Forster (who by that time had taken up residence as a professional trainer at Letcombe Bassett), Baulking Green soon proceeded to dominate the hunter chase scene. He won the *Horse and Hound* Cup at Stratford three times and the United Hunts' Cup at Cheltenham four times (feats achieved by no other horse). For three seasons, between 1965 and 1967, he had the distinction of heading Geoffrey Sale's handicap three times; and the only reason why he didn't head it in 1963 and 1964 was that a horse called Freddie was already there.

As a contrast to Baulking Green there was Worker, a worthy candidate for any gallery of rogues and a true disciple of Hymettus, though perhaps without the latter's endearing character, for to the best of my knowledge Hymettus never refused to start. Worker did, on several occasions, and clearly enjoyed doing so. All the same, he was a horse of no mean ability when he chose to show it, which admittedly was not very often, though he once finished third to Colledge Master and Bantry Bay; and even inspired Geoffrey Sale (I am sorry, Geoffrey) to write in his annual, 'Very promising. Should do well in 1961'. All sorts of jockeys had a go on Worker, including two top-class amateurs, John Bosley and Michael Tory (who managed to finish second on him after being left 100 yards), and a top-class professional, Stan Mellor (who was also left 100 yards and finished second on him). But the person I felt most sorry for was Michael Bates, the young Essex amateur who had visions of reforming Worker and bought him at the Ascot Sales in 1963 for 260 guineas. It was a brave venture doomed to failure. Poor Michael Bates never got as far as the first fence on Worker, who might have been more appropriately named Shirker.

I have left myself with little space in which to deal with other aspects of the 1961 season; and to those of my readers who feel aggrieved – as they are entitled to – I can only reply that I am telling a story and not writing a history.

However, I would just like to say that John Daniell was the season's leading rider, with sixteen winners, followed by Guy Harwood with fifteen, seven of them (all open events) on his wonderfully generous Spinster's Folly; that 'Fizz' Robarts was the leading lady with ten wins, which embraced both divisions of the

Gibbon Bowl at Larkhill, where she was successful on Glenweather and Icy Steel; and that Raymond Johnson and his coalminer jockey Bob Woolley had a great season with two novices, Odd Eyes and Huntley II.

21
1962

In which girls are made to wait, everything's not quite rosy, and a Yorkshire mare beats a Scottish one

The new rule forbidding girls from riding in point-to-points until they reached the age of eighteen was introduced at the start of the 1962 season, and some interesting views were expressed about it. On balance, they were largely unfavourable, at least among the people I talked to myself. Mrs Pat Tollit, who again rode more winners (nine) than any other lady rider that season, made the point that girls of eighteen having their first ride in a race would be totally inexperienced, and her view was that instead of an age bar for riders there should be a rule prohibiting novice horses from running in these races. A male rider, John Daniell, made the same point; while the courageous Sally Haynes, who described her own fearful accident as 'just one of those things', was convinced that a sixteen-year-old with a sound knowledge of horsemanship (and there are plenty of them about these days) would ride better than many women twice her age. Admittedly some men take a different view. 'I regard point-to-point racing as a man's sport,' one of them said smugly, 'and anyway women are much more accident prone than men.' No doubt this is the view taken today by the Jockey Club, some members of which would, I am sure, be delighted to see women sticking to show jumping and horse trials.

The most brilliant, and at the same time the most exasperating, point-to-pointer of 1962 was the ten-year-old Warwickshire mare Everything's Rosy, who will also be remembered for bringing into the limelight a twenty-one-year-old Warwickshireman who was later to head the list of leading riders for four consecutive seasons. I refer, of course, to David Tatlow, whose name has since become a by-word in point-to-point circles, and whose qualities as a rider are only excelled by his genius as a producer (I hesitate to call him a trainer, although that is what he is, because as the proprietor of a livery stable he cannot hold a training licence). It is only a matter of time, I feel, before he becomes a professional trainer. Harry Tatlow, David's father, was famous in the show ring for his expertise with hacks and hunters; and since David now follows suit in this respect, it is easy to see where he learned the art. But he also owes a great deal to the late Mrs Cecily Gaskell, and at one time Everything's Rosy belonged to her. Mrs Gaskell bought this mare for 180 guineas and ran her over hurdles, without any success.

Everything's Rosy was a most impressive winner of the four-mile race at the Heythrop, a worthy follower in the footsteps of Solbay, Cash Account and Major Rushton's Holystone Oak, the 1961 winner; and before that she had beaten Gay Roger at the Beaufort and won a good open race at the Oakley. She won another race at the North Cotswold afterwards; but the trouble started when she was sent to contest the Dudley Cup. When the starter dropped his flag the mare just swished her tail and declined to take any part in the race. Excuses were made for her. It was said that she had come in season and that all would be well when she went up to Yorkshire for the Grimthorpe Cup. But it wasn't. She went off all right with the others but ran such a listless race that David Tatlow had no alternative but to pull her up. The following season it was made all too clear that the daughter of Airborne (a Derby winner) had joined the infamous ranks of Hymettus and Worker.

Some interesting young riders emerged in 1962. The most interesting of all was the young man who won the race for the President's Cup at the Bullingdon Club on Red Squirrel. In view of what he has accomplished since in the professional field, perhaps I may be forgiven for quoting what I wrote about him in *The Sporting Life* after his win at the Bullingdon Club: 'Brough Scott, the nineteen-year-old Oxford undergraduate who rode this winner, was having his first ride in a race. It was an impressive début, displaying perfect timing and considerable coolness.'

Another future professional was also riding that season, sixteen-year-old John Woodman, whose father, Sid Woodman, then running a livery stable at Lavant, Sussex, was once head lad to Ryan Price. Young John Woodman won open races in successive weeks on the Cowdray mare Domahoney. But even he wasn't the youngest rider to win a point-to-point. This distinction fell to a schoolboy at Millfield, Bill Kirkby (son of the famous Laurie), who celebrated his fifteenth birthday with a win on Mickel's Hill in the adjacent hunts' race at the Brocklesby.

Richard Stuart-Hunt, seventeen-year-old son of the Master of the Surrey Union, had his first success in a race in a division of the open race at the Romney Marsh on Enchanted Atom, owned by the late Mr William Harries; and he won again at the Chiddingfold and Leconfield on the same horse. And then there was eighteen-year-old Robert Dickinson who won the maiden race at the V.W.H. (Bathurst) on his Touch and Go II, beating the great Lawrence Morgan on Sabreen. The Australian said of him afterwards: 'The boy rode a very good race and he has a nice horse there.' He was right in both instances.

It was also the season when Josephine Turner (the present Mrs Robert Bothway) had her first ride in a race at the age of eighteen. This was on her father's horse, The Babe II, at the Easton Harriers; and it was a winning one.

There was, too, Christopher Collins, then aged twenty-two and at that time an articled clerk to a firm of chartered accountants. Who would have thought then that the young man who got beaten a mere three-quarters of a length on his six-year-old Wild Legend by Guy Cunard on Sir Gosland in the Old Etonian Association Race at the Heythrop would finish third in the Grand National (on Mr Jones) three years later and become the leading amateur under N.H. Rules? Well, perhaps Bob McCreery might have done. He was a head behind young Mr Collins on his South Grove.

But it wasn't only the season of youth. There were also some shining veterans, both equine and human. Hard Frost, the Purleigh Flyer, was fizzing through the Eastern Counties, where he won nine open races and a confined one. But even that wasn't enough for him, for he paid a contemptuous visit to the Old Surrey and Burstow and saw off a local champion, Prides Crossing, in a division of the Harewoods Cup race. It is true he was beaten once, by the consistent Diogenes at Cottenham; but that was in a blizzard, and no one in his right senses would have argued that Diogenes was the better horse.

Another veteran, Mr H. T. Hartland's Singing Spider, recorded his thirtieth win in the ladies' race at the Cotswold Vale Farmers.

Although he was to make three more appearances before his final retirement, this was the fifteen-year-old's swan song. Diana Guilding won on him twenty-eight times and on the other two occasions her brother Roger had the mount.

Owing to the very firm going only seventeen of the fifty horses entered for the Dudley Cup actually went to the post. But there were still two divisions of the race, with eight horses in the first and nine in the second. Tim Holland-Martin had an easy win in the first division on his Midnight Coup, who put in such a tremendous leap at the open ditch that one enthusiast almost fainted with admiration. This horse had won the Charles Coventry Cup at the Croome over the same course ten days beforehand and that race is usually considered a good dress rehearsal. But I would not put Midnight Coup amongst the best Dudley Cup winners. Pomme de Guerre, who won the second division, was winning his fourth race in a row for twenty-five-year-old Peter Davenport, and this combination were to enjoy a highly successful partnership in hunter chases for several years. I liked Pomme de Guerre very much. He carried his head low, like Colledge Master, in the manner of a true stayer; and although he never managed to win the Cheltenham Foxhunters' he ran in the race five years running and was never further down the field than sixth. He was second to Freddie in 1964 and fourth three times.

As Midnight Coup and Pomme de Guerre were hunted with the North Cotswold and the Radnor and West Herefordshire, respectively, this was the first time since 1955 (when Cash Account and Creeola won) that both divisions of the race had been won by horses from the West Midlands.

Probably the best point-to-pointer – and certainly the best stayer – north of the Border that season was Tipperary Flame, a nine-year-old mare from the Dumfriesshire. Ridden in all her races by her owner, Andrew Spence, a forty-year-old farmer from Lockerbie, Tipperary Flame won five races in a row, including the new four-mile race at the Eglinton; and although she was beaten by the Yorkshire mare Brass Tacks in the Grimthorpe Cup, this defeat was largely engineered by that master tactician Peter Brookshaw, who had seen the way the wind was blowing when Tipperary Flame beat Brass Tacks at the Pendle Forest a few weeks earlier and learnt enough to profit from it.

Yorkshire produced the two best ladies' horses of the season in Archie Thomlinson's Gold Field and Bert Cleminson's Periboy, and it was very fitting that these two horses, splendidly ridden by Brenda Johnson and Carol Cleminson, should end up winning the divisions of the Lord Astor Cup race at Melton, where Yorkshire horses all but swept the board. Croizet, now back again with Archie Thomlinson, spreadeagled the field in the open event; and Guy Cunard, who rode eleven winners during the season (one less than Bertie Hill), displayed all his old mastery to win the members' race on Sir Gosland and the farmers' race on Vindicated. I think it must have been just before the latter event that I overheard the following conversation:

1st Owner: 'I see you've got your horse in the Farmers'. Didn't know you were a farmer.'

2nd Owner: 'Well, if Cunard's a farmer, so am I.'

22

1963

In which No Reward becomes a champion, a £50 wager is struck, the Hunters' Improvement Society enters the scene, and Ida Croxon calls it a day

Up till this time, hunts which staged a ladies' open race had not been permitted to stage a men's open race. Before the start of the 1963 season, however, this rule was relaxed and both kinds of races were permitted on the same card. Although this was undoubtedly a step in the right direction, inevitably the traditional ladies' open events – such as the Gibbon Bowl at Larkhill's Royal Artillery meeting and the Corvedale Cup at the Ludlow – underwent a certain diminution in status, now that ladies' open races were the order of the day rather than the exception.

But there was a welcome innovation up in Yorkshire at the Middleton in the shape of a four-mile ladies' open race sponsored by a firm of Malton brewers, Charles Rose and Company; and this was now the only opportunity the ladies had for racing over four miles, because the North Warwickshire had been compelled to give up their four-mile ladies' open in 1962 when they moved their fixture to the Atherstone course at Clifton-upon-Dunsmore.

Although Hard Frost continued to paralyse his opponents in the East, apart from a single lapse at the end of the season when he was beaten by the Puckeridge horse Two Pins at Marks Tey, the champion point-to-pointer of 1963 was a horse hunted with the Whaddon Chase, Bill Shand Kydd's No Reward, who had been acquired for 450 guineas at the Ascot Sales in May 1961 after an inglorious season under Rules and was kept at livery with Brian Thompson at Swanbourne, Berkshire. This little horse, by the war-time Derby winner Straight Deal out of a Cottage mare, was one of the gamest and most genuine point-to-pointers of the post-war years, and he had class as well. His first season in the yellow and white stripes with blue sleeves and cap which are now such a well-known sight was 1962, when, with his owner riding (in fact, he was never ridden in a race by anyone else), he won five races and finished fourth to Pomme de Guerre in the Dudley Cup and fourth to Croizet at Melton.

No Reward was nine years old in 1963, when he won eight races in five different counties, including a division of the Dudley Cup. The Upton-on-Severn course might have been made to measure for him. It was then – and still is, though it is no longer the setting for the Dudley Cup – the perfect course to ride a waiting race on, and there was nothing No Reward liked better than coming from behind at the end of a testing trip. A sharp course was no use at all to him.

By a strange coincidence – and certainly it had never happened before – the other division of the Dudley was also won by a horse from the Whaddon Chase, Richard Cooper's owner-ridden Foroughona, a lovely mare by Foroughi who did well to beat Miss Lucy Jones's Young Jerry and a good horse from the Portman country, Dick Hunt's Bushwhacker, ridden by Richard Miller.

There was a happy sequel to these two races which revived nostalgic memories of the old days of point-to-point racing. Richard Cooper offered to bet Bill Shand Kydd £50 that Foroughona would beat No Reward in the open race for the Henry Waterford Cup at the Melton Hunt Club the following Saturday. Bill Shand Kydd won the wager but not the race, for over the sharp Melton course No Reward was beaten a head by the unconsidered Dunnock, owned and ridden by Major A. P. Gilks of the 9th/12th Lancers, and Foroughona finished five lengths away third. Dunnock, in fact, was a good little horse who had once finished third in the Spa Hurdle at Cheltenham. So it wasn't exactly a disgrace; and it looked even less so when Dunnock and Major Gilks won a hunter chase at Woore on their next appearance.

By this time, Guy Cunard was fifty-one years old and Christopher Collins was in the middle of his exams in chartered accountancy. Neither, however, was going to be put off by little things like that. The day after being beaten a head on Calypso Mio by Tim Holland-Martin on Hilly Wood in the Old Etonian Association Race at the Heythrop, the Major reached his double century of point-to-point wins, on Sir Gosland in the open race at the Cleveland; and he ended up as the season's leading point-to-point rider with fifteen winners.

As for the youthful Mr Collins, the three races he won on his Wild Legend, a seven-year-old by Bewildered, included the Heythrop four-miler. Unfortunately, after completing his hat-trick in the open race at the South Oxfordshire, Wild Legend met with a setback; otherwise he would have gone up to Yorkshire to contest the Grimthorpe Cup, in which I am convinced he would have proved too good for Harrow Hall and Brass Tacks, who finished first and second, separated by a neck. Curiously enough, these two Yorkshire horses both went point-to-pointing south of the Thames later on. Brass Tacks was sold into the Crawley and Horsham country, while Harrow Hall went first to Gay Kindersley in Berkshire, then to Jack Marsh in the Tickham area and finally to Neil Wates in the Old Surrey and Burstow. Harrow Hall did much the better of the two, and was still winning races in 1969 at the age of twelve.

There were fourteen starters for the inaugural Rose's Cup race at the Middleton, and they included two of the best Scottish ladies' combinations, Mrs Betty Borthwick and Vultern, winners of five races that season and a similar number the season before; and Mary Denise, owned and ridden by Miss Jean Acaster, an Edinburgh school teacher. Vultern gave the better performance but both finished behind a much less-considered Scottish horse, the eleven-year-old Lucky Willie, from the Jedforest, on whom twenty-one-year-old Margaret Usher rode a particularly fine race to beat the experienced Mrs Bobby Brewis on Devon Flame by a head.

There was, however, a notable absentee. Periboy elected to wait a week for Melton, where he duly won a division of the Lord Astor Cup race for the second year running, easily beating Bachelor's Carnation, an eight-year-old from the Old Surrey and Burstow who had won his last three races for his owner-rider, Mrs Ian Phillips (who as Jennifer Robinson had won many races on Mr Claud Hockley's horses in the Essex area).

The season also saw the beginning of the Hunters' Improvement Society races which are now staged at various meetings (mostly in the West). The first one was at the Bicester, where Mr Hugh Sumner, the President of the Society at the time, put up a handsome challenge trophy which is still competed for. The winner, that year, in a field of seven, was Mr Sidney Parker's Erin's Legend (by Erin's Pride) from the Heythrop. Considering how many of the horses running in point-to-points (Halloween, The Callant and Merryman II were three such) have been sired by premium stallions of the Hunters' Improvement Society, it is really rather disappointing that these races haven't caught on more. In 1963, for instance, among the horses sired by the premium stallion Whiteway, whose progeny won three of the five races at the Tiverton Staghounds that season, were Shirley Jones and Myway, who won twelve races between them, Bushwhacker, who won three, and Bertie Hill's Bright 'n Gay II, who added two open events to the eight races he had won the previous season, when he was unbeaten. Needless to say, none of these horses were in the field for the race at the Bicester. Nor, of course, was Hard Frost, whose sire, Winter's Tale, was also a premium stallion.

Another new race in 1963 was the East of England Championship put on by the Suffolk Hunt at Moulton. This, in fact, was no more than a grandiloquent title for their open event, which was run in two divisions. But I think the race may be said to have lived up to the build-up because, although neither division was won by a horse from the Eastern Counties, both winners were scoring for the fifth time during the season. Major Cunard won the earlier division on his Puddle Jumper; and the second was won, in the faster time, by the East Kent mare Cauliflower, owned by the late Tommy Southern and ridden by John Hickman.

The grotesquely-named Cauliflower (Tommy Southern had another horse with a name that was even more monstrous, Scroggins!) who had finished fourth to Sea Knight in the Liverpool Foxhunters', is, assuredly, worthy of being classed with Hopeful Hero and Duty Paid. And this little chestnut mare, by Sir Winston Churchill's old horse Colonist II, had a character that matched her ability. She was an extremely bad traveller – otherwise she would no doubt have won many more races than she did – and as she stood in the paddock before each race the sweat used to pour off her. But anyone who took this as a sign to back something else was nearly always disappointed. After she had won the open race at the East Kent for the third year running, Gregory Blaxland wrote in the *Kentish Express*: 'With sweating flanks and tongue dangling over her bit (as it often does) Cauliflower looked like a hunted deer as she shuffled over the second last . . .'

Meanwhile, up in the North, a young man in his second season of race-riding was partnering the young horse who had given him his first success the previous season in the hunt race at the Buccleuch. The young man was Alan Mactaggart and the horse was Mr Reg Tweedie's Freddie. And after being beaten into second place in the adjacent hunts' race at the Berwickshire, on what was to be their only other appearance in point-to-points together, Alan Mactaggart and Freddie went on to win hunter chases at Carlisle, Bogside, Kelso and Ayr. And it was Freddie who ended up top of Geoffrey Sale's handicap at the end of the season. This was really rather clever of the Newmarket sage because the only horse of much account that Freddie had beaten at that time was Puddle Jumper. Freddie was not only to become outstandingly the best hunter chaser of the following season, when he was unbeaten in these events and won both the Vaux National Hunters' Chase at Catterick (then the richest prize for hunters and worth £1,608 to the winner) and the Cheltenham Foxhunters', but one of the most popular horses ever to run under N.H. Rules. In later years, when he was still trained under permit by Reg Tweedie in Berwickshire, Freddie won eight handicap steeplechases and was runner-up in two Grand Nationals, to Jay Trump in 1965 and to Anglo in 1966.

At the Ludlow on May 4th, Ida Croxon – Ida Marshall as she then was – had her last ride in a race. She rode Vulcan's Flame in the Corvedale Cup and finished fourth to Diana Guilding on Heated Moment. Ida Croxon, who was forty-seven when she hung up her racing boots, had her first win in 1946 on West End II, a horse owned by the man she eventually married, Philip Marshall. In her time, she rode forty-two winners for twenty-two different owners but will probably chiefly be remembered for her association with the late Mrs Cecily Gaskell's grey Don Isle, on whom she won fourteen races; and also, I feel, for the memorable encounters she had with her great rival Pat Rushton between 1949 and 1961. The two competed against each other in no fewer than sixty races and finished either first or second in thirty-one of them, the final score being twenty wins to Pat Rushton, nine to Ida Croxon and two dead-heats.

As a tailpiece to the 1963 season, I can do no better than record the rare treat that was in store for visitors to Melton. Worker and Everything's Rosy appeared in the same race.

Everything's Rosy got as far as the first fence, which she flatly refused to have anything to do with. But Worker declined to move, except in the opposite direction. And some faithful followers backed them, presumably on the principle that miracles do sometimes happen. The bookmakers, I am told, laughed all the way to the dogs on Saturday night.

23

1964

In which a new rule fails to achieve its purpose, Hard Frost signs off, 'The Pointer' signs on, and Guy Cunard wins the Grimthorpe Cup

From time to time, as we have seen, the rules governing point-to-point races are changed in certain instances; and some of these changes are retrogressive rather than forward-looking. Such was the rule introduced in 1964 whereby any horse winning four open races was automatically debarred from taking part in any other such events during the same season. Many people in the Eastern Counties were convinced that this was aimed at Hard Frost; though in fairness to Messrs Weatherbys and the National Hunt Committee one must I think accept the official explanation that it was designed to encourage the best point-to-pointers to go hunter chasing. But it can hardly be said to have achieved its purpose. Only two of the eight horses who won their quota of four open races in 1964, Straight Lady and Burnished Gold, actually won hunter chases, and few of the others even attempted them.

Of this new rule, one owner said: 'I don't need a piece of repressive legislation to help me make up my mind.' Another said: 'If a horse is good enough, I say let him win all the races he can.' And Mrs Louise Barber, the wife of Hard Frost's owner, said: 'I do not think it will make much difference, as there are so few horses who won more than four open races anyway.'

And in 1964, Hard Frost, who was in his last season of point-to-point racing at the age of fourteen, was not one of them. But he did win three open races and two confined events, ending his racing career with a walk-over in the open race at the Enfield Chace. In a point-to-point career which stretched from 1959 to 1964, Mr George Barber's great horse ran in forty-nine races, winning thirty-two open events, five confined races and a hunter chase. This is what Geoffrey Sale had to say about him in the 1965 edition of his annual:

> It has been said that Hard Frost was nothing out of the ordinary, on the premise that he never ventured far out of his country. This is, of course, unwarrantable balderdash, as Mr Barber's gelding has always raced in the Cottenham Opens where any of the critics could have brought their wonderful nags at the beginning of the season – if they had the courage.

At the beginning of the season, a rival to Geoffrey Sale appeared on the scene in the shape of a gentleman from Lincolnshire calling himself 'The Pointer'; and the first appearance of The Pointer's pocket manual, with its ratings by numbers, aroused some stimulating cross-talk in the correspondence columns of *The Sporting Life*, where The Pointer was injudicious enough to make a remark which he was soon to have cause to regret, namely that 'Freddie will have to be in the Mill House class to uphold the reputation which has been accorded to him'. In fact, Geoffrey Sale was the only handicapper – and there were several others operating at the time – bold enough to rate Freddie above Baulking Green . . . until the following season, when Freddie was promoted to the top of all the other handicaps. But by that time, of course, he stuck out so far that even a blind man could have detected his merit.

It was in 1964 that the last of the West Country banking fixtures were held. These were at the North Cornwall, Cury Harriers, Four Burrow, Tetcott and the Western, where the most consistent winner was Kipling Tors, a little twelve-year-old chestnut gelding of dubious parentage owned and ridden by W. E. (Bill) Brooks. Kipling Tors, who had won four races the previous season, won four of the five open events over banks and the hunt race at the Stevenstone over fly fences.

There were some very good horses in the South West that season, and one of them was the 1969 Grand National winner, Highland Wedding, a horse who was given to breaking blood vessels. But fortunately he was in good hands. His owner-rider, Peter Calver, was a Wiltshire veterinary surgeon. Highland Wedding, who had won his last two races of 1963, a season he started as a maiden, was the winner of four of his six races, three of them at Larkhill. But none of these were open events and a much more likely-looking candidate for the Grand National at that time was Quintina, the big bold chestnut mare by Fortina from the Portman country in Dorset. This mare, who had only lost her maiden certificate the previous season, was unbeaten during 1964, when two of her four wins were in open events. Her owner-rider, Richard Miller, who is known in the Portman country as 'The Jolly Miller', on account of his high good humour, has to shed the best part of 2½ stone in order to make the weight in point-to-points. But he still manages to ride a great many winners, and certainly Quintina was one of the best horses he has ever sat on, though he didn't have her for long. Before the 1964 season was over he had sold her into Fred Winter's stable. Under Rules, however, Quintina never fulfilled her promise, although she did win one race for Fred Winter and in 1965 she was second to Honey End in the Withington Chase over four miles at Birmingham and runner-up to Norther in the Welsh Grand National. At the time of writing, she is back again point-to-pointing for John Webber in the Bicester country.

There was another Portman horse who won more races than Quintina although he was twice beaten by her, and that was Richard Woodhouse's Woodside Terrace, who underwent an an astonishing transformation when he came into Dorset from Yorkshire, purchased at the Ascot Sales in September 1963 for 360 guineas at the age of ten. Dick Woodhouse, who is now one of the Joint Acting Masters of the Portman and very well known for his association with Highworth, won six races on Woodside Terrace in 1964; and the following season, to the accompaniment of an enormous Dorset roar, the partnership swept past Prilliard to win the Cheltenham Foxhunters'.

Mrs Andy Frank's Far East II, from the Devon and Somerset Staghounds, and Frank Ryall's Lamerton mare Shirley Jones both won six races in 1964; and the former was still winning in 1970. Mark Goddard-Watts won seven on Easter Elopment, who was also hunted with the Devon and Somerset Staghounds; and Una Brander-Dunbar won eight races on the Mid-Devon mare Myway, one of the most consistent winners in the West for several seasons.

And there was an exciting newcomer in the Puckeridge country. This was Mr Frank Harvey's Duke of Cinchon, a horse who held the record for the Liverpool Hurdle course. After getting the worst of it with No Reward in an adjacent hunts' race at Friars

Wash, Duke of Cinchon finished his season with a hat-trick in open events; and in one of these, over the Friars Wash course, the pace was so hot that Hard Frost was relegated to fourth place in his single defeat of the season.

But the champion point-to-pointer of the 1964 season was Mr W. J. A. Shepherd's Straight Lady, an eight-year-old mare by Straight Deal (the sire of No Reward) from the Cotswold Hunt. This mare won both the four-mile race at the Heythrop and the Dudley Cup, as well as three hunter chases, in one of which she beat Baulking Green. The mare's pilot at the Heythrop was the owner's son, Richard, then a seventeen-year-old schoolboy at Marlborough. But he was unable to get off for the Dudley Cup, in which the twenty-one-year-old Richard Willis (who had been associated with Baulking Green in his early days) had the mount. The field was a particularly good one, but Straight Lady won very easily from Lucy Jones's Ilbesena (John Daniell) and Tim Holland-Martin's Green Parrot, a very promising novice; and among those unplaced were Woodside Terrace (4), Domaboy (5), Pomme de Guerre (6) and No Reward. The last-named, who had won six of his seven previous races, his only defeat being by Straight Lady's stable companion Chaos at Tweseldown, was clearly running much below form.

Another horse to run unplaced in this race was Aria who had been off the course for six weeks. This horse deserves a special mention for several reasons. First, for his looks. A particularly taking son of Tudor Minstrel, he had the presence and bearing of an aristocrat. Aria was a great favourite in the Eastern Counties, where he was hunted with the Newmarket and Thurlow by his owner, Mr G. S. C. Gibson. But he was a very difficult horse to keep sound and it is a tribute to his owner's patience and skill that he was able to keep him at the top of the tree for so long. At his best, Aria was a very fine performer and quite capable of beating anything he came up against in his own area, especially at Moulton, his favourite course. In 1964 Aria was eleven years old.

Another thoroughly genuine horse was Domaboy, who, whilst never quite reaching the top flight (though his connections never minded taking on the best), was certainly at the top of the second flight. He won many races in his own part of the country and some out of it. Bridger Champion, who owned him, and Billy

Champion who rode him so well, are the two sons of Jack Champion, the huntsman to the Old Surrey and Burstow. The irony of the situation regarding Domaboy – and others in the stable – was that Bridger was never able to ride the horse himself in point-to-points because for a very short time he was once employed professionally with horses. If ever there was a case for relaxing the rule in special circumstances, this is one.

The leading riders of 1964 were the two greatest of the two sexes, Guy Cunard and Pat Tollit. Major Cunard rode twenty-two winners, which was more than any other rider had ridden in a single season since the war; Mrs Tollit rode ten winners (two more than Una Brander-Dunbar in the West and Josephine Turner in the East). Eight of Pat Tollit's wins were on the ten-year-old No Duda, but the best race she rode on this little horse was a losing one. This was at the North Ledbury, where she lost both irons at the fourth fence and rode the remainder of the race without them, to be beaten no more than half a length by Heated Moment, a good little horse who won many races with Diana Guilding up but broke a fetlock at the Ledbury five weeks later.

Apart from the fact that Major Cunard had his best season since the war in terms of the number of races won, it was also a highly satisfactory one for him in other respects. He won the Old Etonian Association Race at the Heythrop on Sir Gosland for the second time in three years, after a great duel with Gay Kindersley on Harrow Hall, took in a hunter chase at Folkestone on Vindicated and – greatest triumph of all – won the Grimthorpe Cup on Ferncliffe, who was by no means his best horse (Young Rohan and Puddle Jumper were both superior). Ferncliffe, in fact, owed his success to his owner's brilliant jockeyship. It was a case of impeccable judgment of pace, and, as so often with this brilliant rider, perfect timing. After the Scottish mare Tipperary Flame had exhausted herself trying to make all the running, and Glann (the 1961 winner) had taken over at the second last, the Major struck like lightning round the final bend, reached Glann before the last fence and easily held off a late challenge from the fast-finishing Scalby Sceptre.

For Tipperary Flame it was her last appearance on a racecourse. She had won thirteen races, never fallen, and produced a son. The son was Corrielaw Diamond, the winner that season of the four-mile races at the Eglinton and the Percy; and he too was going to have a crack at the Grimthorpe Cup.

Tailpiece outside the weighing tent
1st Steward: 'Shall we have him up?'
2nd Steward: 'Don't be so bloody silly. He's one of ours?'

24
1965

In which certain ladies are dealt a body blow, David Tatlow shows his skill, a strike takes takes place in the Eastern Counties, and Pat Tollit sends up the 100

Before the start of the 1965 season a rule was brought in requiring all owner-trainers of hunter chasers to hold a full permit. Although this sounded innocent enough, it was a body blow to women, who at that time were not considered eligible for permits and were thus effectively prevented from running their horses in hunter chases. The worst sufferers from this sex discrimination were those highly successful ladies Mrs Jackie Brutton and Miss Lucy Jones, both of whom had winners of the United Hunts' Cup at Cheltenham to their credit. To Mrs Brutton, in particular, it was a bitter situation to be in, because in 1965 she had in her stables at Compton Abdale another potential winner of this race. The horse's name was Snowdra Queen, a seven-year-old mare by Brightworthy bought in Wales for £300. Fortunately, with this brilliant mare, who was hunted by her owner in the Cotswolds, it was only a matter of time; for in 1966, when women were granted permits to train hunter chasers, Snowdra Queen *did* win the United Hunts' Cup; and after being beaten by Baulking Green in 1967, she obtained her revenge and won it again in 1968.

Like Straight Lady before her, Snowdra Queen won both Lord Ashton of Hyde's Cup at the Heythrop and the Dudley Cup, ridden on each occasion by Henry Oliver. At the Heythrop she didn't have much to beat, after Straight Lady and Woodside Terrace had been put out of the race by a horse refusing in front of them at the open ditch the first time round; but it was a different story in the Dudley Cup, where she was opposed by some very good horses who had every chance had they been equal to it. Snowdra Queen had the race already won when Persian Barrier fell at the last fence; and neither Bouffon II, who won five races that season, nor Faruno, who went on to win the

Grimthorpe Cup ten days later, could get anywhere near her.

One of the most stimulating features of the 1965 season was the three-cornered contest between Guy Cunard, Frank Ryall and David Tatlow for the title of leading rider. It was eventually resolved in favour of the Warwickshireman, who finished the season with a total of eighteen winners, as against Major Cunard's fifteen and Frank Ryall's thirteen.

To some extent, both Guy Cunard and Frank Ryall were unlucky, the former with coughing in his Malton stable – though not before he had won seven races with Young Rohan and piloted Ferncliffe to success in the combined Old Etonian and Old Harrovian Race which was then in its first year at the Heythrop – and the latter with injuries to his best horses, the two half-sisters that he bred himself at his farm in Devon, Shirley Jones and Beera Girl. Shirley Jones broke down at the Lamerton towards the end of March and Beera Girl was off the course with a damaged shoulder from mid-April.

But there was no doubt at all that David Tatlow was a worthy champion, and he was to remain one for the next three years. Bouffon, his best horse that season, was rather an extraordinary animal. Although he had won three flat races in Ireland when trained by Paddy Sleator, and two hurdle races afterwards, he had acquired a reputation for being ungenuine, and there were certainly some signs of it when he made his first point-to-point appearance in an open event at Cottenham. Cantering comfortably at the head of the field, he stopped dead in his tracks at the penultimate fence, an open ditch, and let three horses go past him before jumping it from a standstill. He then ran on to such purpose that he made up all the lost ground in a matter of seconds and won by half a length from Cardinal Wolsey. It was an astonishing performance by the rider as well as the horse. But there were to be no more signs of Bouffon's waywardness until he changed hands at the end of the season and went into another stable. It is a great tribute to David Tatlow's skill as a trainer that as soon as he had Bouffon back in his stable, at the end of the 1966 season, he promptly won another race on him.

Whereas Bouffon was brilliant but wilful, Mystery Gold II, who was still running in 1970 at the age of sixteen, was as genuine as the day is long. A smallish bay gelding by Goldwell out of an unknown mare, he joined David Tatlow's string in 1964 and between 1964 and 1969 he never won fewer than four races in a season. In 1965 he won six races in seven appearances. After the two horses had both won at Cottenham, David Tatlow said: 'Mystery Gold is a good horse, but he will never win a Dudley Cup. But this Bouffon is a really high-class animal – just the job for it.' He was proved right in the first instance but wrong in the second.

On the whole, point-to-point riders, unlike some show jumpers I could name, are an obedient lot; but in 1965, in the Eastern Counties, there was a rebellion that was quite without precedent. Six of the leading riders in that area, Michael Bloom, David Wales, Hunter Rowe, Sam Cooper, Ted Harvey and Guy Lyster, refused to ride at the Newmarket and Thurlow because they considered the Moulton fences too dangerous; and this opinion was shared by a number of owners who withdrew their horses. There was a kingsize row when the news got on to the front page of *The Sporting Life* on the day of the races, and an attempt (not entirely successful) was made to have the correspondent of that newspaper up before the Stewards for excessive use of the pen. But the upshot of it all was that before the Suffolk fixture a fortnight later some drastic alterations were made, and two of the rebels, David Wales and Sam Cooper, rode winners there.

Faruno, the Grimthorpe Cup winner, was not a great horse, but he warrants a mention because his time of 8 mins. 45.4 secs. was less than two seconds outside the record set up by More Honour in 1956. A nine-year-old bay gelding by Foroughi out of the mare Miss Bruno, who had bred those redoubtable stayers Bruno's Cottage and Brunador II, Faruno was the first winner of this race from the Meynell country in Derbyshire and Staffordshire, and he was very well ridden by his twenty-five-year-old owner-rider, Richard Perkins, from Burton-on-Trent.

But it was the third horse, Corrielaw Diamond, who really took the eye. Like his mother, Tipperary Flame, he was a beautiful mover, and in the summer of 1965 he won six championships in the show-ring. He was a good horse on anything but very firm going (as it was at the Middleton that year); and his successes in 1965 included the open race at the Berwickshire which Tipperary Flame had won for the last three years; and the four-mile race at the Eglinton for the second year running. Neither he nor Tipperary Flame were ever held after flagfall, and in all their attempts at four miles or more Andrew Spence used to take them down to the start with two bridles. Corrielaw Diamond always raced in a rubber snaffle, which would have been much too frail for taking such a free mover to the post. I doubt if either he or his mother were ever seriously trained in the accepted sense of the word, as they were frequently used for herding sheep and cattle on Mr Spence's farm at Lockerbie. Andrew Spence is a man – and there are many such in the point-to-point world – who believes in racing for pleasure.

With fifteen winners in twenty-one appearances, Pat Tollit was again the leading lady rider, and in the Corvedale Cup at the Ludlow she became the first (and so far the only) lady rider in Britain to achieve a total of 100 winners. The horse she sent up the hundred on was Uncle Coke, a seven-year-old gelding by Silver Pencil bought for 120 guineas at the Ascot Sales in the spring of 1964. Uncle Coke who had won a couple of hurdle races before he came into Mrs Tollit's possession, went through the 1965 season like a dose of salts; until, that is, he came up against Plummers Plain at Melton on the final day and was made to look very ordinary – as indeed was everything else.

But this was hardly surprising, because Plummers Plain was a past winner of the Whitbread Gold Cup at Sandown and his partnership with Gillian Pearce has been one of the highlights of the point-to-point scene in the present decade. In some ways, Plummers Plain was a funny old horse who liked to have things all his own way, and he was not much good in the mud. But when conditions were right – and he wasn't often raced when they were wrong – all his opponents saw of him was his posterior disappearing into the distance.

There are people who think that horses like Plummers Plain should not be running in point-to-points, even if hunted till the cows come home. But it by no means follows that a horse who has won many steeplechases in his younger days will necessarily sweep the board when he goes point-to-point racing. In fact, the majority of these ex-chasers do not make much impact on the point-to-point scene. It is the young horses coming up, not the old ones going down, who make the impact. Quite apart from this, however, a horse such as Plummers Plain captures the imagination of the public in much the same way as a film star, and he puts considerably more into point-to-point racing than he takes out of it.

But if Plummers Plain was the most spectacular horse running in ladies' races during 1965, he had at least one possible rival on the score of ability in the Tynedale horse Minto Burn, the winner of the Heart of all England at Hexham that year, and two years later of the Liverpool Foxhunters'. Minto Burn, whose dam, Cousin Kate, was herself a well-known point-to-pointer and also a Heart of all England winner, was unbeaten in ladies' races; and Brenda Johnson, one of the best lady riders in the North and now the manager of Mr J. M. Turner's horses in Suffolk, won six races on this horse and three on Gold Field.

I must say, I would have liked to have seen Minto Burn and Plummers Plain in the same race, joined perhaps by the Hampshire Hunt's Orchid Moor, who spreadeagled the field on no fewer than six occasions and had a throughly workman-like rider in Sally Baillie.

A more prolific winner than any of these, though against somewhat inferior opposition for the most part, was the South Devon mare Myway, whose ten wins in 1965 enabled Una Brander-Dunbar to finish the season runner-up to Mrs Tollit. The only horse to beat Myway was Over Court; and it is not without significance that this horse was ridden by Pat Tollit's natural successor, Sue Aston, who was also up on the Dufosee mare Miss Surprise when this little horse broke Bantry Bay's course record at Larkhill by winning the ladies' race at the Tedworth in 6 mins. 6 secs.

But for one lady rider there was tragedy. At an earlier Larkhill meeting, Mrs Gillian Matthews broke her back when Sunsketch was brought down by a fallen horse as he landed over the open ditch three fences from home.

The end-of-term Melton Hunt Club fixture at Garthorpe is always an exhilarating occasion; and in 1965 Mystery Gold II won a high-class members' race there; Bouffon II dead-heated in the open race with Scrum-Half, who had taken over the mantle from No Reward in the South Midlands; Plummers Plain and Minto Burn won the two divisions of the ladies' race for the Lord Astor Cup, the former in six seconds' faster time; and in Major Eldred Wilson's six-year-old Salmon River, a horse bred by John Thorne at his stud in Warwickshire, we had the most promising winner of the novices' championship since Croizet.

But alas, it was short-lived promise, for in the autumn of the same year Salmon River broke his leg in an accident at his home in Norfolk. This was a particularly bitter blow for Major Wilson, who had recently lost his good hunter Essandem in a handicap chase at Wye. Another fatal casualty among the top hunter chasers that season was Major John Birtwistle's Leyton Orient, as the result of an accident at Cartmel.

Tailpiece
1st Speaker: What is the best ladies' horse?'
2nd Speaker: 'Whichever horse Pat Tollit rides.'

25
1966

In which several Hunts display their initiative, a post-war record is broken and the Grimthorpe Cup goes to Scotland

In 1966, that irksome regulation restricting the number of open races that a horse could win to four was consigned to the scrap-heap; Guy Cunard was out of action the whole season following an injury sustained at Cartmel in October; Pat Tollit was out most of the season with a bad back; and two riders were killed on successive Saturdays, Douglas Towse at the York and Ainsty and Malcolm Williams at the Ross Harriers.

Malcolm was a remarkable man, a most distinctive figure who rode in a collar as the result of a broken neck. The son of a parson, he ran a livery stable from a converted pub near Hereford, and one of the horses he brought out there was Mystery Gold II, shortly after this horse had come over from Ireland. When Mystery Gold II won his first race in England, the open event at the V.W.H. (Earl Bathurst's) in 1961 as a seven-year-old, Malcolm Williams was in the saddle.

Those splendid veterans, Calypso Mio, Cauliflower, Spinster's Folly, Myway, Domaboy and Periboy, all had the final wins of their careers in 1966, and the first four were making their final appearances.

Calypso Mio was the oldest of them. He was seventeen years old when he won the hunt race at the Sinnington with Mr J. Coldbeck deputising for Major Cunard. In a career which began in 1955, the son of Jamaica Inn ran in over seventy races, winning eighteen point-to-points, ten hunter chases and two steeple-chases. His first success was in the maiden race at the York and Ainsty in 1956.

Cauliflower never quite reached the top flight as a hunter chaser – largely, I dare say, because, she was such a bad traveller – but the East Kent mare, who started by winning the maiden race at the Royal Engineers Draghounds in 1960 as a six-year-old, was virtually unbeatable in point-to-points after her first season. Her only subsequent defeat in these events occurred in 1966, when she unseated seventeen-year-old Peter Southern in the open race at the R. E. Drag; but it was a year in which she won six races in a row. Altogether, Cauliflower won twelve point-to-points, including the open race at the East Kent three years running, and eleven hunter chases. She was third to Baulking Green in the *Horse & Hound* Cup at Stratford in 1962, and to Santa Grand and Royal Phoebe in 1966; and in the Liverpool Foxhunters' of 1963 she was fourth to Sea Knight. The three riders who shared in her successes were John Farrant (who won the first race on her, and two hunter chases), John Hickman (eight point-to-points and eight hunter chases) and young Peter Southern, who won three point-to-points and a hunter chase on her. Tommy Southern, Cauliflower's owner, died in 1970 at the age of sixty-eight. He was forty-four when he had his first ride in a race. One of the most popular sportsmen in Kent, he produced a continuous stream of successful point-to-pointers, beginning with Celtic Cross, who won three point-to-points in 1946 and four hunter chases in 1947.

Guy Harwood's Spinster's Folly, who had his last win at the age of fourteen, in the hunt race at the Cowdray, was a marvellously consistent horse. His first success was in the open race at the Hambledon in 1960; and his twenty-five wins, most of them in open events, included three dead-heats, the most notable being at Melton in 1964, when Guy Harwood forced him up in the last stride to share the spoils in the open race for the Henry Waterford Cup with Puddle Jumper. The son of a Derby winner (My Love), Spinster's Folly was also the grandson, on his dam's side, of an Ascot Gold Cup winner (Precipitation).

Myway, who won ten of her eleven races in 1966, was a model of consistency, after her first season in 1961 as a six-year-old. She was a big mare standing 17 hands high, and she was never ridden by anyone other than her owner. Between 1963 and 1966 Una Brander-Dunbar and Myway had a single defeat in each season, once by Jennifer Barons (formerly Renfree) on Sanscrit, twice by Sue Aston on Over Court and once by Sue Aston on Polar Star. In fifty-six appearances they won thirty-seven races and were placed eight times.

Although Periboy never won with a man on top, the son of

Perion and Laura Gay (by Roidore) was one of the great ladies' horses. He won twenty-seven of these events, the last of them at the Staintondale at the age of fourteen; and Carol Cleminson was in the saddle for twenty-three of them. On the other four occasions, which included his initial win at the York and Ainsty in 1959, Angela Radcliffe rode him. But perhaps his greatest achievements lay in winning the four-mile Rose's Cup race at the Middleton two years running and making five winning appearances at Melton.

The regulations that govern point-to-point racing do not offer much scope for initiative in the framing of races, but there were some welcome examples of private enterprise in 1966. The Wheatland introduced a British Field Sports Society Race for horses that had won neither an open point-to-point nor a hunter chase since the start of the season; both the Essex Union and the East Essex tried the experiment of varying the distances of their races; and, most enterprising of all, the Bicester turned their open event for the Lord Bicester Gold Cup into an optional sweepstake by inviting each owner to wager £10 on his horse, and putting up a tenner themselves, the winner to take all plus the £40 prize money.

The winner of the Bicester sweepstake in its inaugural year was Mr Dudley Surman, for whom there was £120 to come when Mystery Gold II beat Stratford Herald by three-quarters of a length. This was Mystery Gold's fifth win of the season; and David Tatlow, whose twenty-five wins were a new post-war record for a single season, also won five races on Mr John Jordan's Barley Bree and five on Mr W. D. Adams's Amba III. In the 1967 edition of Geoffrey Sale's annual, these three horses were all handicapped within 2 lb. of each other, Mystery Gold II at 10st. 11lb. having a slight edge over the other two.

Barley Bree, a ten-year-old chestnut gelding by Jock Scot out of a Trigo mare, was in his first season of point-to-point racing. But he was a winner on the Flat and over hurdles; and after a single point-to-point win, in a division of the members' race at the Harkaway Club, he started second favourite to the Worcestershire horse Persian Barrier for the four-mile race at the Heythrop. Both, however, were soundly beaten by Bob Sawyer, a fourteen-year-old gift horse from the Old Berkshire who used to be in training with David Gandolfo. Gerald Dartnall (who is now a professional) rode a most intelligent race on this horse, who opened up such an enormous lead that nothing had a chance of getting to him.

The general opinion at the time was that Joe Jackson, Jnr, had waited too long on Persian Barrier, who was noted for his finishing speed; and it was anticipated with some confidence that he would not make the same mistake in the Dudley Cup. He didn't. This time Persian Barrier hit the front a mile from home. But the going that day was exceptionally testing, and the Worcestershire horse was powerless to resist the storming late challenge of the nine-year-old Handsel, owned and ridden by Geoff Cambidge, a forty-year-old Shropshire farmer who had acquired the best horse he has ever owned for under £300 at the Ascot Sales. It must have been a frustrating season for the connections of Persian Barrier, who won six races but lost the two that mattered most; especially in view of the fact that when Persian Barrier met Handsel again, in the open race at the Albrighton a few weeks after the Dudley Cup, he had no difficulty turning the tables on him.

It was a good season for the Puckeridge horses, and for three of them in particular. Although beaten by No Reward at the Hertfordshire and by Oriental Prince at the Cambridgeshire, Duke of Cinchon won five open races for the Harveys of Bishops Stortford in the expert hands of Hunter Rowe; and the fifteen-year-old Two Pins, who was bred by Frank Harvey from his point-to-point mare Pincushion, came out of retirement to celebrate the twenty-first birthday of the course at Wickham Hall and make a successful appearance in the Puckeridge Hunt Race; while Hugh Hodge's game mare Flying East displayed so much stamina winning the new four-mile adjacent hunts' race at the Essex Union that she was taken up to Yorkshire to contest the Grimthorpe Cup. She didn't win it, but she ran a magnificent race to be second to the Scottish horse Banjoe and finish in front of two former winners of the Cup, Glann and Faruno.

Banjoe was, in fact, the first Scottish winner of the Grimthorpe Cup, and but for a disqualification at the Lauderdale for missing a flag he would have been unbeaten that season, when his successes included the four-mile race at the Eglinton, where he beat Corrielaw Diamond, who had finished third to Straight Lady and Puddle Jumper in the Cheltenham Foxhunters'. An own brother to Bandalore, the Champion Hurdle winner of 1958, Banjoe was hunted with the Fife and ridden in all six of his races in 1966 by twenty-year-old John Hutchison-Bradburne, who had his first winning ride on him. But Banjoe was never quite the same horse again after winning that Grimthorpe Cup.

Perhaps this is also the moment to say that Mr Hodge, Snr, the owner of Flying East, is an Ayrshire man who has hunted with the Eglinton; and Hugh Hodge, Jnr, the mare's rider, was only a lad of five when the family moved to Hertfordshire in 1933.

At Larkhill in May there was an unexpected treat for point-to-point goers when Plummers Plain and Orchid Moor came up against each other in the Tedworth ladies' race. But all the race revealed in the end was the tremendous courage of the Hampshire mare. Despite laming herself badly at the open ditch three out, she got up on the post to beat Dunstable by a head, with Plummers Plain a length away third. It was Orchid Moor's tenth successive win, but it proved to be her last race. As for Plummers Plain, who was very far from being himself that day, he went on to Melton and won in a canter.

David Maundrell's Lizzy the Lizard, who won the novices' championship at Melton that year, was another in the line of Croizet and Salmon River. This seven-year-old mare by Romany Air, bred by David Maundrell at his farm in Wiltshire, from a mare loaned to him by his father, was to win the National Hunt Chase at Cheltenham three years later in different ownership. But not before she had been beaten in the same race in 1967 by another of the point-to-point novices of the 1966 season, Mr 'Gilly' Guilding's Master Tammy, who was also bred by his owner.

A third novice of the 1966 season – and one who went on to win many handicap steeplechases – was the five-year-old mare Hal's Farewell; and the man who produced this one from his livery stables in Sussex, Roy Trigg, was the same man who produced Woodland Venture (the Cheltenham Gold Cup winner of 1967) the previous season.

Tailpiece

In Ireland, Mrs E. A. Baker, of Mullingar, won the heavy-weight race at the Naas Harriers riding side-saddle against seven male opponents. All the horses in this race were carrying 15 st. 7 lb., and the indomitable Mrs Baker had to put up five stone of dead weight.

26
1967

In which the ladies take on the men, a new formbook appears, Guy Cunard has a field day, and the first point-to-point dinner is celebrated

For many years the more militant ladies had been campaigning for their right to ride against the men; and in 1967 their ambition was partially realised when permission was granted for them to ride in races confined to the hunt(s) promoting the meeting, so long as they carried the regulation weight of 12 st. 7 lb. This was a welcome move, except perhaps to a few die-hard males. It occasioned so little comment at the time, however, that one lady rider was moved to write to *Horse & Hound* in the following terms:

> Can it be that this change has taken place so easily that it has made little if any difference to the other riders and spectators? If so, what is the chance now for allowing ladies to ride in perhaps Maiden races as well next year?

But answer came there none from the flinthearts of Portman Square.

The first ladies to win against the men were two Scots, Mrs A. P. Forrest on Patricia Jean and Miss Joan Walker on Juliette IV, who dead-heated with each other in the hunt race at the Lauderdale on March 11th. Later the same afternoon, Mrs Jill Ditton won the hunt race at the R. E. Draghounds on Coal Tar and Mrs Gillian Coate won the corresponding event at the Wilton on Four Fivers.

There was another major change in the rules before the start of this season. Hunts were permitted to reduce the minimum weight for their open events to 12 stone, provided that they imposed a penalty of not less than 7 lb. for the winner of a steeplechase or a hurdle race or of an open race at a point-to-point 'within the

Bill Shand Kydd on his No Reward, the champion point-to-pointer of 1963

Richard Woodhouse going to the post on his Woodside Terrace at the Blackmore Vale in 1964

Two of the southern stars – The East Kent mare Cauliflower (Peter Southern). Guy Harwood on his Cowdray-hunted Spinster's Folly

period of the current year and the two years immediately previous to it'. Most, though not all hunts took advantage of this concession. But among those who did not – and rightly so, in my opinion – were the Worcestershire, the Middleton and the Heythrop, because to have done so in their case would inevitably have resulted in the Dudley, Grimthorpe and Lord Ashton of Hyde Cups ceasing to be true championships.

A particularly welcome feature of the 1967 season was the first appearance of *Hunterform*, the weekly formbook that is still with us today. This publication presents the results in far more detail than the old *Raceform* ever managed to do, and even includes comments on the running. It is a sure sign of the growing public interest in point-to-point racing that so ambitious a project is able to survive. There was certainly a time when it couldn't have done.

Other features of this season were a new lease of life for No Reward, who had a hat-trick of wins in open races; a repeat success for Mystery Gold II in the sweepstake race at the Bicester; Master Tammy and Lizzy the Lizard winning on the same day at Larkhill before going on to finish first and second in the National Hunt Chase; and the start of point-to-point racing on Lincoln Racecourse, where the Blankney, the Burton and the Grove and Rufford all held their fixtures.

Sue Aston broke one course record and lost another. On Touch and Go II in the ladies' race at the Staff College and R.M.A. Sandhurst, her time of 6 mins. 20 secs. was the fastest so far recorded at Tweseldown. But when Richard Miller won the open race at the Royal Artillery on Court Gardens in 6 mins. 5 secs. – a time that was equalled later in the season by Peter Cave on his Bronze Miller – the record she had set up at Larkhill on Miss Surprise in 1965 was smashed by a second.

Two young riders achieved notable doubles. Richard Shepherd won both members' races at the Bullingdon Club for the second successive year, one of them on a horse making his first appearance on a course, the six-year-old Poulakerry. Sixteen-year-old Stewart Stevens, who had his first point-to-point winner the previous season, won the hunt race at the Devon and Somerset Staghounds on his father's Mountain Torrent and the open race on his uncle's Madison Square. Two years later this young man was to have a major success in a different field, when he won the Punchestown Horse Trials on Benson, a horse bred on his father's farm in North Devon by a yearling out of a yearling.

Several riders had their fiftieth win, David Gibson on Regal Mist at the Woodland Pytchley, Robert Bothway on Indian Sun at the Essex and Suffolk, Richard Miller on Keysaire at the Portman, Grant Cann at the Hambledon when he completed a hat-trick with a win on Devon Pilgrim. And one rider, Roger Guilding, reached his century with a win on Lady Beware at the Croome.

But for two riders there was tragedy. Jean Morrison died from the injuries she received after a fall on Moneycara at the last fence at the Berwickshire; and Angela Radcliffe fractured her spine in a fall at the Bramham Moor.

For David Tatlow it was another highly successful season during which he rode twenty-four winners, five more than Roger Guilding and seven more than Guy Cunard. The best Tatlow horse was Barley Bree, whose most memorable achievements were a hard-earned win over Court Gardens in the four-mile race at the Heythrop and the thrashing he administered to Bronze Miller in the open event at the Cotswold Vale Farmers.

Bronze Miller – and I am writing of him in the present tense, because he was still operating in 1970 – is one of those spectacular performers who set off like the wind from flagfall with the intention of galloping their opponents into the ground. Another Plummers Plain, in fact; and, like Plummers Plain, he succeeded more often than not. Before he came up against Barley Bree, this pale-coloured chestnut son of Exodus (the sire of Tipperary Flame and Corrielaw Diamond) had won fourteen races in this fashion, seven of them that season. But in Barley Bree the flying machine from the Berkeley found a horse who could beat him at his own game, partnered by a rider who was shrewd enough to vary his tactics for the occasion.

Neither Barley Bree nor Bronze Miller were seen in the Dudley Cup; and for this there was a red-hot favourite in Sunarise, for whom Charlie Nixon had paid 2,000 guineas at the Ascot Sales the previous May after the horse had won seven races in Devon and Cornwall, where he was unbeaten.

The first race for Sunarise in his new colours was the ladies' open race at the Cotswold Vale Farmers in May 1966, when Scarlett Knipe (daughter of the Kinnersley trainer Fred Rimell) was successful on him; and he won his first five races (all of them open events) of 1967 without giving Roger Guilding a moment of anxiety. But in the Dudley Cup he was beaten, partly on account of the very firm going, which he hated, but also because he came up against a horse who had few superiors on this type of going, Mrs Geoffrey Freer's French-bred Tailorman, whose sire, Wallaby II, was an Ascot Gold Cup winner, and whose grandsire, Tourbillon, won the French Derby. Ridden for Mrs Freer by Peter Hobbs, Tailorman mastered Sunarise between the last two fences and went on to beat the course record with a time of 6 mins. 35 secs. This was a second faster than the previous best set up by Culleenpark in 1960 and equalled by Pomme de Guerre in 1962.

Sunarise was also beaten in his next race, by Chris Collins's Titus Oates in the John Corbet Cup at Stratford. But there was no disgrace in this, for Titus Oates was later to fetch the record price (for a N.H. horse) of 14,750 guineas at the Ascot Sales and reach the top class as a steeplechaser.

For the second time in four years, and the third altogether, Guy Cunard won the Grimthorpe Cup. This time he was riding Puddle Jumper, who hadn't been beaten in point-to-points for four seasons; and the twelve-year-old son of Iceberg II won going away from the Essex contestant, Prepotent, who had already won five point-to-points that season and was to win a hunter chase at Fakenham before it was over.

Puddle Jumper was one of four winners for Major Cunard at the Middleton. The others were Ferncliffe in the hunt race, Young Rohan in the adjacent hunts' race and Mr R. A. Bethell's Toy Shop in the Yorkshire Agricultural Society Race. Puddle Jumper and Young Rohan were then Guy Cunard's two best horses. His nine successes on the former (seven of them in a row) included two hunter chases and the Old Etonian Race at the Heythrop which he was winning for the fourth time; while on Young Rohan, a horse who started his point-to-point career in Kent and was bought at the Ascot Sales for 300 guineas after winning a maiden race there as a six-year-old in 1961, Major Cunard won seven races in nine appearances.

One might say with some justification that the Middleton meeting of 1967 was a Cunard benefit; except that there was an extremely good ladies' race, in which two Yorkshire girls, Patricia

Mason on Woodland Maiden and Sarah Bethell on Forty Light, went hell for leather over four miles before Woodland Maiden got the better of the duel. A week later there was a repeat performance at Melton; and this time, over the shorter course, it was Forty Light who emerged as the winner.

The going at Melton was very holding, and neither Tailorman nor Mystery Gold II, two of the principal contestants for the Henry Waterford Cup, were at all happy in it. But there was one horse in the race who positively revelled in the conditions, the South Durham mare Queen's Guide, on whom Geoffrey Wade had won four open races in the North. This was the mare who was to win the Foxhunters' Cup at Cheltenham two years later, an achievement which will have surprised few who saw her come from behind to cut down Cool Autumn at Melton. Except perhaps those who find it difficult to believe that any horse purchased for 150 guineas can win at Cheltenham.

Another horse who appreciated the underfoot conditions that day was Richard Woodhouse's Highworth, the winner of the novices' championship. And he, too, was to go on to make a name for himself as a hunter chaser, and even emulate the feat of his predecessor, Woodside Terrace, by winning the Cheltenham Foxhunters'. A son of Romany Air, Highworth was bred in the Old Berkshire country by Ted Dibble, who sold him to Richard Woodhouse after he had finished second in the maiden race at the Avon Vale in 1966 as a seven-year-old. Highworth's success at Melton was his sixth in the Woodhouse colours.

Of course, there were other good novices of 1967 who didn't run at Melton; and one of them was the Ledbury seven-year-old, Touch of Tammy, a full brother to Master Tammy. On this highly promising youngster, who was to meet a tragic end three years later, Roger Guilding won the maiden race at the North Ledbury and the adjacent hunts' race at the Cotswold Vale Farmers. Another was Devon Pilgrim from Roy Trigg's Sussex stable. This horse, who had won prizes in the show ring under the name of Aintree, later went into training with Ryan Price and Miss Auriol Sinclair, and after winning a race for each of them was much fancied for the Totalisator Champion Novices' Chase at Cheltenham, though he failed to shine in it.

It was another good season for ladies' horses, and in particular for Brenda Johnson's Minto Burn, who at last came up against

Plummers Plain, and beat him fair and square at Melton. Ann Harden's front-running Darnick Tower was busy slaughtering the opposition in the South West; Miss Jacqueline Harries's Appian Knight was doing the same in Wales; and busiest of all was Mr Oliver Carter's Over Court, on whom Mrs Avril Williams won nine races in Devon and Cornwall. There were also two exciting new recruits from the N.H. scene; and one of them, the ten-year-old Golden Wood, who was formerly in training with George Owen at Tarporley and was now being ridden by his niece Denise in her first season of race-riding, went through the season unbeaten. The other was Miss Anne Greenwood's seven-year-old Mister Sunshine, who had been hunted by his young owner with the Pendle Forest and Craven Harriers and gave her five winning rides in six appearances.

And there was Pat Tollit, now I suppose in the veteran class, but riding as brilliantly as ever. On her new horse, Gansy, a winner on the flat and over hurdles, Mrs Tollit entered the winner's enclosure eight times and was seen in the full flower of her genius at the Albrighton Woodland on the final day of the season when gaining a length in the air at the last fence to get home from Mrs Pat Hinch (née Newton) on her father's Cool Autumn and Sue Aston on Lawtonia.

Some five months after the season was over, we had the first of the annual point-to-point dinners which are now a well-established tradition. It was held on the October 27th at the Kensington Close Hotel, London, and attended by 250 enthusiasts from all parts of the country. The toast to point-to-point racing was proposed by Guy Cunard and responded to by Christopher Collins, the leading amateur under N.H. Rules. The occasion was also marked by the introduction of two challenge cups. David Tatlow was presented with the *Daily Telegraph* Cup for the leading gentleman rider of the season; and Pat Hinch became the first holder of *The Sporting Life* Cup for the leading lady rider.

Tailpiece

At the Ward Union and Fingal Harriers' point-to-point in Ireland, women riders filled the first three places riding against the men in the Ward Union Hunt Cup; Miss Fidelma McGivern, who rode the winner, was having her first ride in a race.

27
1968

In which Player's take a hand in things, a West Country veteran rides his 200th winner, Guy Cunard retires, and a son follows in his father's footsteps

In 1968, a season when Foot and Mouth played havoc with the point-to-point fixture list and many meetings were lost altogether, there were two major innovations, one appertaining to the rules and the other to the pattern of the season. The minimum height of the fences was raised from 4 ft. to 4 ft. 3 in., to bring them more into line with N.H. obstacles; and the Nottingham tobacco firm of John Player & Sons Ltd introduced the national point-to-point championship for the Player's Gold Leaf Trophy, which, with its thirty qualifying events varying from season to season, and a final on a professional racecourse, has added an extra dimension to point-to-point racing.

Fears were expressed in some quarters that the Player's venture would turn out to be little more than another benefit for the hunter-chasing brigade, and one correspondent gave these views an airing in a letter to *The Sporting Life*. 'But some will be wondering,' he wrote, 'just how far this generously-endowed fixture is a point-to-pointers' championship and not simply another hunter chase, albeit one confined to horses which have won a point-to-point during the current season.'

In fact, these doubts have proved groundless. Neither Baulking Green nor Cham, the two top hunter chasers of the 1967 season, nor Titus Oates, the leading hunter chaser of 1968, were among the seventeen horses who went to the post over 3¼ miles at Newbury in May for the first Player's Gold Leaf Trophy, worth £1,304 to the winner; and in a memorable duel between the products of two of the most genuine point-to-point stables in the country, Miss Lucy Jones's Bartlemy Boy got home from Mr W. J. A. Shepherd's Poulakerry by a short head, both horses having qualified for the final by winning divisions of the open event at Tweseldown on the first day of the season.

At the Bolventor Harriers in February, Frank Ryall rode his 200th winner when he won the maiden race on Mama's Boy; and at the Cotswold evening meeting in April, David Tatlow, the leading point-to-point rider for the fourth successive year, reached his century with a win on Mystery Gold II in the open race.

And at the Derwent in March, Guy Cunard had the accident which proved the last straw. He was riding his young horse Johnstone in the maiden race, and the crashing fall he had at the sixth fence was one fall too many. He sustained severe concussion and a fractured breast-bone and was eventually compelled to call it a day at the age of fifty-six. It is infinitely sad to think that the familiar cry 'Come on the old Major' will be heard no more on Yorkshire racecourses. But he has had a long and satisfying innings and, aside from the legendary Willy Rooney with his 360 winners in Ireland, his grand total of 268 point-to-point winners is unlikely to be equalled, let alone surpassed.

It was a sad year in other ways. Rosie's Cousin collapsed and died after winning the ladies' race at the North Cotswold. Frank Hobbs, who used to own those good horses Whispering Breeze and Pocket Borough, died in Kent. Jack Castle (the father of George and 'Chubb'), one of the most respected hunter judges in the South Midlands and the 'producer' of two of the best point-to-pointers in the area, Dysie Dumps and Scrum-Half, died in Oxfordshire. Charlie Nixon died in the Croome Country.

And in September, Major Harold Rushton died. Few people have done more for point-to-point racing than Major Rushton, whose name will forever be associated with the Dudley Cup, and of course with O'Dell. Master of the Worcestershire from 1929–33 and Joint-Master with Mr Hugh Sumner from 1933–37, he was also Hon. or Jt-Hon. Sec. of the Worcestershire point-to-point from 1931–67; and during his racing career he rode eighty-seven winners.

Two well-known horses returned to the scene to make positively final appearances. At the Puckeridge, Two Pins, now seventeen years old, emerged from retirement again to run in his fifty-first race and record the win which gave him a grand total of fifteen since his first public appearance eleven years earlier; and at the Dulverton (West), the Taunton Vale mare Spinning Coin II made her first appearance on a course for five years, four years after her first foal, Royal Toss, had finished second in a race at Chepstow. The mare was then fifteen years old and, after being a long way in arrears for the greater part of the journey, she got up to win the ladies' open race by a neck.

At the Mendip Farmers', Bronze Miller broke the record for the Nedge course with a time of 6 mins. 27 secs.; and before the season was out he had won his twentieth race.

For Plummers Plain and No Reward it was the last season, and both are now grazing in the Elysian fields. Plummers Plain made a successful farewell appearance at Melton to win his twelfth ladies' race for Gillian Pearce; while No Reward, at the ripe old age of fourteen, won two races in five appearances to finish his days with twenty-seven wins behind him.

But whereas Gillian Pearce had no replacement for Plummers Plain, or at least not one of anything like the same calibre, Bill Shand Kydd had a worthy successor to No Reward in Matchboard, a five-year-old mare by the same sire, Straight Deal. Matchboard's first appearance on a course was in a division of the maiden race at the Bicester, where she displayed a remarkable turn of foot from the last fence to win very cheekily; and she was cantering home from Flying East in her next race when she hit the top of the second last and came down. But in her two other races of 1968 the Whaddon Chase mare never made the semblance of a mistake. The following season she won four steeplechases.

Matchboard was perhaps the outstanding novice of the 1968 season. But there were several other possible claimants for this title, and three of them were in Scotland. One of these, Border Mask, a six-year-old by Border Chief, went on, like Matchboard, to distinguish himself under Rules. Another was Risky Nap, who won both his point-to-points and the Heart of all England at Hexham. And the third was Jedheads, owned by the same Charlie Scott who produced The Callant. Lintalee, the dam of Jedheads, was The Callant's sister; and Jedheads, like The Callant before him, won three point-to-points in his first season and the Heart of all England in his second. It was also a Scottish horse, Mr G. R. Dun's Bright Beach, a mare from the Lauderdale, who won the Cheltenham Foxhunters' that year.

But it was a horse from the Belvoir who won the Melton Hunt Club's novice championship, which was being sponsored for the

Mother and Daughter – Tipperary Flame and Corrielaw Diamond, ridden by their owner and breeder, Lockerbie farmer Andrew Spence

Mrs Pat Tollit winning on Uncle Coke at the Worcestershire in 1965. This was Mrs Tollit's 99th winner; and three days later she brought up the century on the same horse in the Corvedale Cup at the Ludlow

Sue Aston, the natural successor to Pat Tollit, winning on Tenor at the North Warwickshire in 1970

first time by the Marie Curie Memorial Foundation for the relief of cancer. This was Lance Newton's Roving Lad, a six-year-old chestnut gelding by Poaching who cost 1,000 guineas as a yearling and won three races on the Flat. In the capable hands of the stable jockey, Tommy Philby, Roving Lad showed a clean pair of heels to fourteen opponents and won in a canter. This was a case of a local horse living up to a considerable reputation as a speed merchant.

Another highly promising newcomer was Permit, from Eric Cousins's Tarporley stable; although he can hardly be described as a novice, since he came to point-to-point racing after winning three hurdle races the previous season as a four-year-old. Ridden each time by the trainer's son, Permit won three open races before being sold at Doncaster in August 1968 to Neville Crump for 14,000 guineas, which was only 750 guineas short of the price paid for Titus Oates at Ascot the previous month. Since then, Permit has won four steeplechases.

Bright Willow, the Dudley Cup winner of 1968, was also a newcomer, and a novice at that. This horse, who had won show jumping competitions for Walter Biddlecombe (the father of Terry and Tony) and was running in the colours of Mr Alan Cure, the Chairman of the West Warwickshire Farmers' Hunt came to Upton-on-Severn after two modest successes and a defeat by Pennyalina in an open race at the Ledbury. Not surprisingly, with Pennyalina again in the field, along with such experienced performers as Highworth, Lizzy the Lizard and Tailorman, Bright Willow started at odds of 20–1. But the much-fancied Pennyalina fell at the second fence, Tailorman found the going too soft for him; and Bright Willow, ridden with the utmost confidence by Robert Chugg, was a comfortable winner from River Slave and Highworth. Brightworthy, the premium stallion who sired Bright Willow, also produced the winner of the United Hunts' Cup at Cheltenham, which was won for the second time by Snowdra Queen; and Bright Willow was to win this race himself the following year.

There was also something of a turn-up for the book in the Grimthorpe Cup, which was won by the fourteen-year-old Shandover, who I think must be the oldest horse ever to have won this race, and certainly no other horse as old as that has won it since it was first run over 4½ miles in 1954. As Shandover had won his last three races, as well as a three-mile novices' chase at Carlisle the previous season, he was clearly entitled to some consideration. But others were entitled to more. Banjoe and Puddle Jumper, for instance, even though the latter was without the services of Guy Cunard; while also in the field were Sea Knight, a horse of bottomless stamina who had twice won the Liverpool Fox-hunters', and a very live candidate from East Anglia by the name of Honeybrook, who was being ridden by Michael Bloom.

It was a marvellously exciting race to watch, and it was only by a neck that Shandover managed to hold off the faster-finishing Honeybrook, who had lost valuable ground when he went right through the sixth from home and thus narrowly failed to emulate the feat of his dam, Kitty Brook. A neck behind Honeybrook came Puddle Jumper, who was also finishing faster than the winner.

The race was a triumph for the Dickinson family. Shandover was owned and trained by Tony and Monica, both great point-to-point riders in their day, and ridden by their nineteen-year-old son, Michael, whose performance echoed his father's on Turkish Prince in 1953. For Michael Dickinson it was the second leg of a notable double, as he had previously won the National Hunt Chase on Lord Leverhulme's Fascinating Forties.

But the last word must be for Puddle Jumper, the horse that Guy Cunard bought at the Ascot Sales in June 1961 for 900 guineas. By the end of 1968 (he didn't run in 1969) this horse had won twenty-two of his twenty-six point-to-points and three hunter chases.

And at the annual point-to-point dinner in October, after David Tatlow had been re-presented with the *Daily Telegraph* Cup and Sue Aston, who had equalled Pat Tollit's record of fifteen winners in a single season, had received the *Sporting Life* Cup, there was a special presentation of a silver tray which bore the inscription: 'Presented to Guy Cunard at the point-to-point dinner, October 18th, 1968, to mark his retirement from the sport to which he contributed so much.'

Tailpiece from Guy Cunard

'I was never very popular with doctors or ambulance personnel.'

28
1969

In which the Jockey Club takes over, the Tote relents, and The Dikler gets himself talked about

When point-to-point racing came under the jurisdiction of the Jockey Club in 1969, a loophole was closed. Before weighing out, all riders were required to produce to the Clerk of the Course a certificate of eligibility signed by their Hunt Secretary. Failure to do this – and there were several instances of it, most of them occasioned by forgetfulness – resulted in permission to ride being refused. The object of the regulation, in the words of the statement issued at the time by the public relations office in Portman Square, is 'to ensure that point-to-point riders are all regular hunting people and have paid their minimum hunt subscriptions before the start of the season'. An admirable precaution which has effectively removed the temptation to engage riders with dubious qualifications.

Before the start of the season, a bombshell was dropped by the Horserace Totalisator Board with their announcement that they proposed 'to combat increasing costs' by withdrawing Tote facilities from forty-nine meetings. Since most hunts rely very largely on their annual point-to-point to finance their activities in the hunting field, and many could not carry on without the money collected from this quarter, the news was received with considerable dismay throughout the country; and an impassioned letter in *The Sporting Life* from Mr W. F. Ransom, the Chairman of The Carholme point-to-points, expressed the general feeling on the subject. 'I can see in the very near future,' wrote Mr Ransom, 'point-to-pointing in Lincolnshire and many places being a thing of the past and many hunts closing down.' His plea to the Tote Board to reconsider their decison was taken up by others, and in the end the Horserace Totalisator Board relented, although in 1970 the four meetings in Wales and three in Scotland where the Tote takings had averaged less than £500 over the past three years were cut out and there were to be reduced facilities available over the Easter holiday, when the fixture list is heavily over-loaded and it is difficult to supply staff.

Every point-to-point season has its disappointments. Sometimes, for one reason or another, the brightest stars of the previous season fail to train on; and sometimes they are overtaken by misfortune, as happened in the case of Bartlemy Boy and Poulakerry, the two heroes of the 1968 Player's Gold Leaf Trophy. Poulakerry broke down at the V.W.H. in early March after a single success at Larkhill and little more than a month later he had been joined on the sidelines by Bartlemy Boy. But the latter, at least, had time to spreadeagle a big field in the four-mile race at the Heythrop, where he made the running from pillar to post and caused John Daniell to remark afterwards: 'If he had a turn of foot he'd win the Cheltenham Gold Cup!'

In the meantime, Sunarise and Touch of Tammy went triumphantly on their way. Sunarise was unbeaten in seven open events; and Touch of Tammy, who won four point-to-points and three hunter chases, started a hot favourite for the Player's Gold Leaf Trophy, which this time was being run over 3½ miles at Haydock. Unfortunately, he was far from being at his best, having had a penicillin injection a few days beforehand for an infected foot, and he finished fifth to the northern mare Forty Light, who had earned her qualification through winning the ladies' open race at the Holderness. In one respect, this was a rather appropriate success, because it was the first year that ladies' races had been admitted in the list of qualifying events. Forty Light started at 33–1 and won by 1½ lengths from Bright Willow, who was giving her 7 lb. But the form was made to seem all wrong when, on his next appearance, Touch of Tammy ended his season with a comfortable defeat of Bright Willow in the *Horse & Hound* Cup at Stratford.

Although Roger Guilding collected 11 point-to-point wins by means of Sunarise and Touch of Tammy and finished the season with a total of thirteen, there were three riders ahead of him, Michael Bloom with nineteen, Bill Shand Kydd with eighteen and David Tatlow with fifteen. Tatlow was possibly just a little unlucky not to be at the head of affairs once again, because one of his best prospects, the North Warwickshire mare Amba III, broke down at the West Warwickshire Farmers' at the end of

March; and he also lost out through the cancellation of some meetings.

There was, however, a tremendous duel between Bloom and Shand Kydd for the *Daily Telegraph* Cup, and thousands of people must have found their interest in point-to-point racing sharpened by it; even, I daresay, some who never saw the two adversaries in action against each other, since the Press saw to it that everyone was kept informed of the situation. The turning point came at the Melton Hunt Club fixture on May 22nd, when the East Anglian rider won the novices' championship on Lt. Col. W. W. Arnold's Skygazer. This was Bloom's nineteenth winner, in a season which saw him ride four of the five winners at the North Norfolk Harriers', and it increased his lead over Shand Kydd to two. At the Mid-Surrey Farmers' Club meeting two days later, the Whaddon Chase rider had his last chance to draw level; but although he won the open race there on Musk Orchid, he failed in the club members' race on Star of Arum and so ended his season one behind.

It was nevertheless Bill Shand Kydd's most successful point-to-point season since his move, some years beforehand, to the beautifully appointed stables at Leighton Buzzard where he installed the shrewd Brian Thompson as his stud manager. It is a great partnership that has flowered there over the years and now makes its presence felt on the hunter chase scene.

The most prolific winner from the stable in 1969 was Musk Orchid, the exceedingly tough seven-year-old by No Orchids that Bill Shand Kydd purchased out of Ryan Price's yard for 625 guineas at the Ascot Sales in September, 1968. Musk Orchid won nine races in twelve appearances, more than any other horse.

One of the few horses who managed to beat Musk Orchid was the year-younger Skygazer, on whom Michael Bloom won five races; and this powerful chestnut gelding by Copernicus was certainly one of the outstanding novices of the season. The pity is, since staying is his forté, that this horse is not eligible to run in the Cheltenham Foxhunters', on account of his having been hunted with a pack of harriers.

Two other novices of particular distinction were both hunted with the Meynell in Derbyshire, but they never met each other, possibly by design. One of them was Mr J. M. Spurrier's six-year-old Hilton Gravelle, who ran in four open races and won them all; and the other was Mr F. Sutton's eight-year-old mare Blue Dean, who finished fourth in the Player's Gold Leaf Trophy and wound up a highly successful season with a win in the John Corbet Cup at Stratford.

It seemed that there might also be an outstanding novice in the North, and yet another advertisement for the progeny of Exodus, when the grey Open Road, a five-year-old mare from the Hurworth, won her last three races on the trot. At the end of the season, this youngster was sold at the Ascot Sales to Mr W. J. A. Shepherd, in the Cotswolds, for 4,200 guineas. But so far she has proved a grave disappointment. Which only goes to show that all that glisters is not necessarily gold.

But the star that glittered brightest of all was The Dikler, and no one is going to convince me that this one isn't gold, though several attempts have been made. This enormously powerful six-year-old, who took such a prodigious hold that he had to be hunted in a double bridle, first appeared on a course in a division of the open race at the Beaufort, where he finished second to Touch of Tammy. He then won an open race at Crowell in the fastest time of the day and repeated the performance at Kimble, where even Musk Orchid was made to look like a second-rater. The Dikler's next, and last appearance of the season, was in the open race at the South Oxfordshire, his home meeting; and here, I regret to say, not even that accomplished horseman Brian Fanshawe could prevent him from running out. So, in a manner of speaking, Musk Orchid obtained his revenge, much to the delight of Brian Thompson, who was convinced he would do so anyway.

It was a discomforting moment for those of us who believed that in The Dikler we had seen one of the most exciting prospects ever to appear on a point-to-point course. But though we were sadder, we refused to be wiser. And in view of the eminence that The Dikler has attained since, who is now going to say that we were wrong? Certainly not John Lawrence, who wrote of The Dikler after he had won the Honeybourne Novices' Chase at Cheltenham in November, 1969 from Fulke Walwyn's stable on his first appearance under N.H. Rules: 'I haven't seen many more promising runs at Cheltenham since Tim Brookshaw rode Mill House here as a five-year-old.' It is true that, although he won two more races that season, The Dikler blotted his copybook by parting company with his jockey on three other occasions and, to some extent, by getting beaten by Titus Oates at Kempton, but his potential still stands out a mile; and who is to say that failure in the Cheltenham Gold Cup of 1970 won't be followed by triumph in 1971?

A one-time show hunter, The Dikler towered over his point-to-point rivals in the paddock, where his aristocratic bearing and the majesty of his tread made him the cynosure of all eyes. This uncharacteristically big son of Vulgan out of a Dublin Horse Show winner, Coronation Day (by Grand Weather), came into the possession of his fortunate owner, Mrs Peggy August, on the death of her uncle, Mr Edward Bee, who bought The Dikler for £3,500 and died two days after the transaction was completed.

Hardly less stimulating than the duelling for the *Daily Telegraph* Cup was the battle between Sue Aston and Josephine Turner for *The Sporting Life* Cup. It was not resolved until the final day of the season when Convoys was taken down from Suffolk to the Tiverton Staghounds' to contest the ladies' open race and Josephine Turner got him home by a short head and a neck from two of the local stars, Jack in the Basket and Silver Nutmeg. This was Miss Turner's fourteenth winner and it put her one ahead of Sue Aston, who was without a ride in the race but was present as a spectator! It was a well-deserved success for the best lady rider in East Anglia, one whose split-second timing and fine judgement of pace has gained her a great many admirers outside her own area.

Convoys, the best horse Josephine Turner rode, changed hands as a yearling for 4,000 guineas, and he was a winner on the Flat as a two-year-old. But he was acquired by Josephine's father, through the Newmarket Bloodstock Agency, for the comparatively cheap price of 400 guineas at the Ascot Sales in the summer of 1966 as a four-year-old. His first success in the Turner colours was in the maiden race at the Norfolk & Suffolk in 1968. David Turner won four races on him that season, and Josephine won three; and in 1969 brother and sister won four races apiece on him, two of David's successes being in hunter chases.

Three weeks after being presented with *The Sporting Life* Cup at the annual point-to-point dinner in September, Josephine Turner married Robert Bothway, an Acting Joint-Master of the Dunston Harriers.

Sue Aston's most prolific winner was Hartlands, on whom she

won seven races. This was a considerable achievement, because although Hartlands had won five saddle club races the previous season when ridden by his owner, Christopher Glyn, the man primarily responsible for founding the point-to-point dinner, he was very far from being an easy ride and had to be scrubbed along almost from start to finish. When Christopher Glyn had the terrible misfortune to fracture his spine in a swimming accident in Australia shortly before the start of the season, he cabled home to say that he wanted Miss Aston to ride his horse. It was an inspired decision. In Sue Aston, Hartlands found the perfect partner, and on more than one occasion it enabled him to win a race which would have been lost with any other rider on top.

There was no Dudley Cup in 1969. For the first time since the war, the Worcestershire Hunt's fixture succumbed to the weather conditions and even postponement failed to save it. And there was very nearly no Grimthorpe Cup either. This, too, was postponed, and a somewhat sub-standard field went to the post at Whitwell-on-the-Hill on an evening in mid-week. The race was won by the Grafton horse My Night, who had been runner-up to Bartlemy Boy in the Heythrop four-miler. This horse's only previous success that season was in a division of the members' race at the Melton Hunt Club six days beforehand; and Medicine Bow, the horse he defeated in the Grimthorpe Cup, failed to win a race all the season.

It was also a southern horse who won the Liverpool Fox-hunters', Mr V. H. Rowe's home-bred Bitter Lemon, who I think must be the first horse from the Puckeridge to win this race. Skilfully ridden by the ebullient Hunter, Bitter Lemon never put a foot wrong over the big fences and once he had hit the front it was simply a question of how much daylight he would put between himself and the runner-up.

Tailpiece

In the hunt race at the Heythrop, David Nugent put up so much weight to ride his heavy-weight hunter Clonmellon that there were not enough weights to accommodate him on the scales. 'Surely,' he said afterwards, 'I must be the heaviest man to go to the post this point-to-point season?' At 18½ stone this was too modest a claim. As Clonmellon returned to the paddock after the race, he was heard to mutter: 'He must think I'm a bloody elephant.'

29

1970 and the Future

In which new championships are introduced, a five-year-old wins the Dudley Cup and the Jeremiahs are rebuked

Before the start of the 1970 season the point-to-point scene suffered its greatest loss since the death of Major Rushton. Lance Newton died. An inspired administrator, utterly tireless in his plans for the furtherance of point-to-point racing, and with the capacity to communicate his enthusiasm to others, Lance Newton was the power behind the Melton Hunt Club, and it is largely as a result of his influence that the club's annual point-to-point fixture at Garthorpe has become an end-of-term highlight, an occasion which plays no small part in shaping the pattern of the season. The bright spirit has been extinguished, but the work lives on and the open event for the Henry Waterford Cup at Melton is now known as the R. L. Newton Memorial Race.

We saw, in 1970, the proliferation of the regional championships which were started the previous year in the South East by the champagne firm of Laurent Perrier, who extended their sponsorship to the West Midlands with a championship for owners and riders on similar lines.

Others followed suit. Into the picture stepped the whisky distillers John Dewar & Sons Ltd., with their Dewar's Whisky championships on three fronts, the South of England, the South Midlands and East Anglia. In the North, confined to the counties of Yorkshire, Lancashire, Cumberland, Northumberland and Durham, there was a points championship for lady riders sponsored by Pegus Horse Foods; and in the South West there was even a riders' course championship, sponsored by a firm of brandy shippers, Messrs. Camus, and restricted to performances at the three Nedge meetings, the Mendip Farmers, the Weston Harriers and the West Somerset Vale.

All this might well have resulted in horses keeping strictly to their own areas, which in my opinion would not be a good thing for point-to-point racing as a whole, since the sport thrives on a competition between horses from different parts of the country. This is why races like the Dudley Cup and the Player's Gold Leaf Trophy are of such absorbing interest.

In fact, however, the regional championships did not have the cramping effect that was feared in some quarters. Owners and riders continued to pursue the national awards for performances over a wider field; while the sponsors on the local fronts must surely have been gratified with the evidence of social goodwill engendered by the consumption of their products.

The season also saw the initiation of a national point-to-point owners' championship, launched (in the contemporary tradition) by Marnier-Lapostolle, the makers of Grand Marnier liqueur cognac, who put up a handsome challenge trophy for presentation at the annual point-to-point dinner along with the *Daily Telegraph* and *Sporting Life* Cups for the leading riders.

Since the idea of this new championship was to give the smaller stables an equal chance with the bigger ones, the result was determined, not simply by the number of races won, but by the number of races won with one horse. It worked out beautifully. The issue was in doubt right up to the last day of the season, when the three leading horses, Barty, Far East II and Tenor were all in action, though not against each other. That would have been too much to expect in the circumstances. Barty and Far East II both won their races at the Dulverton (East) and Tenor won at the Melton Hunt Club. Had Barty finished out of a place, there would have been a triple dead-heat for the Grand Marnier Rose Bowl, as each horse would then have ended the season with nine wins and no further placing to give him an advantage over the others. Instead, we had a clear winner and two joint runners-up.

Ten wins in a season is a considerable achievement in itself. But in Barty's case, it was ten wins without a single defeat. And what made it more remarkable still was the fact that this twelve-year-old gelding from the Wilton had only managed to win one race in nine appearances the previous season. It was what one might call a brother and sister triumph, for Barty is owned by Alexander Gordon-Watson, who won five races on him, the other five being won by his sister Mary in her first season of race-riding. Mary Gordon-Watson is, of course, a champion in another sphere. In 1969 she won the individual title in the European

Horse Trials Championship at Haras du Pin on Cornishman V.

Mrs Andy Frank's Far East II, from the Devon & Somerset Staghounds, has been a model of consistency for many seasons. By the end of 1970, when he was unbeaten, as he was the previous season in point-to-points, this thirteen-year-old horse had won thirty-five races.

As for Tenor, whose partnership with Sue Aston yielded nine wins in eleven appearances, this is a case of a discard from a professional racing stable repaying the care and attention lavished on him by a hunting farmer in the Heythrop country. His owner, Kenneth Dale, first spotted him three years ago in a field by the railway line at Moreton-in-Marsh. At that time Tenor was the property of a local milkman who had acquired him for his son to ride in gymkhanas! In 1970 this versatile horse, whose sire Macherio was an Italian Derby winner, won over all distances from three to four miles, his success over this last distance coming when the North Warwickshire reintroduced their four-mile ladies' race at their Lowsonford meeting.

After Sue Aston had won the ladies' race at the Golden Valley on Tenor a spectator remarked, 'Now we know why they reckon this girl is the best in the country'; and after she had won on the same horse at the Heythrop, where she stole the race from Mrs Ann Harden and Darnick Tower on the last bend, another said: 'If Sue Aston was a man, Terry Biddlecombe would be out of a job.' But not everyone feels the same way about this brilliant rider. Some people think she rides too short and are consequently unable to conceal their delight on the rare occasions when she comes off; and to some of her fellow riders any praise of her in print is like a red rag to a bull. This is one of the penalties that has to be paid for reaching the top of the tree in any sport.

With fourteen wins, Sue Aston comfortably regained *The Sporting Life* Cup which she lost to Josephine Turner the previous season. Her nearest rivals were Mrs Pat Tollit and Anne Greenwood, each of whom rode nine winners.

Anne Greenwood, who hunts with the Pendle Forest, was the leading lady in the North, and in Mister Sunshine and Roman Scandal, the latter in his first season of point-to-point racing, though he was the winner of six races on the Flat and two over hurdles, she had what were probably the best ladies' horses in the country. Roman Scandal was unbeaten in six appearances; and the only time that Mister Sunshine was defeated was when he broke a bone in his leg finishing second to Zangavar at the Sinnington and had to be put down.

It was this disaster that caused Anne Greenwood to lose the Pegus Championship to Marie Tinkler, who enjoyed a great season on Zangavar and Flexodus, two horses acquired from the Turners in Suffolk. Mrs Tinkler, whose husband Colin had such faith in her that he wagered £100 at 5–2 that she would win the Pegus, was once a top-class show jumper. In 1953, as Marie Delfosse, she won the Queen Elizabeth II Cup at the Royal International Horse Show on Fanny Rosa.

The leading gentleman rider, and winner of the *Daily Telegraph* Cup, was David Turner, who won nineteen races and reached his half century of wins when he was successful on Birchwood Too (one of his few rides outside the stable) in the open race at the Mid Surrey Farmers' Club. The runner-up to him was Grant Cann, the rider of Far East II, who had 16 wins in the West Country, one more than David Gibson and Bob Davies (no relation to the leading professional of the same name).

'Might with luck go through 1970 unbeaten,' wrote Geoffrey Sale in his annual about Convoys, one of the horses ridden by David Turner. Well, he didn't exactly do that; but he did win seven races in eleven starts, and displayed his qualities as a fighter by winning three of these races by a neck, a fourth by a head, a fifth by three-quarters of a length, and a sixth by getting up on the post to force a dead-heat. Another consistent winner from the East Anglian stable was Billy Larkin, a six-year-old son of Hard Sauce who had won two races on the Flat, and broken his duck over fences the previous season in a hunter chase at Fakenham. After winning four races in a row on this horse, David Turner took him up to Yorkshire on the final day of the season and won at the Goathland.

Despite the bone-hard going for the Middleton & Middleton East fixture at Whitwell-on-the-Hill, there were thirteen starters for the Grimthorpe Cup; and although the best of the Yorkshire horses were conspicuous only by their absence, eleven hunts were represented, ranging from the Dumfriesshire in Scotland to the Enfield Chace in the South. The winner was a horse from the South Notts, Eric Willson's Young Highlander, who was returning to point-to-point racing after an unsuccessful venture under Rules.

Ridden for the first time by David Gibson, Young Highlander, who had won three of his five previous races with his owner up, took over the lead from the Cheshire mare Innismena at the fourth from home and went on to score comfortably from the fast-finishing Clybeg, who passed Slave Knocker, the Enfield Chace representative, in the run-in.

The winner's time of 8 mins. 40 secs. was actually 3½ seconds faster than More Honour's record time in 1956; but as one of the fences was omitted on each circuit owing to the state of the ground, it would be doing More Honour less than justice to credit Young Highlander with a new record.

I would not care to describe the 1970 Grimthorpe Cup as a vintage one. But I have no hesitation about applying this description to the Dudley Cup, which in 1970 found a new home at Chaddesley Corbett, where the course was specially altered to provide a proper test of stamina.

The favourite for this race was Sunarise, who had won his last seven races, which included two hunter chases at Worcester, and whose only defeat was on his first appearance of the season, when he went under to Sally Furlong (one of the top novices of the 1969 season) and Highworth at Larkhill. With Roger Guilding confined to the sidelines as the result of an injury, Sunarise was being ridden by Robert Chugg, who had already won five races on him, including the two hunter chases and the sweepstake race at the Bicester. Among his opponents this time were Sally Furlong again, Lord Fortune (the winner of the four-mile race at the Heythrop and two other races), Bartlemy Boy, Auld Cigar (one of the best point-to-pointers in Wales), and a highly promising five-year-old mare called Frozen Dawn, owned by Mrs E. C. Gaze and ridden by Henry Oliver, who was once associated with Snowdra Queen.

And it was the five-year-old who won, the first horse of this age to win the Dudley Cup since Dust Cap in 1912. The moment of truth for Sunarise came at the formidable open ditch six fences from home. He dug his toes in and tried to refuse it. Robert Chugg pushed him over, but by that time Sunarise had been passed by Frozen Dawn and Bencombe House, and although he re-passed Bencombe House three fences out he was never able to get on terms with Frozen Dawn, who had two lengths to spare at the post. Lord Fortune, coming late on the scene, got the better of a duel with Bencombe House for third place. Sally Furlong, who never showed much interest and was clearly feeling the effects of an old shoulder injury sustained the previous season, finished fifth. Auld Cigar was a faller around the half-way mark; and Bartlemy Boy was pulled up after making the early running.

In Frozen Dawn we had seen an exceptionally good horse, and maybe even a great one. Her Dudley Cup win was her fourth in a row. But more remarkable than this was the fact that it came only three days after she had won the open race at the Tredegar Farmers' evening meeting by a short head, a margin so flattering to the runner-up that the Stewards called Henry Oliver up before them and severely cautioned him for going to sleep. Which seemed an odd way of going about things, considering that he did after all win the race.

Like so many of the young horses running in point-to-points, Frozen Dawn was acquired in Ireland, where she was bred at the Garryrichard Stud in Co. Wexford. Her sire, Arctic Slave, stands at this stud. Her dam, Early Light, is out of Broken Dawn, who bred a number of distinguished N.H. horses, including Brasher, My Fortescue and Even Break. As a four-year-old, Frozen Dawn was placed three times over hurdles when in training with Fred Rimell, but she had never been over fences before starting in point-to-points.

What is such a horse worth? This is a question that nobody can answer with certainty. It is known, however, that Mrs Gaze turned down an offer of £11,000 for her from a well-known N.H. trainer who saw the mare as a potential winner of the Cheltenham Gold Cup.

Four days after her Dudley Cup win Frozen Dawn made her last appearance of the season, in a division of the open race at the Cotswold Vale Farmers' evening fixture, and won that. And just over three weeks later, Lord Fortune set the seal on the Dudley Cup form by winning the Player's Gold Leaf Trophy at Newbury, beating Skygazer by a head in a field of sixteen, with the northern horse Old Oats fifteen lengths away third.

It was nearly the end of a great season for Lord Fortune. But not quite. A week after his success at Newbury he turned out for the *Horse and Hound* Cup at Stratford and went very close to winning it, going under by less than a length to the hard-ground specialist Some Man.

A seven-year-old chestnut son of Fortina out of a mare by

Preciptic, Lord Fortune is owned and trained by Mrs Jackie Brutton, for whom he was purchased in Ireland by Fred Rimell as a three-year-old. He is proving a worthy successor to Snowdra Queen and has a thoroughly capable pilot in George Hyatt.

Melton without Lance Newton was naturally not the same. But the magnetic attraction of this splendid fixture was such that three of the riders who had mounts in the Player's Gold Leaf Trophy arrived by helicopter from Newbury. One of them was the rider of Skygazer, Michael Bloom, who won the Marie Curie Novices' Championship for the second successive year, this time on Rouletto, a six-year-old by Caporetto in his first season of point-to-point racing.

And there was always Ursula Newton, Lance's indomitable widow, who was here, there and everywhere, and whose Roving Lad ran a great race to divide Highworth and Young Highlander in the Lance Newton Memorial. This race was run in 6 mins. 10 secs., the fastest time ever recorded at Melton, the previous best being Plummers Plain's 6 mins. 11 secs. in a division of the club ladies' race in 1965.

What a magnificent replacement for Woodside Terrace Highworth has been to Richard Woodhouse! In 1970 he followed in the footsteps of his illustrious predecessor by winning the Cheltenham Foxhunters', and his seven successes brought his grand total of wins up to twenty-two, achieved in four seasons.

By this time, Bronze Miller, the only horse to beat Frozen Dawn when the mare stood up, had won twenty-eight races, Touch of Tammy had had the accident at the North Ledbury which ended his life, Col. C. R. Spencer (the veteran owner-rider of Victory Spirit) had ridden his 100th winner, and two outstanding campaigners were due for retirement.

For sixteen-year-old Mystery Gold II and fifteen-year-old Puddle Jumper it was a case of *anno domini* catching up with them, and they managed their fade-outs with distinction, Mystery Gold by winning the members' race at the Harkaway Club and Puddle Jumper with an honourable defeat by Scalby Fortune in the adjacent hunts' race at the Goathland. While neither of these two came anywhere near topping Lonesome Boy's post-war record of sixty-five wins, each made a considerable impact on the point-to-point scene. Mystery Gold won thirty-four of his forty-nine races, thirty-two of them while he was stabled with David Tatlow, who rode him in all but one of them; and if Puddle Jumper had been kept to point-to-points instead of making frequent assaults on the hunter chases, he would doubtless have won many more races than he did. As it was, his sixty-six appearances in the colours of Guy Cunard gave him twenty-five wins in point-to-points and three in hunter chases, and on the vast majority of these occasions 'dear old Puddle' was ridden by the Galloping Major himself.

I have heard it said that point-to-point racing is a dying sport. But this I do not believe. What I do believe is that some hunts are finding it increasingly difficult to make money out of it. This, however, is partly their own fault. They have been taking too much for granted. It is not enough these days simply to put on a point-to-point fixture and wait hopefully for people to turn up for it. Much more needs to be done in the way of advertising and promotion. It is no good having something to sell if you don't know how to market it. And it is no good at all putting on a poor programme with poor amenities. The public are much more demanding than they were. They have been given a taste of point-to-point racing at its best by men like Lance Newton and Harold Rushton, and they are hungry for more. Unlike those diehard letter-writers who pepper the correspondence columns of *Horse and Hound* and sign themselves 'Disgusted' or 'Fairplay', they are not much concerned with whether or not a horse has been 'genuinely hunted', and they have no time at all for people who keep bawling 'Pot-hunter'! (Neither have I, for that matter.) They want to see good horses and fair fields running over courses which look as if some money has been spent on them. And they want to be made to feel welcome. Naturally, owners also need to be encouraged; and one way of doing this, as Major Cunard has suggested in his Foreword, is to increase the prize money. But this is not the only answer.

It is astonishing, when one comes to think of it, how much has been done for point-to-point racing by people who are not directly concerned in it. Player's have done a wonderful job for the sport with their Gold Leaf Trophy. The *Daily Telegraph* and *The Sporting Life* have stimulated interest and sharpened people's competitive instincts with their cups for leading riders. Other commercial enterprises have come up with other ideas and awards. The annual point-to-point dinner in the autumn reawakens interest and gets point-to-point enthusiasts together. All these things

Smiles from David and Barbara Tatlow after David had recorded his 100th win, on Mystery Gold II in the open race at the Cotswold in 1968

Michael Bloom and Josephine Turner, the leading riders of 1969, holding the trophies presented to them at the point-to-point dinner. Mrs Jenny Bloom is on her husband's right; and on Josephine Turner's left is the man she married three weeks later, Robert Bothway

Major Harold Rushton photographed with Capt. Brian Fanshawe (now a Master of Foxhounds in Ireland) in the paddock at Upton-on-Severn in 1965

Lance Newton with his daughter, Mrs Pat Hinch, at the point-to-point dinner in 1967. Mrs Hinch is holding *The Sporting Life* Cup, awarded to the leading lady rider of the season

are good for the future health of point-to-point racing. All are an indication of the enormous interest there is in the sport, an interest which is by no means confined to the hunting and farming fraternity. Moreover, the impact of point-to-point racing on the N.H. scene is greater than ever before, and a point-to-pointer in the Cheltenham Gold Cup is no longer an absurdity.

It is true that a number of hunts are being compelled to amalgamate with each other by economic necessity, that courses are being lost and long-established fixtures going to the wall. But fresh ones are springing up in their place, and people are still prepared to spend money building new courses. Inevitably, there will be some pruning of fixtures in the future. But this has long been overdue anyway. Too few horses have been chasing too many courses.

Point-to-point racing a dying sport? Whoever says this has to be joking.

I am getting just a little tired of the ceaseless propaganda that is being poured out by the British Field Sports Society with their incessant warnings that the end of foxhunting would mean the end of point-to-point racing. Nothing of the sort. If foxhunting should fall a victim to the envious machinations of the anti-hunting brigade, point-to-point racing will still survive, in one form or another. After all, there are always the draghunts; and one leading point-to-point rider, whose name might come as a surprise were I to reveal it, tells me that he prefers hunting with draghounds!

As I think this book has shown, the Jeremiahs have been fulminating about point-to-point racing ever since the first horse jumped the first twig. They will continue to do so. It makes no difference. It takes much more than this to put down a beloved sport. Of course, if the farming community, who have done so much for point-to-point racing over the years, were suddenly to lose interest, or be forced out of business by the tax collector, that would indeed be serious. But I do not think this is likely to happen, and as long as farming survives point-to-point racing will continue to take place on the great green back of our native countryside.

So really, Major, it *is* a continuing story.

30

About the Courses

Point-to-point courses vary so much from area to area, and sometimes even within areas, that I feel a closing chapter on their individual characteristics may prove helpful to owners, riders and spectators. I do not pretend to have encompassed every course, but comments about most of them, based partly on my own observations and partly on a cross-section of informed opinion, now follow. Let us start at the top of the country and work down.

Scotland

These courses are usually pretty testing, and some very good horses have won over them. One of the most testing of all is that of the Lauderdale at Mosshouses. This is very much the old type of point-to-point course, best suited to a true stayer. It is a left-handed, up and down course, and in bad weather the going can get very heavy, especially before the last fence. The viewing facilities are good.

The Fife course at Balcormo Mains also needs a stayer, though it is fairly flat, with one drop fence which requires careful negotiating. Left-handed and with good viewing.

The old Bogside racecourse, where the Scottish Grand National used to be run, is the setting for three meetings, the Lanarkshire & Renfrew, the Eglinton and the Ayrshire Yeomanry. This is a flat, right-handed course on old grass, with well-sloped fences and excellent viewing facilities; the grandstand, paddock and boxes are all there still.

The Dumfriesshire course at Lockerbie is also flat and right-handed, and with a sandy soil that seldom gets heavy. Like Bogside, it is a fairly long course and the view is nearly as good.

The Linlithgow & Stirlingshire course at Oatridge is rather similar to the Lauderdale, left-handed and with plenty of undulation. It can be very soft or very hard, and there is occasional plough. The viewing is good.

The left-handed course at Friars Haugh, Kelso, where the Buccleuch & Jedforest and the Berwickshire have their fixtures, is a park course with island fences and a steep climb which has to be undertaken twice. The going seldom gets heavy but the fences are hard and need jumping. Some of them are too close together for the comfort of long-striding horses. The viewing facilities leave something to be desired, and in order to keep the horses in sight all the time it is necessary to run about quite a bit.

Northumberland, Cumberland and Durham

The Percy, West Percy & Milvain course at Alnwick, where the open race used to be run over four miles, is a long, left-handed course with some undulation, but not too steep. Some ridge and furrow. Viewing facilities good.

The Cumberland Farmers have a flat park course at Dalston, with island fences, some of them rather small and soft. The track is right-handed, and the runners are out of sight for a short time on both circuits. The going, on old grass, is usually good.

Horses require both speed and stamina for Corbridge, where the Braes of Derwent, the Tynedale and the Haydon hold their races over a 3¼ mile right-handed course without much undulation. An all-round performer is what is required here. The fences are nice average ones and the viewing is good.

The South Durham and the Zetland use the same course at Sedgefield. This is a short, fast course, left-handed and 2½ times round, with reasonably good viewing.

Lancashire and Yorkshire

The Vale of Lune course at Whittington is a good, galloping, left-handed course that drains well.

The Pendle Forest & Craven Harriers' course at Sawley requires a stayer. This is a 3¼-mile course with the last two fences downhill. The track is right-handed and the horses do two circuits of it. Good for spectators.

Stayers also do well over the Holcombe Harriers' course at Nab Gate, where the track is left-handed with a fair amount of undulation. The same applies to the Cleveland course at Little Ayton, except that this is flatter and there is usually some arable, which can be very deep in wet weather.

The left-handed Hurworth course at Hutton Rudby is rather a

short one. The slowest time recorded here in 1970, on good going, was 6 mins. 43 secs., and the fastest 6 mins. 13 secs. But it is a real switchback course with a rise to the last fence. The fences are not normally very difficult. There is usually a field of arable, otherwise all old turf. The view for spectators is no more than fair.

The Bedale & West of Yore course at Hornby Park is a longish, rather flat, all-grass course, left-handed, with good fences. But it is not a particularly good course for spectators.

The Goathland course at Dunsley, however, has excellent viewing facilities. This is a short and somewhat twisting right-handed course with a downhill finish. Not the sort of course for a Bartlemy Boy or a Poulakerry!

The left-handed course at Wykeham is shared by the Derwent, the Sinnington and the Staintondale. This is a fast, quick-drying course eminently suitable for an early fixture; and the viewing facilities are good.

So they are at Swindon Wood, where the Bramham Moor hold their fixture over a right-handed, galloping course on which the drainage has recently been improved. The fences here are very good.

The right-handed Middleton & Middleton East course at Whitwell-on-the-Hill is one of the best courses in Yorkshire. In fact, I would go further than this and call it one of the best in the country, although it is apt to get very firm after a long dry spell. This is the setting for the 4½-mile Grimthorpe Cup race and the ladies' four-mile open race for the Rose's Cup. But it is a true stayers' course even for the other events, which are run over 3½ miles. And as there is a natural grandstand at Whitwell, the viewing facilities are first-class. The fences are fairly big, especially the open ditch, but they are beautifully sited and falls are usually few and far between.

Another stayers' course is the one at Bretton Park used by the Badsworth and the Rockwood Harriers. This is left-handed and very hilly; and there is a stiff uphill run before the slight downhill one to the finish. The fences are usually fairly easy, and the viewing facilities good.

The flat York & Ainsty course at Easingwold is very sharp, with a sandy soil that usually rules out heavy going. It is left-handed and very good for spectators, in contrast to the Holderness course at Dalton Park, where the view is restricted by trees. This is a flat, right-handed course with its fair share of twists. Not one for short runners.

North Midlands

The Cheshire Forest course at Littleton is a short, right-handed all-grass course without any undulation. Not a course for stayers, and very similar to the disused aerodrome site at Eaton Hall used by Sir W. W. Wynn's and the Flint & Denbigh.

The real stayers' course in these parts is the one at Flagg Moor used by the High Peak. This is ideal for a one-paced hunter who would relish a long pull uphill. Left-handed and with good viewing facilities.

The left-handed course at Eyton-on-Severn, where the North and South Shropshire hold their fixtures, is ideal for a young horse, and for a front runner. The fences are well made and stamina is rarely required, except perhaps in bad weather. The viewing facilities are good but, as the horses go rather far away from the eye, field-glasses are an advantage.

Another front runner's course, unsuitable for long-striding animals, is that of the North Staffordshire at Mucklestone, where the finish has something in common with a roundabout, quarter of a mile downhill being preceded by quarter of a mile uphill. This is a narrow, left-handed course not unlike the one at the Pytchley, with a good view for spectators.

The Meynell have switched courses several times in the last few years. At one time they held their races over a flat, left-handed course at Aston-on-Trent. Then they went to the High Peak course at Flagg Moor for two years, and in 1970 they moved to the South Notts course at Cropwell Bishop. This is a short, fast, right-handed track, with some ridge and furrow and the odd drop fence. I have heard it described as 'a bit of a hunter trial'. But efforts are being made to improve it.

West Midlands

The Croome course at Upton-on-Severn, which was formerly the setting for the Dudley Cup, is a testing, right-handed course that provides a true test of stamina and takes quite a lot of jumping. The wide first fence makes it a good course for large fields, but the landing over the last is not an easy one in wet or hard conditions. The view is reasonably good except where obscured by willow trees in the water meadows.

The left-handed Albrighton Woodland course at Chaddesley

Corbett, which is also used by the Harkaway Club, has always had the reputation for being a short runner's course; but when the Worcestershire moved there in 1970 they got round this by increasing the distance of their races (including the Dudley Cup) by a quarter of a mile and giving the horses a couple more fences to jump. The improvement effectively silenced the critics and further ones are planned for the 1971 season. These will doubtless include a solution to the problem of a particularly awkward open ditch.

The North Warwickshire (who feature a ladies' open race run over four miles), the West Warwickshire Farmers and the South Staffordshire use the same course at Lowsonford. This is an individual, left-handed course that does not suit all types of horse owing to the steep undulations. There is not much joy in running a horse who doesn't come downhill well, and there are some rather sharp bends. But despite the gradients, it is not a testing course and short runners can win over it. The view, from a natural grandstand, is a very good one.

In recent years the Warwickshire have been running their races over the North Cotswold course at Spring Hill. This is a fairly sharp, right-handed course with some undulation. A real country course with a very agreeable atmosphere, but not too good for viewing.

The Cotswold and the Cotswold Vale Farmers race at Andoversford over a right-handed, undulating course with a long uphill pull to the last two fences and some tricky downhill jumps on the way. This is a course for stayers and tacticians. The viewing is excellent, and for the last few years both fixtures have been evening ones, highly enjoyable and with plenty of runners. The bookmakers enter into the spirit of things and their prices are invariably generous.

The Heythrop course at Stow-on-the-Wold, the setting for the four-mile open race for Lord Ashton of Hyde's Cup and for a $3\frac{1}{2}$-mile ladies' open race, is a particularly fine course, with good solid fences that are discouraging to sketchy jumpers. Again a course for tacticians. Races are often won and lost at the bend before the final fence. Right-handed and with excellent viewing facilities from a natural grandstand.

The left-handed Beaufort course at Didmarton, which is also used by the Avon Vale, suits fast horses and front runners, but it takes some jumping. There is a long downhill run to the third fence from home. The going here is usually good and all the fences can be seen without moving.

Another course that takes jumping is the long, left-handed course used by the V.W.H. at Siddington, where there are several drop fences. Fairly good viewing, but not outstanding.

At Woodford, the Berkeley have a course noted for the excellence of the going, which invariably results in large fields. This is a flat, galloping, left-handed track, with every fence in sight. Front runners can win here, but I have seen them beaten.

The Ledbury and the North Ledbury have a flat left-handed course at Upleadon, where the stiff birch fences have been built under the supervision of a top-class point-to-point jockey, Roger Guilding. This is not a stayers' course, but neither is it one for poor jumpers. In bad weather it can get very wet. A fair course for viewing.

The left-handed North Hereford course at Newtown is an undulating three-mile course, which, since the meeting is an early-season one, frequently takes a caning from the weather. The view is fairly good, though the horses are out of sight for a short spell.

The South Hereford share a course with the Ross Harriers at Belmont. This had some alterations made to it before the start of the 1970 season, but although they improved the viewing facilities they were not entirely satisfactory regarding the approach to some of the fences and no doubt further changes will be made before the 1971 season. It is a long, left-handed course, and in 1970 only the ladies' race was run in under eight minutes!

The Ludlow course at Bitterley has only been in use for two years and is still having teething problems, which may well have been ironed out by next season. This is a slightly undulating left-handed course where experience, on the part of both horses and riders, counts for quite a lot. The viewing is good.

The Clifton-on-Teme have a left-handed track at Knightwick with several sharp bends and a road that crosses the course. Some horses are unsettled by this. But the fences are good and the viewing is excellent.

The United course at Brampton Bryan, also used by the Teme Valley, is a flat, right-handed, three-mile course with small fences and, more often than not, some plough. Trees and hedges make it difficult to obtain a clear view.

Bredwardine, the setting for the Golden Valley and the Radnor

& West Herefordshire fixtures, is a flat right-handed course on which horses can go a good gallop, although there is one sharp bend where they have been known to run out. The Radnor & West Herefordshire used to run their open race for the Crudwell Cup over four miles, but it never attracted fields commensurate with the corresponding event at the Heythrop, and in 1970 they reverted to three miles.

Wales

Probably the best viewing course in Wales is the Monmouthshire at Llanvapley. This is a sharp three-mile course, left-handed, with smallish fences and a short run-in.

The Brecon course at Llanfrynach is somewhat similar, except that it is right-handed and with moderate viewing facilities. This course is also used by the Llandeilo Farmers; and the famous Brecon Beacons, often snow-capped, provide an awe inspiring background.

The Tredegar Farmers' course at Machen, where the Gellygaer Farmers held a new fixture in 1970, is an undulating left-handed course, rather twisty and with a stiff uphill finish. The run-in here is the longest in Wales. The viewing facilities are fairly good, but the finish is some distance from the tents.

The Llangibby, who used to hold their fixture at Penhow, now share with the Curre at Howick. This is a sharp, undulating, left-handed course with a downhill run to the last three jumps in the straight.

The new Llangeinor course at Bridgend is a flattish right-handed course with a good view for spectators; and there is some talk, at the time of writing, of this course also being used by the Glamorgan and the Pentyrch, who have been holding their meetings at Cowbridge.

The courses in South Wales are mostly very sharp and easy, and the same applies to the Pembrokeshire and West Wales courses, which are easier still. The exception is the right-handed Carmarthenshire course at Llanbri, which has a slight uphill finish and a fairly long run-in.

East Midlands and The Shires

A much under-rated course, perhaps because it is unfashionably situated, is that of the Brocklesby in Brocklesby Park. The track is a left-handed one and the going is nearly always good, though there is one very sharp bend.

The South Wold course in Revesby Park has some very broad fences which have been repeatedly patched up, rather than rebuilt, and this sometimes causes horses to go 'up and down'. The track is right-handed and all grass.

The old Lincoln Racecourse, otherwise known as The Carholme, is the setting for three fixtures, the Burton, the Blankney and the Grove & Rufford. This is a good, galloping, left-handed track, with small softish fences. The viewing facilities are perfect and the permanent buildings afford amenities which are lacking on many of the 'country' courses.

Another course with permanent buildings is the fashionable and highly professional one at Garthorpe used by the Belvoir, the Cottesmore, the Quorn and the Melton Hunt Club. This is right-handed and undulating, with rather a tricky drop fence on the brow of the hill. Although it can hardly be described as a stayers' course, it is not one for short runners either, and few of the races are won from the front. The view for spectators is an extremely good one, and as there are extensive facilities for watering the course the going is never allowed to get hard.

The Atherstone course at Clifton-upon-Dunsmore is also very good for viewing; but it is not really a course for long-striding horses now that the finish has been moved up over a sharp left turn with ridge and furrow. I have, however, heard it described as 'a true stayers' course'. The fences are strong and well made.

The Pytchley course at Guilsborough is a very individual one, and it sometimes produces freak results. The left-handed oval circuit is almost flat and fairly sharp. Front runners do not often win here. The going, on old turf, is nearly always good and the viewing is excellent.

The Woodland Pytchley course at Dingley, where the Fernie also hold their fixture, is another good viewing course, and there is both an open ditch and a water jump. The track is right-handed and fairly flat, with a downhill run from the start for about three furlongs. The ground rises sharply to the last fence and levels out at the finish. Most of the races are won from three fences out, and it is advisable to be in front rounding the final bend.

The right-handed Oakley course at Newton Bromswold is a course for stayers. Oval in shape, it is an extended three miles with no sharp bends and a strong uphill finish. This course is always well prepared and presented, with good fences on even ground and fair viewing facilities.

Eastern Counties

This area has recently suffered the loss of two of its best stayers' courses, the ones at Moulton and Bishop's Stortford, though I believe the Moulton course may be used for a single meeting in 1971. At the moment of writing, however, Joe Turner, the Master of the Suffolk, is building a new course on his land at Ampton, near Bury St. Edmunds. This will certainly be ready for use by the Suffolk in 1971 and it is more than likely that at least one other hunt will use it. I am indebted to Mr Turner for the following description :

'The course, a right-handed one, very similar to Cottenham but more undulating, is in a park-like setting, enclosed on two sides by trees and on the other two sides by the early stages of the River Lark and a disused railway embankment, the latter having potential as a natural grandstand. There are a few trees here and there over the site, and an avenue of limes down the middle. The land slopes gently from the top end to the river, and the surface is old turf, which has been re-seeded on top; the site has been levelled and drained as necessary. At this stage, something between £3,000 and £4,000 has been spent on the course, which is some 200 yards off the A134 and very accessible. Parking facilities will be adjacent to the secondary road leading off the main one. Dennis Holland, former point-to-point rider and farmer, is to be Clerk of the Course, and he will be assisted by a committee of able farming and racing people.'

The Cambridgeshire Harriers' course at Cottenham was once the setting for a *bona-fide* meeting and is consequently blessed with permanent buildings, including a grandstand, all excellently maintained. The two Cambridge University fixtures and the Fitzwilliam meeting are also held here. The track is a flat, right-handed one, and the three-mile trip does not take a lot of getting, but there is a long run-in. Mr and Mrs Hugh Gingell, who own this course, are tireless in making improvements, and by doing away with the orchard they have made the viewing perfect.

Hethersett, which is now the setting for the West Norfolk and the Dunston Harriers, is a long, left-handed, undulating course with inviting fences and an uphill finish. 'It always surprises me,' writes a well-known rider, 'that a short-running horse can win on this apparently open galloping course.' The viewing is reasonably good, provided that one is prepared to move about.

Higham, which is used by the Essex and Suffolk, the North Norfolk Harriers, the Easton Harriers and the Waveney Harriers, is a very fast left-handed course, and the open races here are almost invariably won in under six minutes. The going is rarely less than good and the viewing is above average.

Marks Tey, where the Essex, the Essex Union and the East Essex hold their races, is a stayers' course, left-handed and with an uphill finish from two fences out. The going here is apt to vary from one extreme to the other, and the viewing facilities leave something to be desired; which is rather surprising, considering the amount of money that is taken on the Tote at these popular fixtures. In recent years the races on this course have been run over varying distances ranging from three to 3½ miles.

Beeleigh is used only by the Essex Farmers for their Easter Monday fixture. This is a right-handed, up and down and round about track, with the worst viewing facilities in the area. But none of this makes any difference to the large holiday attendance.

Whereas a handy horse is needed for Beeleigh, the Enfield Chace course at Northaw usually requires a stayer. This is a good galloping, left-handed course with well-made fences of some substance; but if there is a way of seeing the whole of the course from any one spot on the ground, I have not discovered it.

South Midlands

One course has recently been lost here, the very popular one at Crowell. But a new course is being built on Col. Arthur Clerke-Brown's land at nearby Kingston Blount at the foot of the Chilterns, looking out towards the old Crowell course. This will be a left-handed course, slightly undulating, and with a good view from the hills. It is expected to be faster and not quite so long as its predecessor; one of the two Oxford University fixtures will be held here in 1971; and by 1972 it should be ready for both of them, as well as the hunt club fixture that is hoped for.

The newly-formed Vale of Aylesbury Hunt, resulting from the amalgamation of the South Oxfordshire, the Old Berkeley and the Hertfordshire, will hold their fixture at Kimble, which will continue to be the setting for the Bicester & Warden Hill and the Pegasus Club (Bar) meetings. This is a really first-class, left-handed course with well-made fences and excellent viewing facilities. Fairly testing.

But not so testing as the long, galloping course at Great Horwood used by the Grafton and the Whaddon Chase. This is emphatically a course for stayers, left-handed and with an appreciable amount of undulation. Good viewing, just short of perfect.

The Old Berkshire have a very fast left-handed course at Lockinge with one of the shortest run-ins in the country. There are some sharp bends but the last five fences are in a straight line. This is one of the few courses where there a splendid view from *all* the car parks.

Surrey, Sussex, Kent and Hampshire

The most-used course in this area is the one at Tweseldown, where five fixtures were held in 1970, the Army, the Garth & South Berks, the Hambledon, the Bisley & Sandhurst and the Isle of Wight. This is a fine, galloping course, well suited to stayers, and with a sandy soil that usually ensures good going. The right-handed track has some undulating stretches and the fences are more like N.H. ones than most. There is a close view of the finish but visibility on some other parts of the course is restricted by undergrowth and, unless one is prepared to cross the course and stand on top of it, by a monstrous mound, the necessity for which is a mystery to all but the Army authorities. The permanent buildings which were erected for the old military meetings are still in existence, and these include a grandstand.

Hackwood Park, the only other course now remaining in Hampshire, where it is used by the Hampshire Hunt and the Vine & Craven, is a course for handy horses who can turn quickly. It is left-handed, with rather a long run-in and fairly good viewing facilities.

The course in Peper Harow Park, near Godalming, which was formerly used by the disbanded Chiddingfold Farmers, was taken over in 1970 by the Surrey Union. This is a sharp, left-handed course with an uphill finish and viewing facilities that are none too good.

The Cowdray use a left-handed, undulating track in Cowdray Park, Midhurst. It is not easy for horses to raise a good gallop here as they are forever on the turn. The finish is slightly uphill and the view pretty good, though not from all the car parks.

The Old Surrey & Burstow and the Mid Surrey Farmers' Club have been using a right-handed rectangular course at Limpsfield with a downhill finish over the last four fences. But in 1971 they are moving to a new site on the inside of Lingfield Racecourse, where the track will be a right-handed one with two 1¼-mile circuits and a ½-mile finishing stretch down the centre.

Another course that suits short runners is the left-handed, harp-shaped course at Ightham used by the West Kent. This has two outer circuits and an inner one and is mostly flat, except for a rise between fences 2 and 3 on the first circuit and 8 and 9 on the second. Good viewing.

The Crawley & Horsham have a good, galloping course at Parham which they now share with the Chiddingford & Leconfield and the Southdown. The right-handed, undulating track suits a stayer. An excellent view can be obtained from a natural grandstand and a reasonably good one from the car parks.

The Eridge course at Heathfield, also used by the East Sussex & Romney Marsh, is both left-handed and right-handed, and the sharp track, which is not without undulation, is particularly suitable for a fast horse. The paddock is in the centre of the course, and the car parks on high land afford a good view of the racing.

The Ashford Valley, the Royal Engineers Draghounds and the Tickham all use the long-established galloping course at Charing, where stayers are in their element. This is a left-handed 3¼-mile course with an uphill climb for the first half mile. The lower end of the course is overlooked by the paddock and car parks.

The left-handed East Kent course at Aldington is a bare three miles but, although it suits short runners, horses can get up a good gallop on it, and there is one short hill three-quarters of a mile from home. Paddock and car parks on a hill above the finish give excellent viewing.

Wiltshire, Dorset and Somerset

Larkhill, like Tweseldown, is becoming more and more popular as a centre of point-to-point racing, and in 1970 this left-handed 3-mile course on Salisbury Plain, where conditions can be so Arctic in the early part of the season, was the setting for the United Services, the New Forest, the South & West Wilts, the Royal Artillery and the Tedworth. The stiff fences and galloping track, which includes an appreciable uphill climb before the fifth fence from home, make it an ideal preliminary for Cheltenham, and many Larkhill winners have gone on to win there. There are permanent changing rooms and, although the horses go rather a long way from the eye, it is a good course on which to read a race.

The picturesque Portman course at Badbury Rings, a noted beauty spot which is now also the setting for the Wilton and South Dorset fixtures, is a quick-drying, left-handed course well suited to horses of doubtful stamina, though stayers have won over it. A sharp bend before the last fence makes it a course for tacticians. Near-perfect viewing.

Kingweston, where the Blackmore Vale and the Sparkford Vale Harriers hold their races, is a long, tough course with a substantial amount of plough, left-handed and undulating, with a water jump and one big drop fence. The open race at the Blackmoor Vale was run in 7 mins. 25 secs. last season, on good going; and the races at the Sparkford Vale, held earlier in the season, took a lot longer.

The Cattistock and the Seavington use a flat, left-handed course at Cattistock with a short run-in; but it is quite a testing track and the times recorded here in 1970 did not differ much from those at the second Kingweston meeting.

The Cotley, who formerly combined with the Seavington, now hold a separate fixture at Chard, over a left-handed course embracing a steep up-and-down hill, which has to be negotiated twice. This is not a particularly good course for viewing.

In recent years a great deal of money has been spent on alterations to the Mendip Farmers' course at Nedge, which is also used by the Weston Harriers and the West Somerset Vale; and this is now one of the best-appointed courses in the South West, with a superb view for spectators and well-constructed fences. The right-handed track is very undulating, with a long run-in.

The Quantock have a left-handed, slightly undulating course at Williton. This is a short, sharp course which can get very wet in bad weather, but there is a fairly long run-in.

Holnicote, where the Devon & Somerset and the Minehead & West Somerset hold their fixtures, is said to be Sue Aston's favourite course. It is left-handed and fairly flat, with good fences, including a water jump, and a shortish run-in. I am told there were three lots of plough to go through in 1970. If this is so, the times are remarkable. Both ladies' open races were won in under six minutes.

The two Taunton Vale meetings are held at Jordans, a slightly undulating, left-handed course with good big fences and ditches on the landing side. Not the best of courses for viewing.

The Exmoor meeting is held on the same course at Bratton Down as the West Dulverton. This is a galloping, left-handed course with an uphill finish, an excellent view for spectators and usually with good going.

The East Dulverton have a moorland course at Venford. This is left-handed, very undulating, with narrow fences that have no wings and a long uphill finish.

Devon and Cornwall

Even with the disappearance of the banking fixtures, the courses in this area are highly individual, mostly with rather small fences which I have heard likened to molehills, though not by West Countrymen.

Probably the best course in Devon is the one at Kilworthy used by the Lamerton and the Spooners & West Dartmoor. This is a fine, galloping course, left-handed but with a right-hand turn from the last fence. Stayers do well here and there is a long run-in for them. The fences are bigger than most in the area; and the viewing facilities are very good, though racing takes places rather far away from the spectators.

The Dart Vale & Haldon & South Pool Harriers, the Dartmoor & Modbury Harriers and the Mid Devon all hold their meetings on the old N.H. course at Buckfastleigh. The course here is right-handed and undulating; and it suits a staying horse. The amenities are as one would expect, and they include a grandstand.

The Axe Vale course at Stafford Cross is a flat, three-mile course which gives spectators a good view. It is right-handed and all grass, and does not normally take a lot of getting.

The Tiverton Staghounds used to run their races over a sharp course at Worlington; but in 1970, in company with the Stevenstone, they moved to the testing, up-and-down Eggesford course at Bishopsleigh where the going varies and the bends are left-handed.

Another very undulating course, and with some drop fences and plough thrown in for good measure, is the Silverton & Tiverton course at Shobrooke. This is right-handed, with a long, hard pull up to the finish, and an excellent view.

Very different except that it is also right-handed, is the sharp

Torrington Farmers' course at Horwood, where the fences are mostly met at an angle and part of the track runs below the finishing post. The fences are rather soft and there is often a large area of plough.

The two Tetcott meetings are held at different places. The Tetcott had a new course at Crimp Morwenstow in 1970, left-handed, predominantly flat and with a good view from the car parks. The South Tetcott course at Highampton must be just about the shortest in the entire country. Some unbelievable times were recorded here last season and, since all point-to-point courses are supposed to be at least three miles long, perhaps the less said about them the better. The narrow fences are set very close together and the right-handed track has more than its fair share of twists. A course for polo ponies?

A very popular course with spectators, and one that gives them an excellent view, is that of the South Devon at Forches Cross. This is a right-handed, undulating course with the kind of uphill finish that is always appreciated by stayers.

In Cornwall, at the moment of writing, there are two courses for speed merchants and one for stayers. The stayers' course is at Tehidy, where the Four Burrow and the Cury Harriers hold their fixtures. This is a real hunting course, right-handed, very undulating and with some plough. Three of the five races at the Cury took over eight minutes to run in 1970.

The course at Lemalla used by the Bolventor Harriers and the East Cornwall is almost flat, with two sharp right-handed turns and an exceptionally short run-in. The North Cornwall course at Trewornan is also right-handed and, though more undulating, rides equally fast. The viewing facilities at all three of the Cornish courses are good.

Perhaps I should close on a warning note. Point-to-point courses do sometimes change from season to season, and it does not necessarily follow that all the courses I have written about will be the same in 1971.

Appendix

These Rules are reproduced by kind permission of the Trustees of the Jockey Club. They are those applying to the 1970 season.

RULES OF RACING

1.

Point-to-Point Steeple Chases are held under the sanction of the Jockey Club and are governed by special regulations made from time to time by the Stewards entitled 'Jockey Club Regulations for Point-to-Point Steeple Chases'. If held in accordance with the conditions of these regulations, they are not regarded as 'unrecognised meetings' and are therefore exempt from the operation of the Rules of Racing imposing disqualifications for having taken part in such meetings.

Any Point-to-Point Meeting which has not been sanctioned as above is an 'unrecognised meeting' and every horse which has run at such a meeting is perpetually disqualified for all races to which the Rules of Racing apply. Rule 194 (ii) of the Rules of Racing applies to persons taking part in such Meeting.

The following Definitions and Rules of Racing shall apply to all Point-to-Point Steeple Chases.

DEFINITIONS

'Farmer' is one who resides permanently on his farm, working it himself, and deriving therefrom his principal and ostensible means of subsistence.

'Hunters' Steeple Chase' is a weight-for-age steeple chase confined to horses certified by a Master of Hounds to have been hunted and to amateur riders.

'Racing Calendar Office' is the office appointed for the time being as the Racing Calendar Office by the Jockey Club.

(The present Racing Calendar Office is at Weatherby and Sons, Denington Estate, Sanders Road, Wellingborough, Northants.)

'Registry Office' is the office for the time being appointed as the registry office by the Jockey Club.

(The present Registry Office is at Weatherby and Sons' Office, 42, Portman Square, London, W.1.)

'Subscriber' is a person who has paid to the qualifying Hunt by February 1st of the current Hunting Season, the Minimum annual hunting subscription of that Hunt.

RULES OF RACING NOS. 1 AND 2

POWERS OF STEWARDS OF THE JOCKEY CLUB

1.

The Stewards of the Jockey Club have power, at their discretion.

(i) To grant or to refuse to grant licenses to Race-courses and to make it a condition of a licence being granted that

(a) the Racecourse shall be a member of the association of Racecourses currently approved by the Jockey Club.

(b) facilities shall be afforded on the Race-course for the operation of the Totalisator.

(ii) To withdraw licences to Race-courses.

(iii) To fix the dates on which all meetings shall be held and in the case of emergency or expediency to order the abandonment of any race or Race Meeting or to make any alteration in the date of any such Meeting and to supervise and make such alterations as they may think advisable in the programme of, or the conditions of any race at, any Meeting.

(iv) To sanction Point-to-Point fixtures, to authorise the publication of 'Jockey Club Regulations for Point-to-Point Steeple Chases' and to make any alterations to them from time to time that they consider necessary.

(v) To prohibit the advertisement of any race or meeting in the Racing Calendar, or call upon the Stewards to alter or expunge any conditions, even after advertisement.

(vi) To grant or to refuse to grant and to renew or to refuse to renew licences to officials, jockeys, and trainers and permits to trainers and amateur riders. Every application for renewal of any licence or permit shall be treated and regarded in all respects and for all purposes as if it were the first application by the applicant for such a licence or permit.

(vii) To accept or to refuse to accept or to cancel any registration under these Rules, notwithstanding any implication to the contrary whether contained in Rule 31 or elsewhere.

(viii) To accept or to refuse to accept entries, and in the case of expediency to refuse to allow a horse duly entered to run in any race, in which event the Stewards may direct that the entrance money be remitted to the owner.

(ix) To allow or to refuse to allow any person to act or to continue to act as an authorised agent.

(x) To make enquiry into and deal with any matter relating to racing whether such matters arise in Great Britain or elsewhere.

(xi) To entertain and determine appeals from the Stewards of Meetings as provided for by Rules 176–179.

(xii) To entertain and decide objections lodged under Rule 170(v).

(xiii) To authorise the publication in the Racing Calendar of their decisions respecting any matter and of the decisions and reports of Stewards of Meetings.

(xiv) To publish in the Racing Calendar from time to time such instructions as they may think fit.

(xv) To exercise any other powers conferred upon them by these Rules and to take any such action as they consider necessary for the purpose of carrying out or putting into effect these Rules.

(xvi) In cases of emergency or expediency, to modify the Rules of Racing or Regulations or any part thereof, or to suspend any Rule or Regulation or any part thereof, for such period or periods as they think fit, without giving previous notice, but should they do so they shall report the fact in the two subsequent issues of the Racing Calendar.

2.

(i) The Stewards of the Jockey Club have power if good cause is shown or when any person has committed any breach of the Rules of Racing to withdraw or suspend his licence or permit.

(ii) When any person has committed any breach of the Rules of Racing the Stewards of the Jockey Club have power at their discretion to impose also upon such person any one or more of the following penalties namely—

(a) They may impose any fine not exceeding, £500.

(b) They may declare him a disqualified person.

Save that where any Rule prescribes a maximum penalty they may not impose any greater penalty or any penalty of some other kind and save that where any Rule prescribes a mandatory penalty they shall impose that penalty. Save as aforesaid the powers given by this Rule are not and are not to be construed as being in any way or in any instance limited or excluded by reason of that fact that some Rules do while others do not prescribe penalties for their breach.

RULES OF RACING NOS. 190–195

CORRUPT PRACTICES AND DISQUALIFICATIONS OF PERSONS

190

Any person found guilty of a corrupt or fraudulent practice whether or not his conduct constitutes a breach of any other of these Rules may be declared a disqualified person or otherwise penalised by the Stewards of the Jockey Club in accordance with their powers under Rule 2 of these Rules.

191.

Without prejudice to the generality of Rule 190 every person is guilty of a corrupt practice within the meaning of these Rules who:–

(i) Administers or allows or causes to be administered or connives at the administration to a horse of a substance (other than a normal nutrient) which could alter its racing performance at the time of racing; or

(ii) Gives or offers, or promises directly or indirectly, any bribe in any form to any person having official duties in relation to a race or race-horse, or to any trainer, rider, agent or other person having charge of, or access to, any racehorse; or

(iii) Being a person having official duties in relation to a race, or being a trainer, rider, agent or other person having charge, of, or access to, any racehorse, accepts or offers to accept any bribe in any form; or

(iv) Wilfully enters or causes to be entered for any race, or causes to start in any race, a horse which he knows or believes to be disqualified; or

(v) Surreptitiously obtains information respecting a trial from any person or persons engaged in it, or in the service of the owner or trainer of the horses tried, or respecting any horse in training from any person in such service; or

(vi) Deliberately misleads the Stewards of a Meeting or the Stewards of the Jockey Club at any enquiry; or

(vii) Is guilty of, or conspires with any other person for the commission of, or connives at any other person being guilty of, any corrupt (or fraudulent) practice in relation to racing in this or any other country, or is convicted of any criminal offence in relation to racing in this or any other country.

192.

When a person is warned off, and so long as his exclusion continues, he is a disqualified person.

193.

If any person be reported by the Committee of Tattersall's he shall be declared a disqualified person. On receiving a notification that such report is withdrawn, the Stewards of the Jockey Club shall withdraw their notice of disqualification and notify the defaulter to that effect by sending a notice to his last known address.

194.

(i) Any person on whom disqualifications have been imposed by any recognised Turf Authority, is a disqualified person under these Rules so long as the disqualification continues.

(ii) Any person who owns, trains, or rides a horse at an unrecognised meeting in Great Britain or Ireland, or any person who acts in any official capacity in connection with such a meeting, is a disqualified person for twelve months from the date of such offence, or for such lesser time as the Stewards of the Jockey Club shall think fit, but this Rule shall not apply to pony or galloway races at meetings confined to pony or galloway racing.

(iii) Any person who offers or promises any reward, either by way of fee, present, expenses, or any consideration whatsoever to an 'Amateur Rider' for riding in a race is liable to be made a disqualified person by the Stewards of the Jockey Club.

(iv) Any person, being an owner of horses, who by advertisement, circular, letter, or other means offers to give information concerning his own or other horses in return for monetary consideration, or any owner of horses who connives at such practice, is liable to be made a disqualified person by the Stewards of the Jockey Club.

195.

A disqualified person, so long as his disqualification lasts, shall not:—

(i) Act as Steward or Official at any recognised Meeting.

(ii) Act as authorised agent under these Rules.

(iii) Enter, run, train, or ride a horse in any race at any recognised Meeting, or ride in trials.

(iv) Enter any Race-course, Stand, or Enclosure.

(v) Except with permission of the Stewards of the Jockey Club be employed in any Racing Stable.

POINT TO POINT REGULATIONS

2.

In all cases where printed Programmes, Rules, or Regulations are issued by the Authority under whose auspices the Steeple Chases are to be held it shall be stated therein that the Meeting is held subject to Rules 1 and 2 and Rules 190 to 195 (disqualifications of persons and corrupt practices) of the Rules of Racing and to Jockey Club Regulations for Point-to-Point Steeple Chases.

SANCTION & CONTROL OF MEETINGS

3.

With the sanction of the Stewards of the Jockey Club, Point-to-Point Steeple Chases may be held on one day annually by:—

(a) A Hunt, or two or more adjoining Hunts, being Foxhounds, Staghounds, Harriers or Draghounds (Masters being Members of their respective Associations).

In the case of Staghounds, Harriers, or Draghounds, if the races are to be held in a country hunted by Foxhounds, the written permission of the Master of such Foxhounds must accompany the application.

(b) By the Royal Navy, the Army, the Royal Air Force, or by the United Services, or by a Naval or Military Formation or Unit, or by a Club or other Society approved by the Stewards of the Jockey Club.

The written permission of the Master of Foxhounds or, if in a district not hunted by Foxhounds, the Master of Staghounds or Harriers hunting the same, in whose country it is proposed to run, must accompany the application in these cases.

4.

Hunt Point-to-Point Steeple Chases shall be held under the control of the Master of the Hounds and of a Committee appointed by him.

PROGRAMMES OF RACES

5.

Not more than five Steeple Chases shall be run on the one day, except at a Meeting where two races are confined to the Hunt or Hunts promoting the Meeting or a race under Sub-sections (e) or (f) is included in the programme when a sixth Steeple Chase may be run.

(a) One Steeple Chase, at least, shall be confined to the Hunt or Hunts promoting the Meeting, and, if there be only one such race, Members, Subscribers, and Farmers of the Hunt shall be eligible to compete.

(b) The programme may also include two Open Steeple Chases, provided that one is a Ladies' Open Steeple Chase.

The remaining Steeple Chases may be selected from:—

(c) Adjacent Hunts' races confined to the Hunt promoting the Meeting and not more than six Hunts actually adjoining it which hold Point-to-Point Steeple Chases and, if there are less than this number, the six shall be made up from neighbouring Hunts; except that where a joint Meeting is held by two or more adjoining Hunts the number of such qualifying

Adjacent Hunts may be increased to eight. All Adjacent Hunts to be approved by the Master of Hounds and specified in the Programme.
(d) A Ladies' race (hunt or Adjacent Hunts), but not in addition to a Ladies' Open Steeple Chase, except that ladies may always ride at the same weights as men in races confined to the Hunt or Hunts promoting the Meeting, if so provided by the conditions of the race.
(e) Races confined to Serving Members of any Naval, Military, or Royal Air Force Formation or Unit.
(f) Races confined to the Members of a Club or other Society approved by the Stewards of the Jockey Club.

6.

Point-to-Point Steeple Chases held by the Royal Navy, the Army, the Royal Air Force, or by the United Services or by Naval or Military Formations or Units, or by approved Clubs or Societies, shall be under the control of a Committee appointed by the Service, Unit, Club, &c., and be confined to Members of such Service, Unit, Club, &c., except that:—
(a) One Steeple Chase may be open to the Farmers of the country in which the Steeple Chases are held (or in the case of a Regimental or approved Club Meeting, to the Farmers resident in the Hunts to which the Regiment or Members of the approved Club subscribe).
(b) One Steeple Chase may be an Open Steeple Chase which may be a Ladies' Open Steeple Chase, and
(c) One Steeple Chase may be an Adjacent Hunts' race confined to the Members and Subscribers to the Hunt in whose country the Meeting is held, and not more than six Hunts actually adjoining it which hold Point-to-Point Steeple Chases and, if there are less than this number, the six shall be made up from neighbouring Hunts. All Adjacent Hunts to be approved by the Master of Hounds and specified in the programme.
The total number of Steeple Chases shall not exceed five, except at a joint Meeting, when, with the special permission of the Stewards of the Jockey Club, a sixth Steeple Chase may be run.

HORSES

7.

((a) Point-to-Point Steeple Chases shall be confined to horses certified by a Master of a recognised pack of Foxhounds, Staghounds, Harriers or Draghounds (being members of their respective Associations), upon the Hunter's Certificate form issued by the Stewards of the Jockey Club, to have been regularly and fairly hunted in Great Britain during the current hunting season.
Every such Hunter's Certificate must be registered at the Racing Calendar Office, on payment of a fee of 10s. for each horse, before a horse is qualified to be entered, but such registration cannot be made unless the horse's name has also been registered in accordance with the provisions of the Rules of Racing.
(b) No horse shall be eligible to be entered or run in a Point-to-Point Steeple Chase which has won any Steeple Chase or Hurdle race under the Rules of any recognised Turf Authority on and since July 1st of the current Steeple Chase and Hurdle race season, or which, from November 1st to March 1st, inclusive, of the current hunting season, has run in any

Steeple Chase or Hurdle race under the Rules of any recognised Turf Authority, Hunters' Steeple Chases in every case excepted.

8.

No horse shall receive in any one season a Hunter's Certificate from more than two Hunts, one of which Certificates only may be used to enter a horse in Adjacent Hunts' races.

COURSE

9.

The Course shall be over a distance of not less than three miles, and there shall be:—

(a) Not less than eight separate fences constructed, not more than two of which shall be jumped three times, and the total number of jumps in any race shall be not less than eighteen. In the case of any race run over a greater distance than that of the approved course one more fence may be jumped three times for each completed half mile of extra distance;

(b) Adequate wings to all fences;

(c) At least one open ditch guarded by a rail.

This Regulation shall not apply to courses run entirely over banks or walls, nor to Point-to-Point Steeple Chases run straight across country, except that they shall be of not less distance than three miles.

10.

The Stewards of the Jockey Club, if they so require, will appoint a person or persons to inspect the Course, and all facilities shall be granted for that purpose. The cost of such inspection to be borne by the Hunt promoting the Meeting.

TRAINING

11.

No horse shall be eligible to be entered for a Point-to-Point Steeple Chase which, since January 1st of the current Hunting Season, has been trained by:—

(a) A trainer licensed to train for Steeple Chases and Hurdle races (unless the horse be the property of himself or his spouse).

(b) An unlicensed person (other than his owner, groom, or the proprietor of the stable from whence the horse has been regularly and fairly hunted during the current season as required for a Hunter's Certificate).

PRIZE MONEY

12.

(a) The money or other prize for the winner of an Open Steeple Chase shall not be of a greater value than £40 in all and of any other Steeple Chase £30 in all.

(b) the value of the prizes for second and third horses shall not exceed £10 and £5 respectively. No fourth prize shall be offered.

(c) No further prize from any source whatsoever may be given except that a perpetual Challenge Trophy may be received by the winner and one other perpetual Challenge Trophy may also be given in any race as a special prize for certain contestants. In each case a memento of the Challenge Trophy not exceeding £10 in value may be given in addition to the prizes permitted in sub-sections (a) and (b) above.
(d) No payment shall be made for the transport of horses to or from a Meeting.

GENERAL

13.
Application for fixtures, giving a first and second choice of dates, accompanied by a fee of £15, must be made to the Registry Office by November 1st in each year.

14.
Two copies of the programme giving the conditions of the Steeple Chases must be sent to the Registry Office not less than six weeks before the Steeple Chases are to be run.

15.
There shall be embodied in the programme a condition that:—
'No person or horse who is disqualified under the Rules of any recognised Turf Authority shall be eligible to take part in these Steeple Chases.'

16.
Entries, which must be made in writing, shall close at a specified time on a day to be stated in the programme, which shall be not less than six days before the day of the Meeting, and a list of the entries on the form prescribed, signed by the Receiver of Entries, shall be forwarded to the Registry Office immediately following the time of closing.
Entries shall not be accepted after the specified time.

17.
No charge shall be made for the admission of persons, either before the Meeting or at any gate, stand, or enclosure thereat, but a charge may be made for the parking of vehicles.

18.
Within fourteen days after the Steeple Chases have taken place a certificate in the subjoined form, signed by two Stewards, shall be lodged at the Registry Office together with a race card and a full return of the Steeple Chases showing the runners, placed horses, &c.

CERTIFICATE

19.
We Hereby Certify:—
1. That .... Point-to-Point Steeple Chases took place at .... on .... in connection with the .... Hunt.

2. That no races of any description, other than Point-to-Point Steeple Chases, took place there on that day.
3. That each Steeple Chase was strictly confined to horses which have been regularly and fairly hunted during the present hunting season.
4. That the distance traversed in each Steeple Chase was not less than three miles.
5. That no money or other prize for the winner of any Steeple Chase was of greater value in an Open Race than £40 or in any other race than £30 in all, with the exception of a memento of a Challenge Trophy value not more than £10
6. That no charge was made for the admission of persons, either before the Meeting or at any gate, stand, or enclosure thereat.
7. That in all respects the Jockey Club Regulations for Point-to-Point Steeple Chases were strictly adhered to.

Signed ....
Address ....
Signed ....
Address .... } Stewards

Date ...., 19

ENTRIES

20.

(i) Entries for Point-to-Point Steeple Chases shall be made in the name of one person who must be the Owner of the horse entered.
(ii) The entry shall state the registered name and age of the horse, such allowances and penalties to which he may at the time of entry be subject, and (except for races confined to the Hunt promoting the Meeting) the name of the Hunt from which the horse's certificate was obtained.
(iii) When the name of a horse has been changed or altered on registration, the name under which he has previously run in Point-to-Point Steeple Chases, as well as his new name, must be given in every entry during the current season.
(iv) Any accidental error or violation of the foregoing sections may be corrected on payment of a fine of £1 provided always that the Stewards are satisfied that there has been no fraud and that the identity of the horse is clearly proved, and that the correction be made and the fine paid before the rider is weighed out for that race.
(v) No horse which is the subject of a partnership, lease, contingency, or other joint arrangement shall be eligible to be entered in any Point-to-Point Steeple Chase, nor shall any horse be entered which is less than five years old.

21.

(i) Subject to Army Orders a hired Charger or Troop Horse hired for Hunting may be entered as the property of the Officer or other rank by whom it is hired.
Army numbers must be given in every entry.
(ii) Hirelings for which Hunters' Certificates have been obtained during

the current season may be entered as the property of the hirer in races confined to—
(a) Officers on the Active List of the Royal Navy (including the Royal Marines), the Regular Army, or the Royal Air Force.
(b) Resident Members of the Universities of Oxford and Cambridge.
(c) Cadets of the Royal Naval, Military and Air Force Colleges.

CLERK OF THE COURSE

22.

(i) The Clerk of the Course shall arrange for the publication of an official card of the steeple chases containing the conditions of each steeple chase, the names of the Owners and of the horses, and such other particulars as are given in the entries.
(ii) The Clerk of the Course shall not allow a rider to be weighed out for any horse until the entrance monies for all entries at the Meeting in the Owners' name have been paid.
(iii) The Clerk of the Course shall arrange that a Parade Ring is provided into which all horses shall be brought a reasonable time before the signal to mount is given for the race in which they are engaged.
No person shall be allowed access to the Parade Ring except officials of the Meeting, Owners and Riders of horses about to run in the next race and persons attendant on such horses.
There shall be no other enclosure reserved for persons, except that not more than one enclosure may be set aside for the entertainment of Farmers. This enclosure may have a view of the Parade Ring, providing that it does not obstruct to the general public more than a quarter of the circumference of the Ring.

STARTER

23.

(i) The Starter shall give all orders necessary for securing a fair start, and after he has called over the names of the runners he shall line up the horses at the starting post, raise his flag, and start them from a standing start by dropping his flag.
(ii) The Starter shall have an assistant who will be stationed some 100 yards down the course and will raise a white flag which will be dropped when the Starter drops his. This flag will indicate when the horses are under Starter's Orders, and will also be a recall flag, and riders must be warned that it is a false start if this flag is not dropped.
(iii) Any rider misconducting himself at the post, or refusing to obey the commands of the Starter, shall be reported to the Stewards.

HUNTERS' CERTIFICATES

24.

Where a steeple chase is not confined to the Hunt promoting the Meeting, the name of the Hunt from which the horse obtained its certificate shall appear on the race card after the horse's name.

STEWARDS

25.
There shall be four Stewards, of whom three shall be Acting Stewards, who need not be Members of the Hunt. The names of the Acting Stewards shall be printed on the race card and be exhibited outside the weighing tent. One Acting Steward shall be present at the weighing tent immediately before and after each race.
Ladies shall not be appointed Stewards.

26.
The Stewards have power to regulate, control, take cognisance of, and adjudicate upon, the conduct of all officials, of all owners, nominators, riders, grooms, and persons attendant on horses, and of all persons frequenting the Meeting.

27.
The Stewards have power to punish at their discretion any person subject to their control with a fine not exceeding £5, and with suspension from acting or riding at the Meeting, and to report to the Stewards of the Jockey Club should they consider any further fine or punishment necessary. All fines to be paid to the credit of the Jockey Club.

PENALTIES AND ALLOWANCES

28.
Allowances, and penalties in respect of a previous win or wins, must be declared at entry and be published on the race card.
If a penalty is incurred after the date of entry it must be declared at scale and be posted on the Notice Board and included in the return of the race.

RIDERS

29.
(i) In races confined to Members, Subscribers, or Farmers of one Hunt the qualification for riders shall not extend beyond Members, Subscribers, Farmers, or their respective spouses or children, of the Hunt holding riders' qualification certificates from that Hunt. In Adjacent Hunts' Races the qualification for riders shall not extend beyond Members, Subscribers, Farmers, or their respective husbands, spouses or children, of the Hunts concerned, holding riders' qualification certificates from those Hunts. Serving Members of Her Majesty's Forces on the Active List of the Royal Navy (including the Royal Marines), Regular Army, or Royal Air Force may be permitted to ride in confined races if so provided by the conditions of the race.
(ii) In Open Races riders must be Members, Subscribers, or Farmers of a recognised Hunt, or their respective spouses or children. Serving Members of Her Majesty's Forces (as specified in the above paragraph) may be permitted to ride if so provided by the conditions of the race.

30.

(i) Professional Hunt Servants, grooms, apprentices, stable lads, and persons who are or have been employed as paid servants in any capacity in private, hunting, racing, livery, or horse-dealers' stables, or persons who have ever received payment, directly or indirectly, for riding in a race are regarded as having 'ridden for hire,' and are professional riders and are not eligible to ride in Point-to-Point Steeple Chases.

This Regulation shall not apply to ladies.

(ii) Persons who hold trainer's licences under the Rules of any recognised Turf Authority shall not be entitled to ride in Point-to-Point Steeple Chases except when riding horses the property of themselves or of their spouses. This restriction shall not apply to persons holding steeple chase or hurdle race trainers' permits.

31.

No lady shall ride until she has attained the age of eighteen years. Ladies are only eligible to ride in races confined to lady riders, except that in races confined to the Hunt or Hunts promoting the Meeting, held under Regulation 5 (a), they may ride at the same weights as men, if so provided by the conditions of the race.

WEIGHING OUT

32.

No person shall, without special leave from the Stewards, be admitted to the weighing-room, except the owner and rider, or other person having the care of a horse engaged in the race, and any person refusing to leave shall be reported to the Stewards.

33.

(i) The minimum weight to be carried in a Point-to-Point Steeple Chase shall be 12st 7lb, except (a) in races confined to lady riders where it may be 11st, (b) in Open Steeple Chases (not confined to lady riders) where it may be 12st, provided that by the conditions of the race, a penalty of not less than 7lb is imposed for the winner of a steeple chase or hurdle race under the Rules of any recognised Turf Authority or of an Open Point-to-Point Steeple Chase (Ladies' Open Races excepted) within the period of the current year and the two years immediately previous to it, and (c) in the cases of races under subsection (ii) of this Regulation.

(ii) In countries where a large proportion of the adult followers usually ride ponies, the Stewards of the Jockey Club may give permission for one or more Steeple Chases for ponies provided the Master of Hounds makes special application stating:—

(a) The approximate percentage of followers who ride ponies,

(b) The conditions proposed as regards the height of ponies and the minimum weight to be carried.

34.

(i) Each rider must be weighed for a specified horse by the Clerk of the Scales, at the appointed place, not less than a quarter of an hour before the time fixed for the race.

(ii) No rider shall ride in any race unless wearing a skull cap, and such cap must be secured with a chin-strap.

35.

No rider shall be weighed out unless the name of the race and of the horse and the rider have been given in writing by the owner or duly authorized agent to the Clerk of the Course not less than three-quarters of an hour before the time fixed for the race.

This declaration must be accompanied by a Certificate, signed by the Secretary of a Hunt, which states the particular qualification which the rider has to ride in the race in question, and in the case of a 'subscriber' that the qualification referred to in the definition has been complied with. Serving Members of Her Majesty's Forces must produce similar evidence as to their qualification.

The numbers of the runners shall be exhibited without delay. When the numbers have been exhibited, no alteration or addition can be made without the leave of the Stewards.

36.

If a rider, after he has been weighed for a specified horse, and before he has been under the Starter's orders, is prevented by accident or illness from riding in the race, another rider may be substituted provided there is no unreasonable delay.

37.

(i) If a rider intends to carry over-weight, he must declare the amount thereof at the time of weighing-out, or, if in doubt as to his proper weight, the weight he intends to carry.

If extra weight, or any variation from the weight appearing on the card, be declared at scale for any horse, such weight shall be exhibited with the number.

(ii) If a horse run in a hood, blinkers, martingale, breastplate, or clothing, it must be put into the scale and included in the rider's weight.

38.

No rider's skull cap, whip, or substitute for a whip, bridle, rings, plates, or anything worn on a horse's legs, shall be allowed in the scales, either in weighing-out or weighing-in.

RUNNING

39.

A horse shall be considered as having 'Started' which has come under the Starter's orders.

40.

All red flags must be passed on the rider's right, white flags on his left.

41.

Any horse getting away from its rider in a race may be remounted, but should it have run out of the course or continued in the race before being caught it shall be brought back to the part of the course where it parted from its rider, and shall continue by jumping all fences from that point. Any rider so losing his horse may be assisted in catching it and remounting it without risk of disqualification.

42.

(i) A horse shall, on an objection under Regulation 57, be disqualified—
(a) if his rider, by foul riding, jeopardized the chance of success of any other horse in a race;
(b) if he runs the wrong side of a flag, post, or boundary mark unless he turns back and runs the Course from the proper side of such post or flag;
(c) if he refuses any fence, and it can be proved to the satisfaction of the Stewards that he has been led over it by any of the by-standers, or has been given a lead over by any horseman not riding in the race.
(ii) A horse is liable, on an objection under Regulation 57, to be disqualified or his placing in the race altered—
(a) if he or his rider jostle another horse or rider;
(b) if he cross another horse at, or in the run home from, the last fence, so as to interfere with that or any other horse's chance.
In all cases the Stewards have power to fine a rider for any of the above offences a sum not exceeding £5 and to suspend him until the expiration of the Meeting, or should they consider such punishment insufficient, they shall make a report to the Stewards of the Jockey Club.

THE JUDGE

43.

One Judge only shall be appointed and he must occupy the judge's box at the time the horses pass the winning post, or the race shall be void. He must announce his decision immediately, and such decision shall be final, unless an objection to the winner, or any placed horses, is made and sustained: provided that this Rule shall not prevent a Judge from correcting any mistake, such correction being subject to confirmation by the Stewards. The Judge shall if necessary for the purpose of placing a second and/or third horse remain in the box five minutes after the first horse passes the post.

WALKING OVER

44.

In the case of a walk-over it shall be sufficient if a horse be weighed out for, mounted, and ridden past the Judge's box, when he shall be the winner.

DEAD HEATS

45.

When horses run a dead heat for first or any lower place the owners shall divide.

46.

Each horse running a dead heat for first place shall be deemed a winner of the race, and liable to the penalty for the full amount he would have received if he had won.

47.

When a dead heat is run for second place, and an objection is made to the winner of the race, and sustained, the horses which ran the dead heat shall be deemed to have run a dead heat for first place.

48.

The owners of horses running a dead heat shall divide equally all the monies or other prizes which attach to the place for which they ran such dead heat, together with the monies or prizes (if any) which attach to the place immediately behind.

49.

If the dividing owners cannot agree as to which of them is to have a Cup or other prize which cannot be divided the question shall be determined by lot by the Stewards, who shall decide what sum of money shall be paid by the owner who takes such Cup or other indivisible prize, to the other owner or owners.
In the case of Challenge Cups the Stewards shall determine the destination of the Cup.

WEIGHING IN

50.

Immediately after pulling up, the riders of the first four horses in each race must ride their horses to the place appointed for unsaddling, and present themselves to be weighed by the Clerk of the Scales; the horses shall remain at the appointed place until ordered to be taken away by the Clerk of the Scales. The other riders may dismount within a reasonable distance. If a rider be prevented from riding back to weigh in by reason of accident or illness, by which he or his horse is disabled, he may walk or be carried to the scales.

51.

In weighing in, a rider shall include in his weight everything that the horse has carried in the race, except as provided in Regulation 38.

52.

(i) If a rider cannot draw the weight at which he weighed out, the Clerk of the Scales shall allow him 2lb. If he cannot then draw the weight, his

horse shall, on an objection under Regulation 57, be disqualified.
(ii) If a horse carry less than the weight he should carry in accordance with the conditions of the race and these Regulations, he shall, on an objection under Regulation 58 (v), be disqualified.

53.

When the riders have weighed in to the satisfaction of the Clerk of the Scales, the Stewards shall authorize the All Right signal to be hoisted over the number board: provided they shall not authorize this until—
(i) The five minutes allowed for objecting under Regulation 57 has lapsed;
(ii) Any objection which may have been lodged on grounds mentioned in Regulation 57 has been decided.
No objection on any grounds other than those mentioned in Regulation 57 shall be entertained prior to the hoisting of the signal.
After the signal has been hoisted no alteration shall be made to the numbers of the winner or placed horses on the board.

54.

If a rider be too ill to weigh in, his horse shall not be disqualified provided that the rider weighed out at not less than his proper weight.

OBJECTIONS

55.

Every objection shall be decided by three Stewards, but their decision shall be subject to appeal to the Stewards of the Jockey Club so far as relates to points involving the interpretation of these Regulations, or to any question, other than a question of fact, on which there shall be no appeal unless by leave of the Stewards and with the consent of the Stewards of the Jockey Club.

56.

(i) Every objection shall be in writing, and must be signed by the owner of some horse engaged in the race, or by his authorized agent, or rider, and must in cases coming under Regulation 57 be made to the Clerk of the Scales; in other cases to the Clerk of the Course. A deposit of £2 shall be made with every objection lodged, which, if the case be decided against the objector, shall be forfeited to the Jockey Club, unless the Stewards shall certify that there was good and reasonable ground for the objection.
(ii) An objection may also be made without deposit by a Steward or Official of a Meeting in his official capacity. Such objection shall be in writing and signed by the Steward or Official.

57.

An objection to a horse on the ground of a cross, jostle, or any act on the part of his rider, or of his not having run the proper course, or of the race having been run on a wrong course, or of any other matter occurring in the race, or before weighing in, must be made within five minutes after the winner has been weighed in, unless, in special circumstances, the Stewards are satisfied that it could not have been made within that time.

No objection on any other ground than these shall be heard within this time.

58.

An objection on the ground,
(i) Of any mis-statement, omission, or error in the entry under which a horse has run, or
(ii) Of non-registration of the Hunter's Certificate, or of the Name of a horse, or of any mis-statement, omission, or error in such registration, or
(iii) That the horse which ran was not the horse, nor of the age, which he was represented to be at the time of the entry, or that he, or his owner, or rider, was not qualified by these Regulations or under the conditions of the race, or
(iv) That he has run at any unrecognised Meeting, or that his owner or rider is disqualified by reason of his having run or ridden a horse at, or acted in any official capacity in connection with, any unrecognised Meeting or race, or
(v) Of carrying wrong weight.
may be received within fourteen days of the conclusion of a Meeting.
Pending the determination of any objection, any prize which the horse objected to may have won, or may win, in the race, shall be withheld until the objection be determined.

59.

The Clerk of the Course shall include in his return to the Registry Office a report of any objection which may have been made and the decision of the Stewards thereon.

APPEALS

60.

When leave of appeal has been granted, the appellant shall forthwith notify in writing to the Registry Office or to the Clerk of the Course, for transmission thereto, his intention of appealing, and at the same time deposit the sum of £10; in all cases, except where fraud or wilful mis-statement is alleged, such notice and deposit must be received at the Registry Office within seven days of the decision of the Stewards having been given, or the appellant shall forfeit his right.
Should an appeal be decided to be frivolous or vexatious, the deposit shall be forfeited to the Jockey Club, or, if otherwise, returned to the appellant.

PRIZES

61.

The Clerk of the Course shall, at the expiration of fifteen days after the Meeting, pay over all prizes to the persons entitled.

POSTPONEMENTS

62.

If owing to the weather, the state of the ground or other circumstances a Meeting cannot be held on the allotted day a certificate signed by a Steward and the Clerk of the Course setting out the reason shall at once be forwarded to the Registry Office. A new date may be applied for. If such date be granted and be not more than fourteen days after the original date all entries shall stand good as if the Meeting had taken place on the day originally fixed. If the new date be more than fourteen days after the original date all entries become void and the races must be reopened.

63.

Any point not covered by these Regulations may be dealt with by the Stewards in accordance with the Rules of Racing so far as they may be applicable, or be referred to the Stewards of the Jockey Club.

Index